freedom time

The *Callaloo* African Diaspora Series focuses on literary and cultural productions in the contexts of the history and cultural politics of peoples of African descent in the Americas, the Caribbean, and Europe. Like the quarterly journal *Callaloo*, the *Callaloo* African Diaspora Series is a forum for artists and intellectuals producing challenging and seminal books that help illuminate the African Diaspora as a multidimensional site of evolving complexity, a location speaking, in part, through its literary and cultural productions that are informed by a number of indigenous traditions, which in turn inform and shape cultural productions across the globe.

freedom time

The Poetics and Politics of
Black Experimental Writing

ANTHONY REED

Johns Hopkins University Press
Baltimore

This book has been brought to publication with the generous assistance of the Frederick W. Hilles Publication Fund of Yale University.

© 2014 Johns Hopkins University Press
All rights reserved. Published 2014
Printed in the United States of America on acid-free paper

2   4   6   8   9   7   5   3   1

Johns Hopkins University Press
2715 North Charles Street
Baltimore, Maryland 21218-4363
www.press.jhu.edu

Library of Congress Cataloging-in-Publication Data

Reed, Anthony, 1978–
Freedom time : the poetics and politics of black experimental writing / Anthony Reed.
  pages cm
Includes bibliographical references and index.
ISBN 978-1-4214-1520-8 (hardcover) — ISBN 978-1-4214-1521-5 (electronic) — ISBN 1-4214-1520-8 (hardcover)   1. American literature—African American authors—History and criticism.   2. Literature, experimental—United States—History and criticism.   I. Title.
PS153.N5R45 2014
810.9′896073--dc23   2014011204

A catalog record for this book is available from the British Library.

Special discounts are available for bulk purchases of this book.
For more information, please contact Special Sales at 410-516-6936 or
specialsales@press.jhu.edu.

Johns Hopkins University Press uses environmentally friendly book materials, including recycled text paper that is composed of at least 30 percent post-consumer waste, whenever possible.

For my mother

You know and I know that the country is celebrating one hundred
years of freedom one hundred years too early.
—James Baldwin,
The Fire Next Time

Memory in our works is not a calendar memory; our experience of
time does not keep company with the rhythms of month and year
alone.
—Édouard Glissant,
Poetics of Relation

Contents

Acknowledgments

To begin, I want to acknowledge those scholars and artists whose work and example has sustained and challenged me. I give thanks and praise to Amiri Baraka, Anthony Braxton, John Coltrane, Charles T. Davis, Henry Louis Gates Jr., Stuart Hall, Deborah McDowell, Valerie Smith, Paul Gilroy, Farah Jasmine Griffin, Richard Iton, Robin D. G. Kelley, Jimmy Lyons, Kerry James Marshall, William Parker, Wadada Leo Smith, Henry Threadgill, and the many women and men who have helped establish and expand African American and African diaspora studies, and who have produced the work that has enabled, challenged and sustained my own thinking. *Àshé*.

I began this work under the guidance of Grant Farred, Amy Villarejo, Barry Maxwell, and Jonathan Culler, who have continued to support me beyond my graduate school days. I am very grateful for the care and depth of their engagement and their consistently making me feel I had a contribution to make. In the days since, I want to especially acknowledge Amy for her incisive and generous critiques of my work, and for her friendship. Grant Farred's continued mentorship, advice, and encouragement has been a model. Thank you for your perspective, wisdom, time, and reminders to focus on the work and its integrity.

It is not possible to acknowledge everyone who has had a hand in shaping this book, providing intellectual, spiritual, and in some cases literal nourishment throughout the process. I especially want to acknowledge just a few of the people to whom I knew I could turn for a friendly or critical ear, and who I knew would tolerate my occasional silence or out-of-context excitement about some new idea. That list includes Peter Bailey, Caetlin Benson-Allot, David Coombs, Lily Cui, Violet Hayes, Natalie Léger, Natalie Melas, Angela Naimou, Petter Nordal, and Seth Perlow. I would like to acknowledge Hortense Spillers, whose comments early in the process have encouraged and allowed me to let the work be as complicated as necessary, but no more complicated than that. I finished one stage of this project while a fellow of the Society for the Humanities, where

I was fortunate to regularly engage Mary Ahl, Seeta Chaganti, Mary Jacobus, Prita Maier, Ruth Mas, Timothy Murray, Reeve Parker, and Celeste Pietrusza, and Zac Zimmer.

My colleagues at Yale have been tremendously supportive and welcoming. Hazel Carby and Jacqueline Goldsby both offered timely interventions to this project, and along with Elizabeth Alexander, have provided a model of intellectual rigor, engagement, collegiality, and friendship. Caleb Smith and Emily Greenwood provided tremendously helpful and generous feedback at a critical stage. I've been enriched and energized by my interactions with Jafari Allen, Eli Anderson, GerShun Avilez, Ardis Butterfield, Jill Campbell, Kamari Clark, Ian Cornelius, Joe Cleary, Wai-Chee Dimock, Crystal Feimster, Inderpal Grewal, Lanny Hammer, Jonathan Holloway, Amy Hungerford, Gerry Jaynes, David Kastan, Wendy Lee, Stephen Pitti, Shital Pravinchandra, Ed Rugemer, Alicia Schmitt-Camacho, Vesla Weaver, and Michael Warner (the last of whom has been very generous with his time and encouragement). I would especially like to single out Robert Stepto, Joe Roach, Larry Manley, and Paul Fry for their mentorship and their example. This, too is a partial list: thank you all.

Virginia Jackson and Brent Hayes Edwards read an early version of this book. Their challenging and thoughtful engagement showed me places where I needed to clarify or rethink some of this book's arguments. I'm very grateful for their intervention and to Yale's English Department for hosting our conversation. The present book is substantially better for their engaged attention and engagement.

I also want to thank all the people who have in one way or another engaged the work in progress, especially Houston Baker, Herman Beavers, Jasper Bernes, Emily Bernard, Louise Bernard, Tony Bolden, Joshua Clover, Margo Crawford, Michael Dawson, Erica Edwards, Gabrielle Foreman, Simon Gikandi, Ben Glaser, Tsitsi Jaji, Gene Jarrett, Arlene Keiser, Jamaica Kincaid, Keith Leonard, Fred Moten, Noelle Morissette, Rolland Murray, Mark Anthony Neal, Aldon Nielsen, Howard Ramsby, Shana Redmond, Heather Russell, Sarah Senk, Evie Shockley, James Smethurst, Courtney Thorsson, Nicole Waligora-Davis, Cheryl Wall, Kenneth Warren, Barrett Watten, Alexander Weheliye, and Kevin Young. All of you, and more than I name here, have taught me that though the act of writing is solitary, one never writes alone. Thank you.

I want to thank my editor, Suzanne K. Flinchbaugh, and her assistant, Catherine Goldstead, who have been terrific to work with. I appreciate both of you guiding me through the ins and outs of the process with so little friction. Thanks to the many artists who granted me permission to reprint their work and responded enthusiastically to parts of the book, especially Kerry James Marshall, Terrance Hayes, Douglas Kearney, Nathaniel Mackey, M. NourbeSe Philip, and the family of Norman Pritchard. The anonymous reader the press engaged has been an invaluable resource for the project, and his or her rigorous and exacting reading pushed the book to be better than it might have been. I cannot thank him or her enough for taking such time, interest, and care with this project. I also want to thank series editor Charles Rowell, whose support and belief in this project has been steadfast and whose journal *Callaloo* has been an important resource to me and to our field.

My dear friends Toyin Akinmusuru and Raphael Crawford have been a constant support of friendship. I want to acknowledge my family, whose support and love has sustained me throughout the process and the inevitable ups and downs. My grandmother enriches my life with all of her amazing stories and advice. My brother, Edward Reed, has been a constant source of wisdom and good humor. I still look up to him. My mother, Deborah Reed, has always been there for me with the tough talk or encouragement I need. Thank you for always being in my corner.

The long solitary periods of composition have made me reflect on how important friendship is and has been to me. In this spirit, I would like to thank Emily Lordi, my constant companion, my dearest friend, and my partner in the truest sense of the word.

I would like to gratefully acknowledge permission to reprint works cited within:

Excerpts from "X/Self xth letter from the thirteenth provinces." By Kamau Brathwaite, from ANCESTORS, copyright © 1977, 1982, 1987, 2001 by Kamau Brathwaite. Reprinted by permission of New Directions Publishing Corp.

"Letter Sycorax." By Kamau Brathwaite, from MIDDLEPASSAGES, copyright © 1993 by Kamau Brathwaite. Reprinted by permission of New Directions Publishing Corp.

"DreamHaiti." By Kamau Brathwaite, from DS (2), copyright © 1989, 1994, 1995, 2000, 2002, 2007 by Kamau Brathwaite. Reprinted by permission of New Directions Publishing Corp.

Excerpts from "Hawk." By Kamau Brathwaite, from *Born to Slow Horses*, copyright ® 2005 by Kamau Brathwaite. Reprinted by permission of Wesleyan University Press.

"junt." By N. H. Pritchard, from *EECCHHOOEESS*. Reprinted by permission of New York University Press.

"The Voice." By N. H. Pritchard, from *The Matrix: Poems, 1960–1970*. Reprinted by permission.

"Zong #1." By M. NourbeSe Philip, from *Facture: A Journal of Poetry and Poetics*, no. 2 (2001). Reprinted by permission of the author.

"The Black Automaton in de Despair ub Existence #1: Up Ye Mighty Race!!!" By Douglas Kearney, from *The Black Automaton*, copyright © 2009 by Douglas Kearney. Reprinted by permission of Fence Books and the author.

"The Black Automaton in de Despair ub Existence #2: Our New Day Begun." By Douglas Kearney, from *The Black Automaton*, copyright © 2009 by Douglas Kearney. Reprinted by permission of Fence Books and the author.

"The Black Automaton in de Despair ub Existence #3: How Can I Be Down." By Douglas Kearney, from *The Black Automaton*, copyright © 2009 by Douglas Kearney. Reprinted by permission of Fence Books and the author.

"Between." By Harryette Mullen, from *Sleeping with the Dictionary*, copyright © 2002 by the Regents of the University of California. Reprinted by permission of the University of California Press.

"Sonnet." By Terrance Hayes, from HIP LOGIC, edited by Cornelius Eady, copyright © 2002 by Terrance Hayes. Used by permission of Penguin, a division of Penguin Group (USA) LLC.

Excerpt from "Knotted Highness." By Nathaniel Mackey, from *School of Udhra* © City Lights Publishing, 2001. Reprinted by permission of City Lights Publishing and the author.

freedom time

introduction

Visions of a Liberated Future

[I]f there is no black culture, or no longer black culture (because it has "succeeded"), then we need it now; and if that is true, then perhaps black culture—as the reclamation of the critical edge, as one of those vantages from which it might be spied, and no longer predicated on "race"—has yet to come.   —Hortense J. Spillers

Radically, then, one works not for a future present, but imagining the blank certitude of the future anterior. And the audience *is* the unimaginable.   —Gayatri Chakravorty Spivak

In our era of official "color blindness," where now optimistic, now nostalgic "post-"'s proliferate, conceptualizing and otherwise attending to time is politically urgent. We not only need to consider historical gaps and erasures but also to think about and produce inhabitable futures on terms other than those of the present, generating theories adequate to the complexities and contradictions of black life. Simultaneously a hermeneutic and mechanism for shaping allowable discourse, color blindness incorporates, co-opts, or suppresses difference, narrowing and policing the range of the thinkable and imaginable while presenting itself as the imperfect culmination of past struggles. *Freedom Time* argues that black experimental writing, at the level of form, advances an aesthetic of what Erica Hunt has called "unrecognizable speech" and that the hiatus of unrecognizability can spur new thought and new imaginings, especially the (re)imagining of collectivities and intellectual practices. In short, "unrecognizable speech," which pushes at the ruling order's ideological coverage and disciplines of knowledge, provides an important, positive disruption. In that challenge, I locate a new conception of literary politics rooted in literature's raising new questions, proposing new modes of being together, and offering new conceptions and theories adequate to the complexity of our common pasts and presents.[1]

Recent African diaspora literature and scholarship challenges our ideas of the past, reminding us of the complicity of the historical archive with the violence that produced it and historicizing our present concepts of temporality and value through their emergence in the management of the transatlantic slave trade. Other work, to which the present book owes an intellectual debt, has urged scholars to trace what Robin D. G. Kelley has termed black expressive culture's "freedom dreams,"[2] while yet other scholarship has challenged prevailing conceptions of the avant-garde and blackness as mutually exclusive, demonstrating the centrality of race to the practices and self-understanding of experimental arts communities.[3] In its conjunction of the social languages of "race" and experimental practice, black experimental writing urges an analysis of literary politics that looks beyond familiar terms of critique or protest that treat form as another kind of content in an effort to trace in its aesthetic demands the outlines of new forms of community and thought.

For many writers and intellectuals in the era, the change of legal status following the end of legal segregation and formal colonization fell well short of the freedom so many dreamed of and registered in the moment as requiring new political strategies to win a fuller freedom. Those period names—"post-segregation" and "post-independence"—designate new stages in the struggle for racial justice and autonomy and require, in Larry Neal's phrase, new visions of a liberated future. They also designate a torque in the larger institutional structures governing black authorship, a putative "freedom" from being representative of "the race" that similarly marks a shift in the possibilities of racial politics. The phrase "freedom time" invokes some of the insufficiency of the official responses to popular demands for civil recognition, which proved palliative rather than fully emancipatory. The very "success" of those movements quickened the dissolution of the unstable political blocs that had organized to demand justice in the first place. The last fifty years or so have shown the ways those narrowly defined concessions have limited the possibilities for social justice organizing and, worse, stunted the ability to imagine radical alternatives to neoliberal governmentality, or more accurately its "regime of multiple governmentalities."[4] That regime, meanwhile, has proven adept at organizing power along ethno-patriarchal lines within an officially "color blind" framework while redefining the past to authorize the negation of civil gains and the reorganization of public institutions to achieve analogous effects. Official celebrations of the civil rights movement tend to flatten the organizational and political complexity of those movements; official narratives of success, in turn, make the repetition of that success unlikely, even anomalous, while making larger transformations more difficult, if not impossible to articulate. The present masquerades as the fulfillment, or only thinkable outcome, of the past, making it increasingly difficult to articulate alternative visions to this world. The need for radical new conceptions of community and alternative visions of liberation remains pressing, in literature and beyond.

Through a set of theoretical and historical analyses, *Freedom Time* argues that although critics continue to consider black experimental writing in terms of either race or putatively "raceless" experimental techniques, the two are mutually constitutive. In the face of changing notions of black authorship, I argue that authors who self-identify as black take upon themselves the task of defining and redefining blackness for their own purposes. Producing literature that "worries the line," in Cheryl Wall's phrase, between noise and articulate speech, black experimental writing is "the art of saying the impossible." In this introduction, I also discuss the ambivalence about being a "black poet" that some writers feel by attending to a debate at the 1966 First Black Writers Conference at Fisk University and ultimately through a rereading of double consciousness as a diagnosis of the presumption that black writers' condition of intelligibility is addressing a narrowly conceived social problem. My rereading of W. E. B. Du Bois's famous articulation of double consciousness in *The Souls of Black Folk*, and the ways he works within and against the terms racial "folk spirit" arguments, sets the terms of engagement for the chapters that follow, especially the book's methodological prioritization of poetics—an account of the means through which literature produces its effects.

I want to pause to underscore *Freedom Time*'s historical intervention. Most of the current genealogies of "avant-garde" or experimental writing in English tend to neglect black writing, often owing to the necessary granular attention to particular networks, coteries, and traditions of writers and writing. Insofar as critics draw on a nominally color-blind methodology or the ahistorical and theoretically untenable position that "class" is somehow more important than race, writing that directly addresses such political concerns as identity will seem too topical or too far removed from the relevant traditions to count. Often subtending those genealogies is an implicit transhistorical notion of poetry or of the human (which has always been a cornerstone of racial projects) that by default is white and usually male. In this way, in historical and theoretical terms, experimentation and race seem opposed. In effect, critics can then tell the story as though white-identified techniques "liberated" nonwhite writers from the limitations of race. Simultaneously, traditional genealogies of black writing tend to exclude this experimental subtradition to the extent that scholars rely on notions of "expression." Those genealogies rely either on the idea of "finding

a voice" or participating in a transhistorical racial project. Experimental prac-
tices that fall outside of a handful of master tropes simply tend to be neglected.
In *Freedom Time*, I argue that black experimental writing challenges us to re-
think the relationships between race and literary techniques and by extension
to rethink some of the prevailing assumptions surrounding experimental writ-
ing in particular. My analyses in the following chapters offer new conceptions of
both experimental and black writing.

Among many black writers and others, the post–World War II period has
seen increased distrust of political *and* aesthetic representation, owing in part
to concerns in some quarters that representation is too closely tied to restrictive
norms and presumed white audiences.[5] Especially since the end of segregation
and formal colonization, debates over the politics of literary form have inten-
sified among black writers, breaking down to three rough, overlapping tenden-
cies. The historical coincidence and interarticulation of U.S., Caribbean, Afri-
can and Asian freedom struggles is not a given. The conjunction "and" does not
denote an established or uncomplicated commensurability between these sites,
institutions of authorship, or literary strategies so much as it raises anew a ques-
tion regarding the grounds of comparison in this period. As Natalie Melas has
argued, "postcoloniality, and comparison itself, both centrally involve a medita-
tion on community and collectivity as literature represents its aspirations, and
often indeed, its failures."[6] Throughout *Freedom Time*'s analyses, I emphasize
those aspirations to communities and forms of collectivity that either do not re-
duce to untroubled comparison or that in fact recognize the implication of cer-
tain forms of comparison—of comparing black "immigrants," or immigrants in
general, to black "natives"—within larger structures of global antiblackness.

I do not, of course, intend some ahistorical or naturalizing account of race in
my use of the term "black" (rather than African American or Afro-Caribbean) or
my implicit reliance on the concept-metaphor "diaspora" (I limit my comments
on the latter to methodological concerns). As Melas argues regarding the texts
she discusses, they "hail from diverse traditions and have no necessary or intrin-
sic connection; the point of postcolonial comparatism here, thus, is precisely
to bring them into relation over a ground of comparison that is in common but
not unified."[7] Though the current use of the term "diaspora" emerges through
interactions among colonial and African American subjects, it is not coexten-
sive with "postcolonial." Nonetheless, African diaspora authors share a ground
that is common but not unified. Indeed, such unity was an explicit concern that
drove the transition from Pan-Africanism to conceptions of the African dias-
pora. Brent Hayes Edwards notes that "*diaspora* becomes necessary partly be-

cause of the increased contestation over the political scope of *Pan-Africanism* in the independence movement" and traces the connections between the emergence of the term "diaspora" and the institutionalization of black studies in the U.S. academy.[8] Contemporary uses of "diaspora," as Edwards argues, emerge in response to internal differences in the material existences of different black people in the United States, the Caribbean, and beyond. The value of the "use of the term *diaspora* . . . is not that it offers the comfort of abstraction, an easy recourse to origins, but that it forces us to consider discourses of cultural and political linkage only through and across difference."[9] Diaspora, then, is a concept-metaphor of articulation in Stuart Hall's sense, a rhetorical-conceptual figure that designates a " 'complex structure,' a structure in which things are related, as much through their differences as through their similarities."[10] The common structure linking writers is the crisis that follows independence and desegregation, in neither case accompanied by the necessary shifts in the power structures affecting race that would allow their promises to be fulfilled. My point is not that all of the authors proclaim and articulate diaspora but that the perspective of diaspora allows us to see commonalities between heterogeneous sites at this historical juncture.

Freedom Time discusses black experimental writing in terms of its literary effects rather than efficacy within an already defined discursive and political situation. I outline a transnational archive of black experimental writing since the moment of what critics and scholars of the late 1960s called "the new black poetry." Arguing that these texts use literary experimentation to reconfigure the possibilities of both literature and race, without taking either to be static or transparent, I develop a methodology for reading beyond conventional preoccupations with issues of representation and conceptions of literature as a model, drawing out the political possibilities of literature *as* literature. I use the phrase "literature as literature" in a restricted sense to signal the centrality to my analysis of *poiesis* as literature's means of expanding the domain of the intelligible and thinkable. In my analysis I try to recover what is oppositional rather than resistant or subversive in the experimental: its holding open a place for the unthought, for what is unassimilable to the prevailing regime of power and, most generally, its positive claims and demands. How does our understanding of literary possibility change, for example, when we consider dissident practices of citation of texts and forms as transformative of those forms rather than as rejecting or mocking them?

Black experimental writing occasions a reconsideration of a more radical literary politics that are not rooted in the biography or politics of the author or in the determinant political situation to which the work "responds." It also announces a challenge—and opportunity—to disarticulate race as a pseudo-ontological category from the ethico-political obligations thought to derive from race as "lived experience." Here, I depart from those norms of literary analysis that see the work as a reflection of social conditions in order to attend to literature as a mode of *self-production*. I understand the text as a set of differential significations, set in relation but positioned differentially with respect to others owing to the social positions of the authors and their texts, on one hand, and the anticonventional strains of the writing on the other. Most of the texts I consider here are poetry, but they are all generically promiscuous, drawing on and transforming older traditions of poetry and other art forms. Part of my critical task is to make sense of textual diversity without reducing such apparent contradictions to an underlying unity. In other words, I do not aim to show the coherence or unity of the text but rather what Pierre Macherey terms its "free necessity": "A literary work, then, is never entirely premeditated; or rather, it is, but at several levels at once, without deriving monolithically from a unique and simple conception."[11] Form is neither a purely creative act nor a predetermined set of significations that bring to consciousness—through replication or estrangement and critique—the dynamics of the social system with which it is contemporaneous, but something in between.

What I am calling *literary* politics, which are related to other modes of politics within which any given text participates without being reducible to them, derive not only from literature's making legible the outlines of its time, its framing of legible speech and illegible noise, and its injunction to think beyond present strictures of "allowable thought" and forms of value. Literary politics also depend on poetics, the shareable techniques that mark the site where literature touches the social and historical. Techniques are central rather than adjunct to literature's self-production, which is irreducible to intention or historical determination (the ideological limits of the institutions through which authorship emerges). Literary texts respond to concrete historical situations, but texts continually shift the terms of their own reception, so the most radical statement of one day can become a platitude over time. Yet, as I argue via examination of W. E. B. Du Bois's concept of double consciousness, to which African American poets returned in the 1960s's, shortly after Du Bois's death, even familiar writing can retain unthought components that are recoverable from the demands of disciplinary reading or that are renewable within the terms of a contemporary crisis.

Critics' prevailing tendency to approach black literature exclusively through thematics of race or the social narrowly conceived, is one factor that has persistently led to the exclusion of the authors considered throughout this book and other black experimental writers from genealogies of presumptively white avant-garde writing, on the grounds that its concerns seem insufficiently "universal."[12] The relative lack of attention to this experimental, often intergeneric writing allows for the perpetuation of the notion that black writers (and other writers of color) are valuable insofar as they offer testimony or legitimate narratives about so-called race relations, a perspective that largely suppresses or minimizes potentially radical forms of black politics. Simultaneously, the abstractness of black experimental writing and its push for what I call "radical unlearning" of the preemptive understandings of black life tends to result in its being excluded from disciplinary genealogies of African American literature except through claims remarking the text's "resistance" to the material conditions that shape black life. The romance of resistance leaves largely unthought further connections between race and aesthetics as a mode of—and way of understanding—perception.

I refer to this particular kind of misreading, which locates texts within a preemptive black tradition or black social location, as "racialized reading." It effectively sidesteps or precludes other forms of analysis while setting the terms for the ways critics read, teach, and canonize black writing.[13] The connection between race and literature is not immanent to texts, but long-term disciplinary practice has produced the terms within which racially marked literature is read, produced, and analyzed. Racialized reading emerges from the historically specific factors that shape black writing as a project—its appropriation, understood as an externalizing operation that gives it meaning in other domains.[14] Racialized reading reduces black culture to a set of properties, then "appropriates" those properties for other discourses and projects, such as promoting social sympathy, or for restrictive, preemptive ways of misreading. Appropriation enabled those white avant-gardists near the turn of the twentieth century who assumed the "mask" of black dialect as a sign of their own elective countermodernity. Racialized reading similarly relies on the processes of making objects metonymic of cultural practices and on making cultural practices discursive objects. One sees something of this process in the critical reception of black experimental writers first ignored (with the notable exception of Amiri Baraka) or dismissed as derivative (as with Melvin B. Tolson's modernism) or else anthologized and praised for creating art that is about "more than race" (that is, locatable within white-identified traditions) while nonetheless speaking to a certain notion of "the black experience."[15] As a result, racialized reading provides a selective, occasionally prescriptive account of the project of black aesthetics as one of rejoinder, protest, or commentary, figuring black writing as reactive rather than productive.

Racialized reading is thus connected to the reductive, commodity versions of black "folk" culture whose verbal forms, especially, functioned for white modernist authors as rhetorical totems against bourgeois modernity throughout the twentieth century. Fred Moten's provocative chiasmus "blackness is an avant-garde thing . . . and the avant-garde is a black thing" is historically accurate, if analytically insufficient on its own.[16] According to common, romantic nationalist notions of expression and spirit, which I elaborate in the following pages, black texts are always singular and exemplary, signs of a particular writer and a window onto the conditions of life for black people in general. The conjunction of these two perspectives produces the sense that the black text is necessarily oppositional because it is equally necessarily external to modernity: the position of black subjects makes their speech seem necessarily subversive, if only because the conditions of life for so many black people continue to be informed by the singular barbarism of slavery and its aftermath. That may make blackness "an avant-garde thing" to the extent that it continues to figure a disruption of unmarked notions of the human, but to avoid reification it requires Moten's subsequent qualification that to "say that Blackness is intrinsically experimental is not the same thing as to say that Black folk are intrinsically experimental."[17] One must still consider the ways black experimental poetics set their own agenda, articulate conflicts and politics in the present, posit alternative modes futurity and community, and require new modes of thinking.

Like many powerful hermeneutics, racialized reading obscures as much as it reveals, even as it powerfully resolves the question of black literature's distinctness and relationship to politics. To resist the lure of such reading, I engage a situated formalism that remains attentive to the specificity of the moment of a text's emergence, the events to which it refers, and the formal conventions or techniques the work repurposes or reconstitutes. Reading for those three, as the situation seems to require, I attempt to move beyond literary politics as scholars of African diaspora literature customarily conceive them to a new mode of criticism mindful of the radical implications of formal innovation as a mode of social engagement. "Experimentation" in this book thus does not refer only to the aesthetic category of innovation as typically conceived but also to the use of literature to reconfigure blackness and of blackness to reconfigure literature. It names the literary response that occurs when thinking comes up against what W. E. B. Du Bois termed the "limitations of allowable thought," norms of racialized reading, and the contemporary racial order. In the phrase "black experimental writing," therefore, "black" modifies "experimental," and "experimental" modifies "black." I offer "black experimental writing" as a term that describes both the formally innovative writing practices of black writers and the ways such writing transforms our understandings of race, starting from the assumption that the literature does something other than produce knowledge or answer, for example, an implicit "how does it feel to be a problem?" Not exactly providing a differently hued narrative of the avant-garde, *Freedom Time* draws attention to the theoretical implications of black experimental writing, guided in part by the notion that the literature produces its own acts of theory and self-differentiation rather than providing a vanguardist model to follow or confirmation of some broader truth "in the real world" or some theoretical stance. The shifts in the kinds of questions texts ask and the claims or demands texts make on readers is the place from which I interrogate the politics of literature.

For minoritized writers, race exists as part of a larger articulation of social contradictions at work simultaneously inside and outside the text—it is the condition of its speech being intelligible and unintelligible at once.[18] Black experimental writing worries that line, engaging readers at the threshold between speech and noise that philosopher Jacques Rancière refers to as the "distribution of the sensible": a partition or "redistribution of space and time, place and identity, speech and noise, the visible and the invisible."[19] Expanding on Rancière's argument, literary politics lie in the means through which literature articulates new aesthetic communities, addresses itself to an encounter with audiences not yet known or imaginable. Apprehending literature's function within that larger domain of politics requires an analysis of poetics—the specific means through which literature operates most as literature and self-differentiates from the field of the literary.

The phrase "freedom time" invokes that vision, the projected time of the encounter, and the fact that liberation has not yet happened. The disappearance of the term "freedom" (or "liberation") from the common language of black politics should be mourned, especially as this disappearance marks "the disappearance of the *pursuit* of Freedom as an element of black vernacular culture" in the overdeveloped world.[20] Reclaiming the term "freedom" is especially urgent at a time when the Right and neoliberal regimes have conspicuously co-opted "freedom" and "liberty" as bywords for the erosion of the welfare state and complicity with capital's demands as a response to the threat of "totalitarianism." Part of my ambition is to resituate the thinking of freedom in the field of recent literature. Privileging that address to a future anterior audience, I understand the literary text to reach beyond its time to a place that is always just out of reach and away from view until the advent of genuine human freedom.

THE PITFALLS OF BLACK GENIUS

Racialized reading has its roots in a confluence of late nineteenth-century understandings of race and nationalism that W. E. B. Du Bois, whose influence loomed significantly in midcentury discussions of black literary politics, at once exemplifies and transcends. Though Larry Neal sought to distance himself from Du Bois, his utopian "vision of a liberated future" names a moment of radical unlearning rooted in aesthetics that is commensurate with Du Bois's call that black art must "let this world be beautiful."[21] Like Melvin B. Tolson, in his exemplary debate with Robert Hayden at the 1966 First Black Writers Conference at Fisk University, Neal sought to locate the relationship between art and race in the interstices between historically verifiable facts and an interpretation of race as an engine of history. However, Neal rejected the idea of black art as "propaganda," directly challenging misrepresentations and stereotypes, in order to understand black art as autonomous.

Neal, Tolson, and the early Du Bois broadly agreed that part of art's politics rests in *expression*, specifically in the sense that Du Bois had in mind when he declared the "sorrow songs" to be "the sole American music," "the singular spiritual heritage of the nation and the greatest gift of the Negro people."[22] To hear this music, in other words, was to hear the authentic spirit of the land that had produced it. James Weldon Johnson would make similar claims for ragtime and the cakewalk in his preface to *The Book of American Negro Poetry*, while Amiri Baraka would claim that claim that Bob Dylan's "Blowing in the Wind" is "immediately transformed when Stevie Wonder sings it because it becomes about something that is actual in the world and is substantiated by the life of the man singing it."[23] Baraka's argument makes clear the degree to which the concept of black expression—or what I term "black genius"—and the underlying claims to authenticity function within a context of mass media, where such claims have monetary as well as political implications.

The philosophical notion of expression, in its varied senses, has been enormously influential in discussions of African American and African diaspora literature and culture, serving as a key philosophical component of racialized reading. At its extreme, the romantic-nationalist notion of expression solidifies race and, effectively, closes it off, depriving it of its undecidable textuality by rendering it a concept and making possible transhistorical, spiritual/metaphysical accounts of black culture. The term belongs to the long legacy of the Enlightenment, especially to a keen interest in Europe and the United States to link the spirit of a place with the people of that place. *The Souls of Black Folk* and the American enthusiasm for a Hegelian interpretation of history and racial destiny bear the trace of this interest, albeit in different ways.[24] In calling the "sorrow songs" the only "true American music," Du Bois strategically negotiates folk spirit, or *Volksgeist*, arguments, making African Americans (as well as Native Americans, whom he mentions in the next clause) central to the unfolding of U.S. national spirit. Folk spirit is double edged: on the one hand, that concept allows him to speak on behalf of the Negro, because as "flesh of the flesh and bone of the bone of them who live within the Veil" he can claim legitimacy and authenticity as spokesman for the remote "massed millions of the black peasantry." Simultaneously, operating within a cultural situation where the "coon songs" claimed a connection to that same peasantry, that notion of legitimacy drew on and reinforced African American separation: folk spirit's claims to racial particularity thus ran counter to his larger political aims.

Du Bois's concept of the veil, like the structures and strategies of racial differentiation to which it corresponds, is not so much "natural" as natural*ized* and naturalizing. Through repetition and ideological necessity, insofar as race emerges as a justification for exploitation, the veil comes to seem a feature of the natural world, a permanent, unassailable structure, one that cannot be thought, since, being part of the ideological substrate that structures discourse, it is intimate with thinking itself, at once internal to and external to expression. It is also the figure prior to the notion of racial or national expression that has often been central to the authenticating norms that govern cultural production and the project of racial leadership, beginning with the very problem of designating the people of politics. In his account of Du Bois, Robert Gooding-Williams defines "expression" as the presentation and participation in black folk spirit ("avow[ing] and express[ing] the ideals that define the folk ethos of slave culture and antecedently unite black Americans"); on this account, every artifact and performance carries black spirit within itself as form and content.[25] As Robin D. G. Kelley and others have pointed out, the idea of a black folk spirit precedes any actual black people as "*bricolage*, a cutting, pasting, and incorporating of various cultural forms that then become categorized in a racially or ethnically coded aesthetic hierarchy."[26] It has no content apart from its particular use in this counterracist hermeneutic circle and as such marks blackness as *textual*: "Negro" does not refer to an onto-phenomenological object, but it is also not strictly an "ideal" or fantasy.[27] Its value always seems to precede its appearance.

"Textual" here does not refer to script or writing but to the indeterminacy (and overdetermination) of "blackness," that is, the theoretical impossibility of any fixed meaning of blackness. Here, I draw a parallel with Gayatri Spivak's argument regarding the textuality of a vital concept (e.g., the notion of "value" within Marxist discourse): namely, that some pivotal notions resist simple translation from one domain to another because of the "the fields of force that make them heterogeneous, indeed discontinuous." "Negro" and other terms of racial positioning mean different things in different discursive domains, owing to their relative power and position within a larger set of social contradictions. "Textual" indexes the open-endedness of race—its resistance to enclosure within a single, transhistorical concept. Being irreducible to a single concept makes contingent any relationship between represented and representation by insisting that no such folk spirit or *Volksgeist* preexists its expression, reattuning us to the dynamic processes of racialization and the shifting sites of race within cultural production.

Du Bois negotiates the problems of black expression, or, aligning this view of expression with notions of "spirit" in contemporaneous nineteenth-century philosophical discourses, the problems of a narrow view of "black genius" that links black cultural production in the present to an imagined preindustrial folk culture still present in black people. Though it seems to be an analysis of some "pure" expression of the black folk, I argue that Du Bois shows the ways expression participates in a broader process of appropriation that gives black texts their meaning. More forcefully, the process of appropriation is, he suggests, the fight over the meaning of black culture itself. "Black genius" is simultaneously metonymic (rooted in the imputation of a common culture of resistance forged in the crucibles of slavery and capitalist modernity) and metaphoric (referring to the "spontaneous" response of black people that does not require conscious agency or awareness of black culture or black history but that nonetheless "inspirits" black expressive acts). Black genius creates a hermeneutic circle: blackness authorizes the analysis and the outcome of the reception and interpretation of black writing and culture, creating the sense, as Kimberly Benston put it, "that the work's meaning may be located in some standard prior to and external to the expressive act itself."[28]

The opening pages of *Souls* stage this problem in literary terms that would come to inform key debates of black writing in the United States and elsewhere.

Because of the preemptive framing of blackness as a problem, to speak of "the Negro" is to make her appear and disappear in the same gesture: she fades away into the veil of advance knowledge, legend, myth, distortion, and ideological containment that condition her visibility. In their form, the early sections of *Souls* point to a more radical solution than the ways we often read Du Bois, emphasizing the time of the encounter rather than the being of the Negro. Recuperating that radical kernel, the attempt to surpass the "limits of allowable thought," illuminates the sense of politics in this book and especially the ways by which I argue that the analysis of black experimental writing must separate itself from a politics of expression. Here, I want to draw renewed attention to Du Bois's narrated refusal in *The Souls of Black Folk* to answer how it feels to be a problem as a clue to some of his formal strategies and as a key to my own mode of analysis throughout this book. That question, along with the refused reply, shows the limits of expression in a context where the presumptive link between race (the "souls" or spirit of the black *folk* are at issue) and a narrow set of ethico-political obligations can easily make race destiny. The temporality of expression in *Souls*—where one "finds" or "invents" a voice that retroactively produces a proper, self-possessed subject—makes literary selfhood an effect of this dissemination.[29] Central to this is the notion of the veil as a figure of articulation that draws together while separating in order to make expression possible on different terms. The subject of the veil is neither phenomenology's intending subject nor the psychological subject of cognized experience; rather, Du Bois's narrative presents the veil as the limiting historical mediation of subjective experience. The veil is a figure for the dead time that haunts each articulation of the world "as such," a dissimulation of "organic" or "natural" totalities.

This book advances an understanding of literary politics based on such visions and the forms of community that become available as a result of them. The organicism that "black genius" depends on is not new; one can trace it to Samuel Taylor Coleridge's proclamation that "such as the life is, such is the form" and the philosophy of Enlightenment thinker Johann Gottfried Herder, whose work helped to inspire interest in collecting folklore.[30] As Oren Izenberg observes, "Language has been the first resort of cultural nationalism since Herder. Armed with two convictions—that language is the precondition of thought, and that each individual language emerges from nature by design—linguistic nationalists believe language coextensive with the forms of life (beliefs, literatures, practices, institutions) that thought produces."[31] In modernity writ large, language has been—and continues to be—central to articulations of national belonging, insofar as it authorizes rejection of and distancing from linguistic others. Language, of which literature is a privileged domain of contestation and invention, becomes indexed to the health, viability, and value of a culture and ultimately of national or racial belonging.

Giving a sense of the power of racialized reading, however, Izenberg distances his analysis of the "role that poetry can play in social thought" from the social languages of difference and concrete political struggles, emphasizing instead the more abstract, formal category of personhood.[32] Though one might argue that a romantic notion of "the people" replaces "the folk," Izenberg's "new humanism" suggests the highest possible level of generality. However, he explicitly bars literature that can be "understood to be part of an ethical or political project aimed at expanding the sphere of attention or social sympathy."[33] Presumably this prohibition has to do with narrowly conceived "identity politics," of which Herderian cultural nationalism is an example, that that might otherwise overwhelm or complicate his Shelley-derived notion of "poetry in the general sense" and abstract, universal personhood. His racialized reading substitutes an ideal of poetic expression for textual analysis, while Euro-American poetry outlines the extent of his humanism and his canon remains almost exclusively white and male. Language remains the precondition of thought in his account, but his particular effort to disarticulate poetry from immediate social concerns is beset by an insufficiently historicized account of the human and an ahistorical understanding of poetry that nonetheless links it to expression. The challenge is to see the ways experimental writing relates to "poetry in the general sense" while having as one its immediate concerns the contested grounds of social life, using as material the social languages of race, gender, or class and their articulation. To see beyond the veil of expression or black genius requires seeing the ways socially marked writing engages topics not directly related to identity in that narrow sense.

From a different perspective (but voicing a similar wariness toward certain forms of "identity politics" and cultural nationalism), Kenneth Warren has argued that the end of Jim Crow, the institutionalization of white supremacy that continues to be the paradigmatic instance of "identity politics" in the United States and beyond, produced a crisis for African American literature. His account of literature provides in capsule form the evolution of the concept of black genius and its pitfalls. During Jim Crow, Warren argues, black literature functioned either "instrumentally, in terms of whether or not it could be added to the arsenal of arguments, achievements, and propositions needed to attack the justifications for, and counteract the effects of, Jim Crow," or as an "index" of black genius, which was itself instrumental in the same fight.[34] For Warren, culture as *institution* necessarily becomes political in situations of open political antagonism like Jim Crow. The "success" of the midcentury civil rights movement (the end of de jure segregation), like the "success" of black culture (its recognition and mainstreaming), has changed the conditions of black authorship. While arguments like Izenberg's suggest it is too soon to mark the end of "African American literature" as a semiautonomous phenomenon, Warren's polemic challenges us to develop new ways to read black writing. Some readers and critics still turn to black writers for knowledge of life "behind the veil," but that knowledge has a different place within larger political struggles and (ideally) is no longer directly tied to proving the worthiness or humanity of black people. However, the status of black literature as an institution tells us very little about the operations of black texts, even within the era of Jim Crow.

This brings us back to Du Bois, whose negotiation of writing as at once singular (because it tells his own story) and exemplary (because readers would have understood him to be typical of the black folk he wrote about) in *Souls* retains a radical notion of voice that informs my analyses of black experimental writing and its address to an unknown audience. Rather than understanding double consciousness exclusively as an epistemological problem that can be overcome through revolutionary action or liberal reform, I argue that it also temporalizes expression in its multiple senses to address a world to come.[35] It is not an appeal for recognition but an analysis of race as perpetual misrecognition. Du Bois insistently refers to the *historical* rather than pseudo-ontological uniqueness of race: to be both Negro and American requires a revision of both terms—and the institutions that support them—into something more capacious, and "the Negro's message for the world" requires that she be a "co-worker in the kingdom of culture."[36] Playing on the terms of Herderian nationalism, the text mingles its plural "souls" (i.e., spirit or essence) with funerary metaphors right from the first lines of its "forethought," a link that becomes even more peculiar given Du Bois's use of the autobiographical "I" in *Souls* and throughout his writing. That autobiographical gesture links him to his nominal object of study—black folk— through a shared historical horizon and retrospective orientation, typified by the asymmetry of access to the means of literary production.

The opening metaphor of the book as grave—"Herein lie *buried* many things which if read with patience may show the strange meaning of being black here in the dawning of the Twentieth Century"—marks the book as a kind of elegy for something already apparently passed rather than the enduring spirit of a group. In this light, the deployment of death to establish the dawn of a new racial era is not incidental. *Souls* endeavors to articulate a collective spirit and unifying ethos of African Americans as an autonomous, self-expressive group and break from past misunderstandings and misrepresentations of the African. The appeal to readers' patience indicates that presumptive understandings of black life as a problem make temporality—especially the disjunction between repressive appropriations of black culture and untimely demands for black autonomy—central to the book's project of untangling the "strange meaning" of being black. Implicating white readers and their interest, this second sentence, like the first, highlights a temporal rift, a nonsynchronism of contemporaneous elements that allow one to speak of a Negro Problem that was not necessarily a crisis of legitimacy for a nation founded on liberal ideals. At stake, then, is not just the accommodation of African Americans within U.S. civil society but the very constitution of the present and meaning of the past: in Jacques Derrida's phrase, "a certain complicity or co-implication *maintaining* together several current nows [*maintenants*] which are said to be the one past and the other future."[37] *Now* is *Souls*' primary question. At bottom, Du Bois articulates a politics of time and sharing time, indicting at every turn the uneven division of time and challenging the ways the "now" of black life is adjunct to the more general or "universal" now.

Therefore, the opening preposition of "Of Our Spiritual Strivings" is also a question of unequally shared time and social location. "Between me and the other world there is *ever* an *unasked* question," he begins, insisting that "to the real question, How does it feel to be a problem? I answer seldom a word."[38] Beginning the book this way, this mute drama—refused answer to an unasked question—shows both of the pre-texts of any black writing. To speak *as* the Negro, to allow one's own experience to stand in for all Negroes, is to make the Negro vanish. Simultaneously, speaking *as* a Negro is, in that situation, the only condition under which speech is possible at all, even as the situation predistributes the sense of Du Bois's reply, premaps it according to the prevailing consensus that the Negro is a Problem. Asked or not, the answer to the question is partially encoded in the question. This moment, effectively, is an allegory of authorship—of the authority bestowed on the signatory of the book as the one who will provide answers to the questions asked, on the condition that the question predicts the response. Du Bois's performative silence, ironically drawing attention to the issue he paraliptically declares he will not discuss, doubles the initial silence of the unasked question that asks without asking. Though Du Bois claims to answer "seldom a word," he submits in his book to the implicit interpellative demand that he *narrate* his having come to racial consciousness, of having recognized the veil: a tall new-come girl refuses his visiting card, "pe-remptorily," with a wordless glance:[39]

> It is in the early days of rollicking boyhood that the revelation bursts upon one, all
> in a day, as it were. I remember well when the shadow swept across me. I was a lit-
> tle thing, away in the hills of New England, where the dark Housatonic winds be-
> tween Hoosac and Taghkanic to the sea. In a wee wooden schoolhouse, something
> put it into the boys' and girls' heads to buy gorgeous visiting-cards—ten cents a
> package—and exchange. The exchange was merry, till one girl, a tall newcomer,
> refused my card,—refused it peremptorily, with a glance. Then it dawned on me
> with a certain suddenness that I was different from the others; or like mayhap in
> heart and life and longing, but shut out from their world by a vast veil.[40]

The tall newcomer's rejection of the young Du Bois's visiting card marks a mo-ment at which the contingency of racial difference becomes ontologized (or rei-fied), with the outcome being that Du Bois then has to reinterpret it as rooted in history. Better stated, the parody of Hegel's philosophy of history that famously follows, culminating with the description of the Negro as the "seventh son," suggests the need to reinterpret history to find a place for the Negro.[41] The re-sult is a repeated scene of writing and revision.

Du Bois figures double consciousness as a problem related to expression, turning on the impossible imperative to speak simultaneously *of* and *on be-half of* the Negro, making Du Bois's own position an explicit theme of the text. His articulation of double consciousness stresses the nonsynchronism of the black subject with the world, which appears as already marked by differential and differentiating power relationships. Writing, insofar as it privileges a den-sity of references and meanings, offers a space where transformation may be prefigured, refigured, or promised. The veil figures a discrepancy that haunts articulations of the world "as such" and dissimulates the sense of time as "natu-ral," undermining the very authority on which the text apparently rests. *Souls* formulates a problem that will inform the work of black experimental writers that follow him: the textual nature of "blackness," whose meaning and value are determined to a large degree in advance by the ensemble of historical, social, and affective relations.

The visiting card—bearing the visitor's name and signifying the intention of a future visit by indicating that the visit required by protocol in order to secure an invitation has happened—operates in the structure of a promise, figuring a time of fulfillment in the future. The point is not the fulfillment of that moment but opening a new set of possibilities. The visiting card is an allegory for the several forms of textuality, and for my book, *Souls*' play with textuality, citation, and temporality is an allegory for black experimental writing. The visiting card is also an injunction, a claim on us to anticipate that future moment that I stop short of saying is messianic. This scene and the promised encounter dramatize the scene of listening as well as techniques of response, and through its self-reflexive rhetoric it figures writing as generative of those ecstatic moments in which the text is liberated from its referential or representational functions, enabling it to affect some imagined receivers who are constituted as a people or a community. The fundamental conflict takes shape around differential time—the before and after the event, the event's recursive nature, the event's always having happened out of time serving, in this case, to mark the difference between an "I" and a "them." The visiting card establishes the necessity of founding a different time in which the Negro's "message for the world" will be intelligible, allowing and occasioning a different conception of the past and present, and thus of the future. Black experimental writing "speaks" with what is at once a singular and plural "voice," and through that act it lays claim to yet unfigured visions of a liberated future.

SAYING THE IMPOSSIBLE

Black experimental writing, seeking through form to expand the range of the thinkable and sayable, is one way of responding to the presumed conjunction of race and expression. I have lingered over Du Bois in part because of his continued influence in the period of the "new black poetry" in the Black Arts era. One exemplary exchange is the debate between Melvin B. Tolson and Robert Hayden at the First Black Writers Conference at Fisk University in April 1966, at the beginning of the period of this book's study.[42] For both, race was an overdetermined site of social contradiction, distinction, and discipline; the difference between them was in the way they articulated the problem and whom they imagined as audience, which tells us something about the larger political terrain each imagined. This First Black Writers Conference, which brought together established writers like Tolson, Hayden, Gwendolyn Brooks, J. Saunders Redding (who delivered the keynote), and more politically radical novelists like John Oliver Killens and William Melvin Kelley sought to address the shifting possibilities for relating politics, race, and literature in the midst of the civil rights movement. In a sense, however, the more radical writers had returned to the work of the recently deceased W. E. B. Du Bois. Every era, it seems, must inherit its own Du Bois, for the problem of modernity remains the problem of the color

line, which overdetermines significance in advance and limns the "limits of al-
lowable thought." Killens's call for black writers to develop ways of writing and
valuing literature that did not require looking "into the eyes of the white master
for an image of ourselves" echoes Du Bois's account of double consciousness
as "looking at one's self through the eyes of others, measuring one's soul by the
tape of a world that looks on in amused contempt and pity."[43] Part of Killens's
point, I take it, is to challenge black writers to make different decisions about
the kinds of stories they chose to tell, about the themes or lives they privilege.
His comment also questions, at least implicitly, the social function of authorship
as Foucault discusses it (that is, those stories white publishers would publish,
what black authorship meant within larger political discussions, the standards
by which white critics would evaluate black texts). The notion of "black genius,"
which made one's work valid insofar as it participated in a larger unfolding
folk spirit and elided any discrepancy between race as ontology and as ethico-
political fidelity to historical experience, was a counter.[44]

Margaret Walker and Arna Bontemps joined Hayden and Tolson on a panel
entitled "Poetry from the Negro Renaissance until Today," which proved to
be the centerpiece of David Llorens's retelling of the First Black Writers Con-
ference. Hayden made the politics of expression, and black genius, an urgent
political question. Opposing black nationalist arguments, he declared those in
attendance should "quit saying we're black writers writing to black folks—it
has been given importance it should not have," labeling himself "a poet who
happens to be a Negro."[45] Hayden's locution and aspiration echo Gwendolyn
Brooks's foreword to Langston Hughes and Bontemps's 1964 anthology *New
Negro Poets: USA*: "Poets who happen also to be Negroes are twice tried. They
have to write poetry, and they have to remember that they are Negroes."[46] If
"they could solve the Negro question once and for all," they might turn to "the
composition of textured sonnets or buoyant villanelles about the transience of
a raindrop, or the gold-stuff of the sun."[47] Absent definite historical conditions,
writing is simply a way of relating to the world and literary institutions. The bur-
den of race as they understood it is that the conjunction "Negro poet" seemed
to disproportionately affect the available (allowable) range of topics, while
literature should be able to say anything. While Brooks, who would famously
profess black nationalist politics at the Second Black Writers Conference the
following year, seems to argue that the resolution of the Negro question is the
precondition of the poet's freedom, Hayden seemed to claim poetry in a roman-
tic sense, shaped by but more importantly shaping contemporary political con-
tradictions. He defined poetry as "the beauty of perception given form, . . . the

art of saying the impossible"; in concluding, he anticipated detractors (and assured them of his commitment to black culture), using the black vernacular to tell them that should they object to his position, "Baby, that's your problem, not mine."[48]

If Hayden worried about the narrow range of topics one might be committing oneself to in declaring oneself to be a black writer addressing a relatively stable black community, Tolson fully embraced a politics of expression, making the literary act itself a matter of racial—that is, historical—specificity. He asserted that "nobody writes in a vacuum or out of a vacuum" but rather under historically definite circumstances that tell "which way he went in society." Tolson further argued that the poet's "tridimensionality" (biology, sociology and psychology) shapes one's decision to become a poet and what one writes. A Negro poet is qualitatively different from other poets not in essence but because of the specificity of her or his experience. Taking issue with Hayden's casual use of "happens," whose meaning is related to "chance" or "fortune," Tolson ended with a flourish: "I'm a black poet, a Negro poet. I'm no accident, and I don't give a tinker's damn what you think."[49] Blackness, in other words, is not one contingency among others but also is not strictly a transhistorical "folk spirit." Whereas Hayden wanted to sidestep the problematic of representation that Du Bois wrote about by making it a matter of authorship, Tolson accepted it as constitutive of both writing and authorship. Neither, ultimately, located the blackness of writing in explicitly "black content"; respectively, Hayden and Tolson understood the blackness of writing to come from social position or objective experience, which are not exclusive terms.

In different terms, Tolson recapitulated and revised Du Bois's earlier arguments for the historical specificity of blackness, transforming them into a more direct ethical commandment not fully commensurate with the debates surrounding black literature that would follow.[50] Stuart Hall has famously argued that race is "the modality in which class is 'lived,' the medium through which class relations are experienced, the form in which it is appropriated and 'fought through,'" but Tolson sought to fix the center of race more definitely, defining in positive terms what in his moment was a negative.[51] It would be easy, but mistaken, to understand Tolson to have been making a narrow argument about political commitment or "identity politics" or to understand the debate in familiar universalist/particularist or authentic/inauthentic binaries. Tolson's position points to, but does not entirely resolve, the conflict between the black writer as singular and exemplary in his turn to race as a pseudo-ontological category that informs both what we think black writing *does* and what it *ought* to do. For both Tolson and Hayden, the authorial position "black poet" results from a refusal to decide between race and writing, which ultimately amounts to a choice for both. How does one change the valences of the burdens of black writing in a society where people presume to know in advance what one will say? What role can poetry play in changing the terms of racialization? In short, the question is not whether one can be a poet and not be black but whether one can be both black and a poet in a situation where race seems to frame what one will say in advance.

Among other things, the Tolson-Hayden debate reveals that the conflict is not merely intergenerational, an older generation disagreeing with a younger about the meaning of freedom, but also intragenerational. Where Tolson wanted the freedom to define race, Hayden claimed the freedom to define writing as separate from the meanings attached to being a Negro poet and to black poetry, that is, separate from black authorship. Hence Hayden's complaint that race as means of shaping literary content and address "has been given importance it should not have" refers to the ways black writers have positioned themselves and been positioned within the literary marketplace. Tolson insisted that racial experience left an indelible mark on composition, and, as Aldon Nielsen puts it, allowed no separation of "his identity as a poet from his social being as a black man in America."[52] Combining Hayden and Tolson's respective arguments, at the risk of flattening the difference between them, shows the way race is at once inside and outside of the text: textual, a site of conflict rather than a stable concept.

In the arguments that prefaced anthologies of the "new black poetry," black writers produced knowledge about "the black experience" or "the inner crisis of black reality" while being charged with transforming that reality with a revolutionary new vision.[53] Without resolving the debate, these writers made poetry an act of "saying the impossible," producing a statement intelligible only in retrospect. Read together, Hayden and Tolson define a more general issue surrounding black (experimental) writing and the moment of its emergence. Race is one means through which a textual surface seems to make legible some more fundamental meaning or claim, even as it has no meaning apart from the claims one makes for it. Attention to that surface itself—the techniques through which it "says the impossible" and brings into existence thinking obscured by dominant ideologies and ideologies of race—stresses complexity, the ways this writing does not make itself available to epigrammatic resistance or expression.[54] Every text addresses both its own moment and an unknown future readership. My attention to the typography, phonology, and other elements in literature's ensemble of signifying elements keeps the focus on the "literariness" of literature—the habituated norms of writing and reading that govern its production at a given time—as an address to that unknown, future anterior.

That is another way of understanding "saying the im*possible*," which I adapt as one slogan for experimental writing. The possible is a codification of the present and a calculation based on present knowledge that figures the future as a future present. To "say the *im*possible" is to produce a statement that interferes with the existing forms of thinking and knowing in a given moment. Experimental texts differ in and defer their own legibility, flaunting racial and literary conventions to produce sentences not yet heard before. Black experimental writing's dense textual surfaces and surplus of meanings disrupt a politics of expression, stressing the contingent, textual nature of race and the different simultaneous meanings it can have or not have. It inscribes itself in the margins of the possible, invoking a now at once out of reach and immanent in the present, producing and destabilizing its own contexts for meaning.

That destabilization itself, I argue, marks the ways black experimental writing breaks with the aesthetic and political regimes that separate speech from noise, addressing itself to an emergent community that, drawing again on Rancière, I understand in aesthetic terms: "Human beings are tied together by a certain sensory fabric, a certain distribution of the sensible, which defines their way of being together." The writer "weaves" this fabric to create "a form of common expression" through which the community can recognize itself as community, and through which meanings of the human can be contested and reimagined.[55] Forms of common expression codify a consensus and common sense that they then seem to express: all of those unconscious decisions that shape and predict our responses, including our rejection of some texts as too far "out." As a deconstruction of the possible, black experimental writing promotes dissensus with the calculable present, an aesthetic break that anticipates new forms of community. The political value of black experimental writing, therefore, does not lie in its advocacy or its themes but its commitment to the "aesthetic break" where consensus slips away and new thinking breaks through.[56] Consensus names a certain way of being together that can become unconscious, unthought, and simply procedural. The moment of dissensus is a moment of desubjection, of dedisciplining knowledge and promoting thinking as radical unlearning.[57]

I use the term "radical" to underscore the sense of consensus as a disciplinary grid that determines in advance the kinds of thoughts that are allowable and the kinds of responses acceptable and sensible at a given moment, while effacing its origin in order to appear inevitable, natural, permanent. The radical is a re-marked beginning of thought. The consensus of "the Negro Problem," or of "diversity" in our moment, is that for all the celebrations of "difference," that "celebration" justifies the tacit maintenance of racial boundaries and a hierarchical structure that encodes the normative "same" as white, heterosexual, male, and bourgeois. Thinking as radical unlearning refers to thinking at its limits, beyond the point where rote learning and pat understandings can tell one what to think, to thinking that goes out of its place, leaves its boundaries, and becomes undisciplined, open to the coming of the new.

CHAPTER SUMMARIES

The book consists of two sections and a brief postscript. The first part of the book, "World Enough for a Figure," a phrase I take from the poet Jay Wright, analyses the links between the graphic texture of writing and expression, considering three different insistently material poetics. The first chapter, "Broken Witness: Concrete Poetry and a Poetics of Unsaying" argues that N.H. Pritchard and M. NourbeSe Philip synthesize two roughly contemporaneous understandings of concreteness—involving idealized notions of words and black experience —to "unsay" commonsense notions and reopen horizons of thought. The second chapter, "Establishing Synchronisms: Sycorax Video Style and the Plural Instant," offers an account of Bajan poet and scholar Kamau Brathwaite's Sycorax Video Style, which treats language as a medium through which one can produce a temporal poetics that modulates the singular and plural, thereby establishing new synchronisms between the individual and the collective rooted in the incomplete processes of colonization and decolonization. The section's final chapter, "Between Now and Yet: Postlyric Poetry and the Moment of Expression," argues that the work of Claudia Rankine and Douglas Kearney marks the emergence of a "postlyric" poetics whose graphic images and allusions to mass culture draw attention to the dimensionless moment of expression in a period during which commodified black expression is celebrated even as black lives remain precarious.

The second section, "Above Where Sound Leaves Off," develops the book's interest in the intergeneric through music as explicit referent and as formal principle. In the fourth chapter, "Sing it In My Voice: Blues, Irony, and a Politics of Affirmative Difference," I argue that Harryette Mullen and Suzan-Lori Parks have developed an abstracted blues poetics rooted in a form of irony as a nondialectical conception of difference, affirming the groundlessness of meaning and form. Nathaniel Mackey's work occupies the final chapter, "Exploding Dimensions of Song: The Utopian Poetics of the Cut," which traces Mackey's play with serial poetics, grammar, and a musicality that underscores the open-endedness of texts. The book concludes with a short postscript that collects its arguments for black experimental writing under the sign of "playing out," returning to Du Bois's politicized account of beauty to make more explicit the book's overall argument that black experimental writing fundamentally *thinks* differently, reworking past techniques and understandings to new ends.

The authors considered in *Freedom Time* are necessarily diverse, representing a broad range of regions, approaches, and concerns, which I group together around conceptual and formal knots such as the political valences of silence, concreteness, language and print as media, reconfigurations of poetic expression and, most generally, the graphic texture of writing. By considering their diverse poetics I hope to encourage new pathways for theorizing the black aesthetics, plural, of the contemporary moment, an aesthetics informed by the faith writers have had for black writing as globally transformative. Rather than offering an account of literary or cultural history, I draw out the political and theoretical implications of experimental form, attending to the ways specific poetic practices—rhetorical and syntactical—work and rework grammars of reading, especially the tendency toward "racialized reading."

As will be clear, this book does not offer a new conception of time. Rather, it draws attention to the still unrealized visions of a liberated future of the past and our own moment. *Freedom Time* refers to social and artistic freedom, the right of literature to "say anything," and a vision of the world that is based on logics other than those of our time. "Freedom Time" is a question, an insistence, a plea, a command, a description of a time yet to come, and a reminder that the definition of "freedom" is not given or limited to present enunciations.[58] As the visiting card promises and asks for a return at some unspecified moment, "Freedom Time" is the hope and promise of that time yet to come.

part 1 world enough for a figure

one

Broken Witness
Concrete Poetry and a Poetics of Unsaying

Words are ancillary to content.   —N. H. Pritchard

The politics of black experimental writing results from intervals—between experience and meaning, between "sense" as sensation and "sense" as meaning—that under the prevailing norms of the ruling order ordinarily appear to be in strict concordance.[1] That concordance not only describes ideology, understood as a species of eternity (things have to be this way by various laws of necessity), but also the disciplinary logic of common sense that governs the meanings assigned to experience. Making those intervals sensible *temporalizes*—puts in time—those prefiguring concepts and shortcuts to meaning, reanimating the need for predisciplinary thinking insofar as temporalization makes the disciplinary processes of common sense apparent *as* process rather than figuring them as the encoded truth of phenomena. This first section, interrogating a variety of experimental graphic and spatial poetics, considers the work of another kind of interval, the spatial arrangement of letters and other graphic signs, as a means by which to animate the first kind.

Written poetry depends on both spatial and temporal arrangements of its elements—linguistic and extralinguistic characters, syntax, space—to achieve its literary effects. The columnar regularity of a sonnet's fourteen lines, for example, provides a surplus pleasure and is one of the form's visual markers. Spatial arrangements can take on a greater, semiautonomous function, becoming a supplemental form of content. We might think here of such shape poems as George Herbert's "Easter Wings" or John Hollander's "Swan and Shadow." The effect of shape poems is most often one of recognition, joining the poetic "image" to its pictorial counterpart. Following W. J. T. Mitchell, one might say that the effect depends on spatial form "as a quality of things" and as "an explanatory model." Its function is both "literal" and "metaphoric," and if "spatial form is the perceptual basis for our notion of time," then visual poetics disrupts the accord between sense and sense, multiplying pathways of meaning.[2] I argue in this chapter that unorthodox spatial forms read with and against themes can spur new conceptions of time and relationality, of aesthetic experience generally, and of specific historical understandings and senses of time.

This chapter is specifically concerned with concretism, which has played an important role in the development of experimental writing in the twentieth century. The mid-twentieth century avant-garde poetic movement linked spatial arrangement as a semiautonomous signifying element related to an underlying, "authentic" truth about the capacities of language and signification. For those writers, making shape a signifying element challenged rationalist understandings that linked the poetic act, as expression, to a self-sufficient, self-transparent subject or language. For midcentury black thinkers and writers, "concrete" also referred to the transcendent "content" of black genius: the "authentic" truth of language "in itself" also related to its performative power to shape history and self-perception, avowing and expressing the ethos of an underlying racial culture. This chapter, focusing on N. H. Pritchard's neglected experimental writing, Terrance Hayes's provocative "Sonnet," and M. NourbeSe Philip's long poem *Zong!*, understands each writer to leverage typographical innovations associated with the international poetry movement against the paradigms of black concreteness assumed by black nationalism and multiculturalism alike. The result is an alternative concrete poetry that puts "content" in question.

All three poets practice a form of *broken witness*: not "giving voice" or speaking on behalf of another or the self but voicing the silence, what conventional language does not allow, that makes such witness impossible.[3] Their experiments with concretism conflate two senses of concreteness I've outlined to produce a poetics of unsaying, a poetics that temporalizes concrete techniques in order to transform and extend the expressive possibilities of black writing through a process that at once introduces and rewrites familiar tropes. For the texts considered in this chapter, the text's effects depend on an arrangement of letters and space that cannot be reduced to mimesis or thematic illustration. The orphaned syllables adrift across the surface of *Zong!*'s pages, which draws its words from the lone surviving court record documenting an instance of mass murder during the Middle Passage, may recall bodies drowning at sea and the drift of histories that have refused to claim their dead, but that resemblance on its own allows readers the false comfort of a history and historiography the poem deconstructs. Similar to Pritchard's textual arrangement, Philip's discontinuous lines and fragmented words explode the dimensions of the page and the history that it draws on through a position of broken witness. In different ways, each of the poets here rely on the intertwined nature of space and time in literature such that combining and recombining sequences of letters and words also combines and recombines sequences of time. Reconfiguring spatial arrangements transforms the project from one of expression into one of deconstructing the conventions and authenticating norms governing that govern the relation of personal experience or testimony. Those norms, prevalent in the proliferation of first-person accounts of everyday life and formal legal situations alike, can tend to obscure the past and ultimately make it difficult to think our present as historical. Rearranging the elements of poetic language—emphasizing even the spatial arrangements of letters within words—makes visible, as it were, other ways of arranging texts, knowledge, history, bodies, and the social order.

Rejecting or deferring the phenomenological presuppositions of both notions of "concrete," while drawing on each, these texts emphasize the "hauntological": something present but not apparent in the presence of the printed word or performance that marks the "untimeliness of the present." The hauntological is a figure for the unfinished event, for conceptualizing—bearing witness to—the coincidence of multiple presents in one present and forms of futurity and ancestrality for which we lack an adequate name.[4] It keeps a place for the anticipated return of what seems not to belong and maintains an obligation to that specter. Rather than stressing more adequate representations of the ancestors, the politics of broken witness derive from the glimpse of something on which each of these concepts rest, a glimpse of alternative arrangements of lives and literature not quite but nearly free.

CONCRETE POETRY: FOR INSTANCE, A SONNET

The term "concrete poetry" came into wide circulation in the 1950s, in conjunction with an international group of poets including Bolivian-born Eugen Gomringer, the Brazilians Augusto and Haroldo de Campos, and their influential Noigrandes group. Augusto de Campos asserted that concrete poetry "begins by assuming total responsibility before language," and in treating historical idioms and words as something other than vehicles of communication, the concrete poet "goes directly to their center, in order to live and vivify their facticity."[5] Facticity, a phenomenological concept associated with Martin Heidegger, marks the relationship concrete poets imagined between poetry and language and positions the movement for some critics as an antecedent for Language poetry. Critical analyses of concrete poetry tend either emphasize the poem's presence or a more directly politicized notion of the "facticity of language" and claim that the poem "dissolve[s] the very structure of perception in order to make room" for some form of expression less bound up, for example, with the imperatives of consumerism.[6]

Something akin to facticity bears on contemporaneous phenomenological notions of "concreteness" important to subsequent critical accounts of the relationship between black writing and black life. To think the facticity of black life has tended to require a hermeneutic of the inmost being of blackness "as such" that recovers its authentic destiny apart from extant political and historical regimes; the facticity of words requires an analogous hermeneutic aimed at understanding words "as such," abstracted from ordinary use. Black literature, among Black Arts theorists and other black nationalists, was concrete to the extent that it provided a window onto racialized subject positions or engaged in a project, as Haki R. Madhubuti puts it, of "defin[ing] & legitimiz[ing] Black people's reality."[7] Madhubuti's notion of expression requires neither the sovereign, self-identical subject that hears and understands itself, nor the modernist autonomous artwork. Instead, it grounds itself in a model of black life, a totality considered from the standpoint of the authentic destiny from which slavery and imperialism has detoured it. A hermeneutic grounded in the facticity of blackness can find in black expressive culture the truth of that authentic being apart from the distortions of history. As Amiri Baraka had remarked in 1967, black artistry "is no description. It *is* the culture."[8] Alluding to Baraka's "Black Art," Stephen E. Henderson would make the most direct statement, praising black poets' "miraculous discovery that Black people are poems."[9]

Both the Noigrandes group and Black Arts theorists echo Heidegger's distinction between "facticity" and "factualness," which he ultimately related to his notion of "authenticity."[10] For Heidegger, "facticity" does not refer to concrete "factualness"—the relationships between facts in authenticating regimes of knowledge—but to the being-in-the-world of that Being that becomes the subject of facts. Just as the facticity of black life requires a hermeneutic of the authentic destiny and inmost being of blackness, the facticity of words requires an analogous authentic knowledge of words "as such," abstracted from use. Heidegger distinguishes between phenomenal appearance—factuality—and the "factuality of the fact of Da-sein."[11] To refer to the "facticity" of the word is to refer to a truth of the word that subtends its phenomenal appearance in sight and sound. Thus, for concretists like de Campos, the poem is always an anticipatory encounter with the word and thus, potentially, a new experience of the world. Likewise, for Black Arts theorists the poem relies on the transcendental facticity of words to achieve its reconstructive work: the encounter with the poem reactivates and participates in the inner lives of words and those who use them.

However, the phenomenality of words—their sublime visual and phonic physicality—suspends the poem between the textural and the textual, between worldliness and wordliness. Ineluctably, poetry temporalizes words: suspends them between the retention of past association and anticipation (what Edmund Husserl called the "protension" of new associations). As an expansion of the notion of referentiality so as to link every aspect of signification to racially specific lived experience, concreteness in this sense refers to the assumption that all black writing is at once exemplary and singular, and rooted in "concrete" (i.e., immediate) rather than abstract concerns. It requires seeing blackness as somehow self-defining and necessary rather than contingent, natural rather than textual.

As a "material poetics," R. P. Draper observes, concrete poetry "intensifies our awareness of the relation between a word and its literal components and recovers for us something of the child's experience of the uncertainty and unpredictableness of letters."[12] Rosemarie Waldrop further argues that concretism is "first of all a revolt against the transparency of the word."[13] These and other accounts of concrete poetry share a tacit assumption that elevating the shape (and sound) of the word and the poem to the level of semantic content *temporalizes* words, suspending them between the retention of past associations and the "protension" of new ones. While the concretists' ambivalence toward language and in a different way Black Arts theorists' similar misgivings derive from slightly different historical bases, they come together in this desire to reactivate language—and the communities it implies—so as to imagine oneself writing as if from the very sources of language and culture. Pritchard and Philip's poetics work between both senses of concreteness and its emphasis on creating new figures to further confound the regime of common sense and thereby promote new ways of thinking and, ultimately, new configurations of community, even as their work also evades the idea of an uncontaminated origin. Hayes's poem, which I discuss shortly, poses slightly different, illuminating problems.

The international concrete poetry movement's version of concretism represents a "revolt against the transparency of the word," and Black Arts theorists saw in black facticity an analogous revolt against the ideological transparency of black experience—that is, the idealized thinking of words or racialized experience having some "as such" or "in itself." Pritchard's and Philip's concrete poetics mark an anticipatory encounter with words as always already unstable because always already embedded within processes of power. In the place of an idealized moment when the sensation of letters has been freed from socially mediated sense, their poetics of unsaying temporalizes language, making significant the interval between sensation and meaning, which introduces a detour in the formation of concepts or schema. Their temporalizing poetics encodes the supposed rift between facticity and factuality as a moment in a larger project such that at the point of its discovering an origin of language, that origin recedes, preventing the enclosure of concepts. The facticity of language exists only as an abstraction, a hermeneutic rooted in a belief in some originary wholeness of the Word. In contrast, the poem becomes an exemplary signification that allows us to interrogate at one level the semantic relations drawn on and anticipated and at another level to ask fundamental questions about the founding of a regime of sense making, facts, and poetry.[14]

Concrete poetry thus becomes a poetics of reconfiguring the relationship of the facticity of language to its historicity (or "factuality") in order to expand the possibilities of thinking blackness and writing poetry. For Pritchard, "words are ancillary to content"; that is, words (or something in the words) are vehicles to some more fundamental but ambiguous and ephemeral meaning related to the opacity of language and experience. In *Zong!*, Philip writes about a slave massacre whose story "cannot be told" and "must be told," told and untold. *Zong!* is in part a series of meditations on the nature of historical facts. What is the efficacy of reporting facts in a language and truth regime that delineates and predetermines any possible resonance of "facts" about slavery? How does one find and make resonant the immensity of the Middle Passage beneath and between the lines of a legal language that conjured away murder without falling back on the preemptive knowledge of what we call, too quickly, the "horrors of slavery"? To explore the "facticity" of a discourse that shapes the factual validity of language—to explore a truth that does not emerge from the historical record within which this event is hardly represented—is to raise questions about being in history and the ways stories and history always haunt what seems like language "as such."

Through their different approaches to concrete poetry, both Pritchard and Philip experiment with spatial arrangements to forge practices of expression for which there is no model. While Pritchard's poetry, as critics have noted, seems more paradigmatically concrete in the ontological sense, both his and Philip's work confront the aesthetic, epistemological, and ontological senses of concreteness I have outlined. Both invite readers to witness the "facticity" of sense making, along with the narrative and epistemological conventions that obscure the history of slavery. Reading them together makes legible the epistemological claims of Pritchard's work and the ontological claims of Philip's that we might otherwise miss. Considering the ways Pritchard's work unsettles assumptions about the nature of poetic expression and experience, we can see that *Zong!* both provides and refuses to bear witness to a massacre of slaves at sea, ultimately calling into question the nature of such poetic witness and of historical fact. Although Hayes also occasionally uses concretist concepts and techniques, his poems more frequently accent the unbearable weight of "content" in Philip's *Zong!* rather than Pritchard's ambiguous "content." All three highlight a central claim of this book: experimentation is not coterminous with innovation that is tied to the protocols of individual or group genius but often entails repurposing, reinterpreting, and redefining older techniques, themselves made legible through multiple traditions. Stripping concreteness of an epistemological and moral content by playing off two different traditions dialectically interrupts the disciplinary reading norms associated with each. Terrance Hayes's "Sonnet" is a more ambiguous instance of concrete poetry in both senses of the term that I have discussed so far. Like most concrete poetry, it cancels its own referentiality, yielding a poetics of unsaying and incomplete resignification. His "impure" concrete poem discredits the idea of the transparency of form and racial signifiers. "Sonnet" occupies a space of betweenness related to Pritchard and Philip's work, belonging as it does to multiple, seemingly autonomous traditions while exemplifying the dual sense of concreteness I have been outlining. That betweenness, speaking and unspeaking its own conditions of legibility, directly relates to my overall analysis of a poetics of unsaying. "Unsaying" underscores that the term "concrete" does not describe a unified or internally consistent practice but an ethos that sees in language and literary conventions something fatally trapped in ideological "common sense," in need of revision.

The sonnet form is one of the most technically demanding fixed forms, is perhaps most associated with the expression of specific ideas, and it is also among the most immediately recognized poetic forms. Usually lyric in mode of address, sonnets move us through a defined set of affective and intellectual concerns, usually resolved after the volta, or turn. Hayes's "Sonnet" has fourteen lines and repeats the ten-syllable, alternate-stressed line "We sliced the watermelon into smiles" fourteen times, in three quatrains and a couplet with three line breaks:

We sliced the watermelon into smiles.
We sliced the watermelon into smiles.
We sliced the watermelon into smiles.
We sliced the watermelon into smiles.

We sliced the watermelon into smiles.
We sliced the watermelon into smiles.
We sliced the watermelon into smiles.
We sliced the watermelon into smiles.

We sliced the watermelon into smiles.
We sliced the watermelon into smiles.
We sliced the watermelon into smiles.
We sliced the watermelon into smiles.

We sliced the watermelon into smiles.
We sliced the watermelon into smiles.[15]

The poem at once fulfills and violates the conventions of the sonnet. Its geo-metric regularity, typically a surplus pleasure, is central to the poem's effect: read aloud, its use of space, especially those stanza breaks, would be difficult to reproduce. The stanza breaks break the solid surface of the text, as if mimicking the act of slicing, though not into smiles. For some, this poem will recall a con-tinuum of American avant-garde poetry traceable to, say, Ron Padgett's proto-Language "half sonnet" "Nothing in That Drawer" (each of its fourteen lines, repeating the title, is five-syllables long) or to Gertrude Stein's earlier play with repetition. Seeing it in this lineage, we could emphasize the relative banality of the action, the grammatical, prosodic, and geometric regularity of the lines, and its refusal to resolve the narrative and emotional tension of the event. Similar to Padgett's poem, Hayes's "Sonnet" is opaque: the occasion of the poem suggests a "deeper" meaning, but its inscrutability, which monumentalizes an appar-ently banal moment, refuses to lend any further significance. Thus, "Sonnet" seems to be a playful statement on lyricization, the process by which almost all poems have come to be read in terms of the lyric genre, figured as the expression of a historically situated subject's "mind alone with itself."[16] The poem reveals the facticity of the sonnet form and the habits of reading associated with it. Al-ternatively, readers may read this as somehow earnest, though strange, tribute to a tradition of African American formal verse that includes Claude McKay's "The Harlem Dancer" and Countee Cullen's "Yet Do I Marvel," a reminder of the ways African American writers have repeatedly negotiated the tropes of the minstrel stage. In either case, a formal, intertextual precedent makes the experimental work legible.

Reading it in terms of both concrete and traditional metered poetry would put emphasis on "watermelon," the word that most invokes race in the U.S. context. Prosodically awkward, situated in the middle of the line, and, like the rest of the words in the poem, without hard consonants, the word seems to accumulate significance through repetition. Further, seeing it as homage to past writers (and commentary on the present), one could consider the poem a sharp critique of U.S. "racial formation," "the sociohistorical process by which racial categories are created, inhabited, transformed, and destroyed," and the relationship of aesthetic excellence and servitude: we sliced but did not eat the fruit.[17] "Watermelon" is a hinge between levels of the poem and forms of concreteness insofar as the pluralized meanings emphasized through repetition cancel the referentiality of its language, thereby making appearance and meaning of words almost simultaneous.[18] "Watermelon," a set of letters and sounds arranged in a vertical column, at once condenses and disseminates the specificities of African American culture and common experience (including that of racist misrepresentation).

The poem only ironically fulfills our understanding of the lyric as the expression of an individual mind or of the sonnet as, to cite Dante Gabriel Rossetti's famous definition, a "moment's monument."[19] Hayes's "Sonnet" meets the requirements of the sonnet form so exactly—if perversely—that the choice of form appears to be arbitrary, a commentary on the form as an inherited set of procedures. Reading the poem as defining and legitimizing black experience would account for the near rhyme that connects "sliced" and "smiles," which can be seen as an index of concrete experience, invoking the threat behind the smile and linking the threats of violence to the legacy of minstrelsy that governs some aspects of black public life. Understanding it strictly in terms of formal concreteness, where spatial composition is indispensible to the poem's effect and the poem's effects are not only "created through time and sound" as with traditional sonnets but also "through space and the seen image" reads the content as essentially void.[20] While it discredits the apparent transparency of literary formal traditions, it also discredits the apparent transparency of racial signifiers.[21] "Watermelon" both is and is not a token of blackness, the smile both is and is not redolent of the minstrel stage, the poem is and is not an example of the sonnet, and "Sonnet" is and is not a concrete poem. Hayes's poem suggests the difficulties of desublimating concept-metaphors like watermelon if only because of the ways other networks of pleasure and other configurations of the social may be active alongside what appears to be the dominant associations.

If we read it as simultaneously concrete in both senses I have discussed—legitimating and expressing the fundamental truth of black life and "revivifying the facticity of words"—then we get a sense of its play with something apparent but not present. Race is here a way of reading—a textual concern indexing disjuncture between the "strange meaning" of blackness and any black person, the former having come to precede the latter. The case for Hayes's poem as a concrete poem would begin by noting that were it not for the title, we might read the blank spaces as erased or canceled lines. Moreover, it lacks the "I" or focalizing consciousness typical of the sonnet form. That absent "I," however, becomes a kind of pun if we reconsider the proximity of "smile" and "simile" as purloining a missing "i." The slice of watermelon is, after all, *like* a smile. The fourteen lines of the poem describe a single visual simile. The "I" that one might expect in a sonnet is thus instead that missing "i" of the simile between sliced fruit and facial expression. The missing "i" is not the speaking "I" but registers as the effaced sign of the poet's presence. It produces a kind of void where a transcendent meaning would ordinarily be, confronting us instead with the processes by which we endow acts and objects with meaning. In the racialized context of the United States watermelon serves as a racial ideologeme: the smallest intelligible unit of discourse at the intersection of blackness as a constative and a transaction of difference—a performative.[22] A narrative in miniature, the poem marks the problem of making difference disappear into brute "appearance" while barring any "facticity" or "in itself-ness" of blackness. The poem's watermelon is one site, invested with desire, where people live their relation to relations of racial difference.

The poetic text understood in these two senses of the concrete exceeds the imperatives of literature to convey "voice" in both the lyric and black expressive senses, exploiting the surface of the poem as a space of inscription to deconstruct a binary between the graphic mark and what the words "really mean." The concrete is one means of finding a politics of literature elsewhere, defined in other than expressive terms. Opening the "closed circuit of the sign," concrete poetry requires that the reader feel her responsibility for the labor of producing meaning without falling back on the artifactuality or evidentiary properties of the lyric or black genius.[23] Though notions of "voice" and "silence" are overdetermined, I have nonetheless risked using those metaphors to get at the interplay between what we typically think of as voice and what we typically think of as silence, categories that concrete poetry's seeming rejection of lyric categories such as subjectivity and recollection extends and challenges. In their place, one finds in the works of these black experimental writers a poetics of broken witness, of witness without the witness, and of unsaying that, in drawing attention to the "facticity" of words, suggests the possibilities of unsaying—speaking of the world and history without repeating the already said. Witness does not transparently relay information but produces knowledge about the event according to existing codes of acceptability, narrative convention, and legal permissibility. Broken witness produces disallowed knowledge of an event that has been electively forgotten and that can only be recalled through codes that erase it again. "Sonnet" evacuates, but does not eliminate, the position of the speaker, leaving the empty site of locution without inviting readers to imagine themselves either as audience or speaker, who cannot be sure they belong to this particular "we." Neither participants nor addressees, readers *witness* the poem and their own processes of making sense of the poem, which demands that we endeavor not to read strictly at the level of the referent. Witness from an evacuated, but persistent, site of enunciation even more forcefully informs N. H. Pritchard's work, which can seem like a form of ghostwriting: writing written for another, or writing that points to the effaced speaking subject.

SPACING AS ERASURE AND REVISION: N. H. PRITCHARD'S UNSAYING AS GHOSTWRITING

While Hayes's "Sonnet" leaves the surface of the poem intact, N. H. Pritchard's concretism more radically challenges our conceptions of what a poem is and how it means. Pritchard, associated with the Umbra Workshop, issued two collections of poetry with prominent presses—*The Matrix* in 1970 with Doubleday and *EECCHHOOEESS* with New York University Press in 1971—and then effectively vanished. His absence from critical accounts of black experimental writing of the 1960s and 1970s is frankly puzzling, and the difficulty of his work may discourage recovery efforts. I understand Pritchard's ambiguous epigraph (from *The Matrix*) that "words are ancillary to content" to refer to the creation of poetry as a visual field in which words do not determine the effect of the poem. In his work, the spacing of letters always threatens to cancel or unsay any semantic content. Neither silence nor inarticulacy, unsaying pushes the text to the point of its unintelligibility, alerting us anew to the mechanisms by which writing ordinarily conveys meaning. I read N. H. Pritchard's concretism as a form of writing that "ghosts" meaning: analogous to the "ghosted" notes in a jazz idiom, his spatial poetics implies additional meanings that remain elusive. The critical tendency to cite his disappearance is in part an effect of a poetics that thoroughly effaces authorship and promises an ancestrality yet to materialize. I would, therefore, describe his poetics as an abstraction of earlier traditions, with the caveat that his work also seems attentive to the mechanisms through which those traditions reproduce themselves, the means through which they are handed down, the temporalizing acts of inscription that subtend them.

The suggestive opacity of Pritchard's work, which helps to engender the sense of something just beyond articulation, is key to its effects. I use the word "ghostwriting" also to capture that sense of the sensual nature of the printed word decoupled from its meaning and granted an unassimilable autonomy. Anticipating my discussion of Philip, which similarly revolves around notions of haunting, I argue that Pritchard performs a spectralizing inscription, drawing on fragments and shards of language that can appear to us as if from the past as a harbinger of a future. His poetry pushes toward an almost "purely" visual poetry in which the presence of words seems almost accidental. Kevin Young, in an assessment of Pritchard's work, suggests that Pritchard's writing may have been "too abstract for a largely white avant-garde trying to simplify and internationalize" poetry "by making graphic" (the assumption being that graphic poetry could be a poetry without a "native tongue") and too "abstract, even highfalutin," to satisfy Black Arts era "vernacular and political aims."[24] In different terms, Pritchard's race may have been too concrete for the international avant-garde that developed around concrete poetry, and his version of concrete poetry represents a path mostly un followed by other black writers.

His abstraction derives from a teasingly specific, antitranscendental use of language that presents the text as depthless surface. It seems to withhold the information or frame necessary to make sense of it. A good example is "FROG," in *EECCHHOOEESS*, which repeats first the preposition "as" and then the phrase "as a" in a vertical column on successive pages, using the phrase as a stem for invention and variation (e.g., "as bowers hour in the sun," "as a hoo," "as a hoo hooz"). Other poems in that collection experiment with typography or utilize unconventional spacing in ways that defy reading, but none are as thoroughgoing in their investments in "wordliness" as "junt":

mool oio clish brodge
cence anis oio
mek mekisto plawe[25]

Neither Hayes's nor Philip's poetry create a "visual and aural syntax by a carefully calculated placement of their verbal elements in the space of the page" as effectively as the austere "junt" does.[26]

This poem typifies Pritchard's poetics insofar as it frustrates habituated reading habits, hinting at a transcendent, but ultimately obscure "content." Its materiality is "ironic" insofar as it exceeds the signifying situation that would animate it: in playing on the desire to produce meaning out of orthographic and phonetic components that ought to be words but stubbornly persist as "pure" sound, it risks decomposing into "mere" material, noise rather than intelligible utterance. The word "junt," (which may be a QWERTY keyboard transposition of "love," although none of the other "words" work that way) turns out to be a little-used English word meaning "trick," "cheat," or an arbitrarily large, irregular quantity of something along the lines of the more contemporary "hunk" (*OED*). The sense that the poem is a play of outmoded vocabulary continues with what is apparently the first word, "mool," which refers to "the soil used to fill a grave" as a noun and "to crumble" as a transitive verb. One could, therefore, mool a junt of bread, say, especially into a bowl to soak it in a liquid. This game of historical reconstitution does not govern the whole poem: "oio," like many of the other combinations, has phonetic value without semantic content. That there are words at all seems accidental to the visual field the poem creates, but one cannot ignore the coincidence of apparently arbitrary groupings of letters and historical words. Readers inclined to pursue the kind of philological game I have suggested may find instead a poem that mocks the search for origins or even common language. At the limit, Pritchard's self-undermining poems ask us whether poetry needs words at all.[27]

Citing Pritchard's poetics as a neglected stylistic forerunner to Language poetry, Aldon Nielsen praises his "ironic materiality," which undoes the critic's "usually unacknowledged reliance upon these mimetic fictions" of black genius that link the poem to a politics of expression and a putatively "unmediated experience of black, nonverbal realities."[28] While Lorenzo Thomas praises Pritchard for investigating "the African underpinnings of 'Black English,'" arguing that his early experiments "lead to a 'transrealism' that resembles concrete poetry," whose "combination of sounds approximated vocal styles and tones of African languages," a poem like "junt" makes clear the contingency of mimeticism.[29] Instead of a logic of origin, we get a graphic "decomposition" of transparency and transcendence, an interrogation of the limits of sense making, a ghostwriting that deconstructs the vernacular into a turning of language whose origins are irretrievable.

If Pritchard's work does uncover and deploy African retentions, it does so without a key, making his obscure signifying practice essentially self-canceling. That sense of unsolvable enigma and antitranscendence is central to Pritchard's poetics of unsaying, through which he refigures the possibilities of poetry as an expressive act. Poems like "junt," which rely on the spatiality of the page to undermine any more primary content, make up the bulk of his two collections. While these poems do not have *definite* content, they nonetheless insist on themselves as poems and impress on readers the need for new protocols of reading and new tasks for poetry apart from expression. Fittingly, one such poem, from his second collection, *The Matrix*, is called "The Voice":

s talk s t oo in t rude

up on t his d une

s till ness b rush e s the sea

c alm t oo s oo n g r e w

c alm ab out the s and

a few gu ll s drew in t heir w in g s

a h us h

be s ide t hem

t he r us h

l in g e r in g

fr om the v o ice

of a dr op f all in g[30]

"The Voice" raises questions about the privileging of that oral aspect. Presented more conventionally, this reads, "stalks too intrude | upon this dune | stillness brushes the sea | calm too soon grew | calm about the sand | a few gulls drew in their wings | a hush | beside them | the rush | lingering | from the voice | of a drop falling."[31] Presented in this way, the poem is relatively straightforward, seeming to represent a lyric recollection of a quiet moment at a beach, contrasting the vertical "intrusion" of stalks with the largely horizontal image of the sea and the beach. Note the several figures of quiet as noun and verb—stillness brushes the sea, a hush, a drop falling. The "voice of a drop falling" is a voice on its way out of being, making the poem a chronicle of its own undoing. Owing to the lack of punctuation, enjambment creates puzzles: does "stillness" brush the sea until it is calm? Does "calm too soon grew" mean "calm also soon grew" or "calm too prematurely grew calm"? Are there two senses of "calm" at play? Knowing that Pritchard is African American (a photo of his face serves as the book's cover image), the sea imagery takes on the added freight of the legacies of slavery, of bodies buried at sea. Finally, though these preliminary postulations are far from exhaustive, treating this work as lyric, one could try to reconstruct the dramatic situation, emphasizing the presumed overlap between the poem's speaker and the biographical writer that such lyric invites. Then we would want to know whether this poem is commemorative, whether it refers to a particular stretch of beach, and so on, in order to create a richer backdrop against which to understand the poem's affective investments. It highlights the interval between experience and meaning, presenting us with that suspended moment, in progress.

Its graphic presentation makes it a commentary on the forms of mediation that inform black realities, verbal and nonverbal. The presentation reveals the way the word "rush" sits in "brush," or "till" in "stillness," endowing "till," read as a colloquial form of "until," with the tension of anticipation (read as a verb, there's a sense of reaping what one has sown). The spacing draws out the proximity of "soon grew" and "song." The "voice of a drop falling" has something to do with the physicality—the weight and wait—of the "voice" in Pritchard's poetics, the sense of the page as a space not taken lightly, a metaphorical "silence" not lightly broken. The blanks of the page seem to be as much an object of composition as the words. As with "junt," the experience of this poem is we have too much or too little detail to make sense of it. There is just that drop falling—a mise-en-abyme or descent that continues seeking some "deeper meaning" "behind" the written work but continually encounters instead more inscription. Neither the voice nor the authentic being of language or letters quite materializes; we witness this failure. Witness, then, can refer to that sense of something happening in which one cannot intervene, of something that has already happened to which one can only testify after the fact. "The Voice" leaves only the sense of a voice cast out that disrupts or retraces the calm.

If my language verges on the religious, this is because I have in mind W. F. Lucas's book jacket blurb, which claims there is something "pristine" about Pritchard's sensibility, Lucas having elsewhere claimed Pritchard's poems "decompose the reader by sight and sound."[32] The decomposition at the level of the word amounts to an extreme form of parataxis and recombination that serves as an allegory for the poems' larger effects. At a glance, one senses that something fundamental has broken down that threatens the integrity of the specialized reading competency with which we would attempt to read the work. Rather than black expression, we witness language denuded as an ensemble of social relations that, suddenly, seem negotiable. Insofar as the kind of reading and thinking Pritchard's poetry requires would not qualify us for most of the jobs that "WE NEED PEOPLE," the poem that follows "junt," pretends to advertise, it has a utopian dimension, enacted, in Fredric Jameson's words, through its "*analogon* for nonalienated labor and for the Utopian experience of a radically

different, alternate society."[33] Such a fantasy of unalienated labor, key to under-
standings of Language poetry and the French New Novel, seems less viable at
a moment when our media culture easily represents and appropriates even the
most radical style as entertainment, which is indexed by the increasing idiom-
atic usage of "random" to describe a proliferation of avant-garde techniques of
epistemological dislocation in mass culture.[34] However, I would stress the latter
part of Jameson's account: Pritchard's poetics offers the conditioned thought
of an unconditioned future. Understanding oneself to be the friend to whom
the poems could be passed on requires taking seriously a de- and redisciplining
of the act of reading where what is utopian, or proto-utopian, is the newly vis-
ible frames that separate kinds of reading.

As a mode of broken witness, Pritchard's poetics of unsaying refers to the re-
vised and evaded link between poetry as expression and the ideas of personal
testimony or witness by turning poetry to nonprescribed ends. "Witness" names
both an externalization of perception and openness before and responsibility to
others. The act of witnessing is conventionally rooted in and routed through the
consensual institutions of governing where relationships between subjects are
relatively fixed and stable; it turns on the need for truth and the possibility (and
conventions) of fiction, that is, false accounts. Witnessing in this sense also
posits information about an event, in this case the event of an aesthetic break:
Pritchard's enigmatic surface of words encodes an alternative arrangement of
the relationship between aesthetic experience in general and its meaning.[35] One
function of his graphic displacement is to draw out unseen relationships between
words, forging a novel relationship between the sound and sight of words.

But this does not fully account for the hesitation the technique creates re-
garding the beginnings and ends of words or for the purpose of the demand that
readers reconstitute—recompose—words. To cite an example from "VIA,"

f   oru   msofru   inedwi   ll[36]

can easily be decoded as "forums of ruined will," but one might need several
readings to feel confident one has read correctly. Pritchard's redistribution of
space and spacing is part of his project to elide the distinction between oral or
written words and "content." The form of the letter and use of the page become
part of the content, as with his treatment of the word "echoing":

ing   echo   ing
    echo

                                              echo[37]

This mock mimesis is particularly playful, with the parts of the words occurring across a whole page, upsetting the relationship between event and repetition, as in an echo chamber. But this mimeticism (the combination of "echo" and "ing" repeating across an entire page before yielding to the word "still" repeated in reverse across two pages with no spaces between words) does not seem to capture the full effect, even if it is difficult to name that other "content."

The effort of constructing conventional meaning or content can seem punitive in Pritchard's work, and the techniques of close reading seem unavailable to the extent that close reading assumes a stability of subject. For example, ".d.u.s.t." begins with the line ".m.a.w..o.f..w..a.n.i.n.g..w.r.u.n.g..t.h.e.i.r..l.i.k.e. ." The periods mostly function to space letters from each other, with two periods marking a boundary between words, and each line beginning and ending with a single period. The possessive pronoun "their" is missing an object. The poem ends ".t.a.t.t.e.r.e.d..a.n.d..s.t.i.t.c.h.e.d..b.o.n.e.s. . | .s.p.r.i.n.k.l.e.d..b.e.c.a.u.s.e. . . ." again denying the final referent—sprinkled because *what*? Even in *The Matrix*'s "N OCTUR N," whose "b odies spra wling in gu tt er's d ank," evokes both alcoholism and the Middle Passage (we later find "shat tere d | c arcass | of ac as que o nc e d run k"), the referent is unavailable. If concrete poetry generally works by canceling referentiality, Pritchard's unsaying begins from solid ground that it decomposes. Pritchard uses concrete poetry's generic cancellation of referentiality as a kind of lever on political notions of black concreteness and black genius, unsaying the very conditions that would authorize speech.

Pritchard's "ironic materiality," often suspending referentiality, continually defers the possibility of a final, transcendent referent, defers the possibility of an ultimate meaning, especially one that would tell us something about the black experience, unless we read the work as allegorical of the attempt to construct meaning in a new tongue. The cultural knowledge and critical consciousness that ought to provide a key instead come up short, often leaving us just at the threshold of meaning. The act of searching for meaning, the confrontation with all that "we" are already too late to recover, remains. The spatial distribution of letters and series of ambiguous correspondences marks an instance of what I have referred to as a poetics of unsaying. Words such as "though," "hush," "dusk," "must," "shall," "will," "such," spatiotemporal words like "as" and "still," and warnings that "[t]here are only pebbles | NOW | NOW | NO | w | soft | Beneath | our feet" recur throughout *EECCHHOOEESS* and *The Matrix*.[38] They limn the place of desire in assertions like Madhubuti's about the concrete nature of black expression—the desire for there to be a "we."

If concrete poetry unites the temporal and spatial axes of poetry to vivify the facticity of words—the "wordliness" of words as at once transcendental and phenomenal—Pritchard's contribution to the form is his emphasis on temporalization—the recollection of past uses and the protension of future associations. His contribution to black experimental writing is to advance an oral/aural poetics that does not depend on or presuppose a concept of voice as the singular/exemplary authorizing instance of black expression or black genius. The many refused, canceled, or indeterminate references delineate a poetics of unsaying. This poetics denaturalizes the social world and disciplines of reading and interpretation that set the meaning and direction of black writing in advance. Readers become aware of language and poetry as historical, instruments of discipline and objects of desire. We see, finally, a revivification of the dead letter of black writing without subordinating the graphic mark to oral performance, and typography as a mean to undermine or deconstruct the very notion of a transcendent, self-revealing logos.

Flirting with the ever-vanishing horizon of meaning, Pritchard's poetics make us bear witness to our efforts at sense making as a protopolitical act. His work makes us aware of the regime of representation that preemptively assigns meanings and marks the iterable conditions under which black writing is legible and authorized. The "break" then is with the pattern of reference, which is accompanied by the construction of new, incomplete patterns that mark the challenge of reading. Rejecting the transparency of poetic form and racial logics produces that thrilling, vertiginous sense of a "drop falling," of the non-self-sufficiency and nontransparency of the voice to itself. There is something utopian in this process, even if I do not want to conflate rearranging or exposing (to whom?) the means of signification with the transformative work of politics. To deconstruct the norms of voice, revealing the dependence of the voice on an authorizing predication, takes on a different resonance when what the poem refers to is not, or cannot be, canceled in the ways Pritchard's seems to. Likewise, the immediate politics of performing mastery change when the poem's topic is the historicity of that language, when one writes from the perspective of "one who has 'mastered' a foreign language, yet has never had a 'mother tongue,'" when one associates that language with one's exclusion from "speaking" as a universal subject.[39] Making these observations, I mean to draw attention to the networks—and archives—of power encoded within the English language that I have only gestured toward so far but that we may well conclude to be at stake in Pritchard's deformations of poetry and in M. NourbeSe Philip's poetics, to which we now turn.

THERE IS NO TELLING THIS STORY:
FUGUES IN A FREE TIME

Memory carries within it forgetting.　　—M. NourbeSe Philip

Forgetting is a way of misremembering the present.

Dawn Lundy Martin

Each past association suggests its own protensions, its own future associations, which sit side by side in Philip's poem, created out of a disarticulated court record. I have been arguing that concretists and Black Arts theorists arrive at the need for new hermeneutics from different historical vantage points but that they come together in a desire to reactivate language—and the communities it implies—so as to imagine oneself writing as if from the very sources of language and culture. Yet, in both cases, the notion of a "pure" or "original" language or sociality requires policing against the inauthentic—that which is too much in thrall to the falseness of appearance and misrepresentation. Philip's poetics are an obverse to Pritchard's: *Zong!* operates between the related senses of concreteness; it stands closer to the Black Arts notion, recovering and resituating the history of slavery and the ways we can speak of it, with an emphasis on creating new figures to confound the regime of common sense. *Zong!* is not a "better" representation of slavery, I argue, but a demand to rethink the nature and spaces of history and what gets occluded in representation, avoiding the twin romances of "resistance" and "uncontaminated" origin. Through this, her work offers new concepts of ancestrality, the protension of new associations with the ancestors for which we lack an adequate name.

Philip's investment in the "facticity" of English is inextricable from its historicity as an important site of struggle that was not only foreign but "etymologically hostile and expressive of the non-being of the African."[40] She argues that

> speech, voice, language, and word—all are ways of being in the world, and the artist working with the i-mage and giving voice to it is being in the world. The only way the African artist could be in this world, that is the New World, was to give voice to this split i-mage of voiced silence. Ways to transcend that contradiction had to and still have to be developed, for that silence continues to shroud the experience, the i-mage and so the word.[41]

The concept-metaphor "i-mage" resonates with Madhubuti's nationalism, referring at once to "the essential being of the people among whom and for whom the artist creates" and that which, "allowed free expression," could "succeed in altering the way a society perceives itself and, eventually, its collective consciousness."[42] Where the former proposition refers to the *expression* of some underlying truth or essence of a people, the latter proposition suggests an unsaying that works toward a "free expression." Philip argues more for developing an adequate "i-mage" from within English than for recovering some lost consciousness or way of being. Unsaying, then, names a means of working toward that "free expression." Since writing in English is self-negating under these circumstances, her poetics becomes one of "voiced silence," writing with a split voice, listening to the "silences—the interstice/s of time."[43] Her poetics concern the temporalization of language: the resources it retains from the past and its directedness toward an uncertain future.

The "i-mage" does not so much recover as invent the "mother tongue," locating ancestry in a future that will have been rather than a past to which one must be faithful. The "i-mage," I would argue, only apparently participates the Herderian nationalism I discussed in the introduction; indeed, it expresses a deeper truth about the lives of "New World Africans." It requires, in Linda A. Kinnahan's phrase, the "transformational making of 'I,'" an experimental deauthorization of language most fully elaborated in *Zong!*[44] The polemic thrust of Philip's argument rests in her analysis of slavery and its afterlives in the period of colonization. One such afterlife is the lack of autonomous "i-mage-makers" who could begin the work of "revers[ing], interrupt[ing] or dismantl[ing] the cultural mythologies" that reinforce (or enact) the disciplinary processes of embodiment that have informed the varied experiences of black women.[45] Related to Pritchard's ghostwriting, the i-mage is a term for the incomplete processes of acculturation, the space left for the writer to "impress her experience on the language," wherein "formal standard language" is "subverted, turned upside down, inside out, and even sometimes erased."[46] The transformational making of "I" is an intertextual recoding, using "a variety of verbal techniques and methods" to translate the i-mage "into meaning and non-meaning."[47] The i-mage does not name a need to create new, positive self-images in which people can see themselves reflected but an obligation to make images and selves new. Thus, Philip squares the difference between writers like de Campos and Madhubuti, seeing the black life Madhubuti discussed as stunted and distorted as still being merely potential.

In the absence of an "i-mage"—a self-erasing, antidisciplinary way of using language and poetic techniques—the colonial language simply confirms "the non-being of the African" as a predicate of the language. The "i-mage" con-

fronts the ideological misrecognition of black life that informs black concrete-
ness by attending to the lives of words to authorize black expression on differ-
ent terms. The need for such unsaying is especially acute in *Zong!* and takes on a
different ethico-political import. This long poem takes as its point of departure
the story of a Middle Passage mass murder aboard the ship *Zong*. The familiarity
of such ghastly stories at once generates and annuls their power, reducing them
to the background of unthought knowledge and facts. The banality of an archive
of slavery that fails to produce the names or testimonies of the dead threatens
to make the event, a drowning at sea, disappear. In writing to bear witness to the
1781 murder of 133 kidnapped and unnamed Africans who were drowned with
the expectation that insurance would cover the loss of capital, how does one
avoid the comfort of cliché (which "humanizes" those whose humanity history
has denied) or romance, the comfort that one knows the story in advance?[48]
How does one, as Saidiya Hartman challenges, "write a new story, one unfet-
tered by the constraints of the legal documents and exceeding the restatement
and transpositions," a story that "disorder[s] and transgress[es] the protocols
of the archive"?[49] How does one write the story in English, given its complicity
in conjuring or consigning the African to "nonbeing," a nonbeing that is not dis-
appearance, a silence that is not silent?

The "absence" in Philip's phrase "the absence of writing" becomes inde-
terminate, referring equally to her first not seeing writing as holding a pos-
sible future for her and to what writing in a colonial language (or "l/anguish")
leaves unaddressed. Philip's experiments in her first collection, *She Tries Her
Tongue, Her Silence Softly Breaks*, move between the play on the lyric typified by
Pritchard's play with spacing. *She Tries Her Tongue*, especially the title poem,
also makes extensive use of citation, presenting passages from the Acts of the
Apostles and the *Book of Common Prayer* alongside stanzas like this one:

oath   moan   mutter   chant
          time grieves the dimension of other
babble   curse   chortle   sing
          turns on its axis of silence
praise-song   poem   ululation   utterance
          one song would bridge the finite in silence
syllable   vocable   vowel   consonant
          one word erect the infinite in memory[50]

From "oath" to "consonant," one can read the nonindented lines either as di-
minishing in ceremony until finally ending with (words describing) the compo-

nents of speech or simply as a catalogue of kinds of speech ranging roughly from the most formal to the most basic. The indented lines, meanwhile, work out a more complex set of propositions, from time "grieving" and turning on "its axis of silence" to what appears to be an appeal for the one song, then one word that can "erect the infinite in memory": the "i-mage," the temporalized counteruse of language grounded in group memory and desire. Thus, again, we square our two senses of "concrete." The poem ends—or almost ends—with what seems like a resolution:

> Ashes of once in what was
> . . . Silence
> Song word speech
> Might I . . . like Philomela . . . sing
> continue
> over
> into
> . . . pure utterance[51]

The phrase "[a]shes of once in what was" is almost unreadable. Is it "ashes of once," another time, or "ashes of 'once,'" the concept of another time? Philip's earlier work consistently presents words on one syntactic "level," leaving the possibilities of recombination open but not infinitely so. Whatever way we read it, this "once" or its ashes suggests multiple streams of time and pastness that sit unevenly inside of or with each other. Part of the work of the "i-mage" is to invent or articulate a relationship to the ancestors and forms of ancestrality that have otherwise been broken or foreclosed. The "i-mage" is a modality of unsaying, confronting the "free necessity" that shapes black writing and black concreteness. Rather than avoid the histories of dispossession, silence, and erasure that inform the lives of "New World Africans," it reconfigures those histories from within. While Philip laments that "Afro Saxon culture" cannot "describe its own reality," its reality paradoxically is "expressive of a dissociative state—a fugue state. A state of amnesia."[52] Where N. H. Pritchard's poetics deform English to the brink of a concreteness wrenched from temporalization, Philip highlights the interplay of memory and forgetting. At the end of the *notanda*, an appendix to *Zong!* drawn in part from her writing journals, Philip reinvokes her own poem to explain the exclamation point in the title:

Zong! is chant! Shout! And ululation! *Zong!* is moan! Mutter! Howl! And shriek! *Zong!* is *'pure utterance.'* *Zong!* is Song! And Song is what has kept the soul of the African intact. . . . *Zong!* is the Song of the untold story; it cannot be told yet must be told, but only through its un-telling.[53]

Context modifies the meaning of song such that it comes to focus instead on something in the untold story, something neither present nor recoverable: the conditions of song's production, erasure, modification, circulation, and reproduction. The dissociative (dissociating) and polyphonic song in which stray bits of melody and counterpoint are "repeated in different keys and at different intervals"; at the same time, the song and the utterance it subtends are pure in their sociality. The temporalizing song aims to move the line between song and noise so that what was unheard or misheard can be acknowledged. Insisting on the exclamation point—itself unvoiced—the graphic texture of her writing is key to the poem fulfilling all these other verbal and preverbal functions. "Pure utterance" ultimately refers to a practice of inscription rooted in fidelity to what has been lost, a fidelity to the sense of blackness as open and negotiable that is inscribed in the text of history.

Such utterance, then, is central to Philip's poetics of unsaying. As she insists, the story of ship captain Luke Collingwood's decision to murder Africans by throwing them overboard alive rather than allowing them to die on board of "natural causes," shifting the cost of their death from ship to underwriter, requires that she "not tell the story that must be told." The *notanda* opens with the proclamation "There is no telling this story; it must be told," which introduces a version of the narrative of "the most grotesquely bizarre of all slave cases heard in an English court."[54] However commonly the court heard tales of barbarities surrounding slavery, *Gregson v. Gilbert*, the *Zong* case from which Philip extracts her poem, involving the insurers' legal responsibility to honor the ship's claim, was not, strictly speaking, "a slave case, and did not hinge on the definitions of freedom or slavery."[55] On the one hand, it was paradigmatically a slave case, one that tells us something about the legal status of slavery, perhaps about the lived experience of slavery or the imbrication of the institution of slavery and the "ontopology" of the law, what the law covers and assumes.[56] The trial record does not mention "murder"; the only question rather is the soundness of Collingwood's decision. On the other hand, it was not a "slave case" because it required that the institution of slavery be assumed in order for the legal matter to be raised: "It has been decided, whether wisely or unwisely is not now the question, that a portion of our fellow-creatures may become the subject of property."[57] The drowned Africans appear only as abstractions, if not props, in a legal framework that continually conjures them away. The violence of slavery is intrinsic to the case and its archives, shaping in advance what statements are permissible, what the proper interests of the law are. To tell the story of that ship without reinscribing and naturalizing that violence, without safely enclosing it in the past as a moment in a larger dialectical unfolding of Time and Progress is the impossible. Not to tell it is to shun the responsibility of telling the history of the present and of seeing the present as historical. Philip's solution is to drawn, etch, and explode *Zong!* from the text of the *Zong* trial report in order to catch the stories it misses.

If the poetics of unsaying figures an antitranscendental encounter with words that fashions a utopian, anticipatory encounter with language by temporalizing the supposed moment prior to letters being yoked to meaning, then in Philip's serial poem the status of texts, invented ancestors, and the movements between speech, song, syllables, vowels and consonants takes on an additional resonance that "unsettles the lyric subject" by tampering with it, rendering it as a voice "in process." Philip describes it as "speaking over my own voice, interrupting and disrupting it, refusing to allow the voice, the solo voice, pride of place, centre page, centre stage. Where words are surrounded by and trying to fill all that white space, negative space, black space—where the silence is and never was. Silent."[58] It is a subject dispersing itself as the effect of textual invention rather than a representation of human consciousness. Formal strategies carry out the figurative dispersals that "disassemble the ordered" text of the surviving court document and increasingly redistribute syllables by sight and sound across the page so that the story is "released" to "tell itself."[59] Compositing an ancestor, Philip figures herself as the one to whom the story is told and who therefore has an ethical imperative to tell the story in its singularity—the story of *this* event—and its exemplary generality—*these* kinds of things are constitutive in the construction of Western capitalist modernity.

The volume *Zong!* consists of the poem (in six sections); a glossary; a "manifest" of the African groups and languages, crew, women who wait, body parts, animals, food and drink, and figures of nature mentioned throughout the poem; the *notanda*; and the text of *Gregson v. Gilbert*. Except for the last section, "Ẹbọra" (Yoruba underwater spirits), the sections of the poem all have Latin names. The first, "Os" ("bones"), consists of twenty-five numbered "Zong!"

(number 7 is absent), which Philip refers to as the "bones" of the overall proj-
ect. The other sections—"Sal" ("salt"), "Ventus" ("wind"), "Ratio" ("reason"),
"Ferrum" ("iron"), plus "Ẹbọra"—she refers to as the "flesh" of the poem. An
earlier version of "*Zong! #1*" begins with a blunt, almost narrative unfolding of
the central events, conflicts, and terms of the *Zong* massacre:

> captain slaveship
> Hispaniola Jamaica voyage
> > > water
> slaves want water
> > overboard
> facts statement declaration
> perils
> > > seas winds currents
> ship voyage water board
> negroes want sustenance
> > > > preservation
> > > > > rest
> action policy insurance value
> slaves overboard[60]

Even from this fragmentary, paratactic presentation, one can trace a narrative
thread: the ship travels between Hispaniola and Jamaica, water becomes an
issue. A proleptic intrusion of the court document rewrites the "perils" as the
repeated testimony of the Negroes (not "slaves") want of sustenance, preser-
vation, rest. The circumstances are not clear, but we can deduce that the slaves
are thrown overboard to recoup as insurance value what threatened to be lost as
the projected value of their labor power, which cannot be extracted from dead
bodies.[61] Revised for publication in *Zong!*, the first poem is much more frac-
tured, unavailable to narrative:

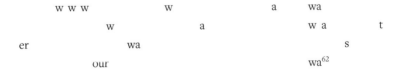

The dispersed arrangement omits any mention of "insurance value," leaving
us with what may be "water was our good," "won," "dey," "one day" "one day
s," and "water of want," among other combinatory possibilities, and anticipat-

ing the dominant textual strategies and thematic contradictions of subsequent parts of the poem.

"*Zong! #2*" is more typical of the "Os" section. It begins:

> the throw in circumstance
>
> the weight in want
>
> in sustenance
>
> for underwriters
>
> the loss
>
> the order in destroy
>
>
> the that fact
>
> the it was
>
> the were
>
> negroes[63]

In just ten lines, the underwriters are analogized to the sharks known to swim alongside slave ships, certain there would be bodies for them to eat. The order to destroy finds an order in "senseless" destruction. Want is understood as a physical presence, or perhaps now as the absence of the dead, and like those enslaved, "that fact," "it was," and "were | negroes" are hypostasized, made into mere objects available as narratemes (the smallest narrative units) or ideologemes. Dawn Lundy Martin argues that "[t]he it was" gives us "the subject-verb relationship stripped to its bare form, drawing our attention, instead, to language itself as the subject, or at least one possible subject," but I would stress the ways this presentation draws attention to antecedentless "it" in the conventional formula "it was."[64] It draws attention to the ways language marks being and nonbeing, the way the poem refuses the information unavailable in the official story. "The were negroes" amounts to the casual accounting of a murder that does not register as murder in the courts and barely registers in our language. Less clear is "the throw in circumstance," which seems at once to be a pun tying together the changing immediate circumstances under which slaves were thrown overboard and to the facticity or "thrownness" of circumstance— the subtending sociohistorical arrangements that made drowning slaves for the insurance money seem an available option under the right circumstances.

While much of the text is, at least nominally, in English, Philip breaks words along phonemic and morphological seams, yielding a fugue-like polyvocality that interrupts "the voice" by finding terms from French, Spanish, Portuguese,

Latin, Hebrew, Yoruba, Italian, Fon, Arabic, Twi, Shona, and West African Patois within English—the languages of a world connected by colonialism. Running along the bottom of the page in the "Os" section is 228 mostly Yoruba names that represent those who died aboard the *Zong*.[65] Read together, the overlap of languages and names sketches a genealogical account of the history of our present and the present of the event, the interrelation of lives brought together through the transatlantic slave trade, emancipation, colonialism, and neocolonial periods. The histories linking these disparate sites and peoples are dramatized on the page, overlaid with each other, without any internal master key or trope to sort out their relationships. Produced through the breakages and breakdowns of English, heightened by shifting typefaces, the overlap shows the ways at a very literal level that some trace of that history is immanent within our concepts, or vocabularies, or orthographies. This too is an act of "vivifying the facticity of the word." It does not posit the word in some pure state but analyzes the nature of the word's situatedness in concrete milieu, the obscuring nature of our regimes of factuality that make it difficult to see and hear the past or think of the present as historical. Broken witness: it does not "give voice" to the enslaved in a way that would then be subject to verification but voices the silence required and generated by the ruling order's common sense that makes such witness impossible.

Simply to settle on this history, and the tacit assumption that history has passed, is to risk seduction by the false reassurance of a progressive narrative that moves silently but inexorably, that replaces the imagination of a "free state" with a narrative of emancipation and the official narrative of the state's continuing improvement.[66] We miss the event—in both its singularity and its exemplarity—by locking it safely in the past, limiting the extent to which it continues to haunt the present. *Zong!* asks us to consider the reverberations of the event of the massacre and its aftermath, the legal and political relations forged in that moment, the relationships and notions of subjectivity, the pathways of desire. To unsay the story of the *Zong* is to peel away everything that comforts or consoles, everything that makes the story familiar. We must abandon our faith in modes of witness imagined to follow from a subject to another, with both of their positions already fixed and secured in advance.

Any recovery of this story also re-covers it, yielding to available legal and ontological concepts governing humanity that were largely formed during this period. How does one recover the drowned Africans into a notion of life at once within but also transcendent of those notions that foreclosed black humanity? How does one claim humanity when the very concept of humanity is haunted by the ineluctable contingency of humanity before the law and the fictions that support it? The poem implicates readers in the process insofar as some passages make us fully responsible for constructing the text's meaning. Whereas the method of "Os" largely consists of a project of recombining and re-sequencing of words from the court document, the "flesh" sections decompose those words, releasing the "words within words," fragmenting words into ever smaller semantic units, so that "king," for example, yields "kin." A phrase that reads "time is tardy late in time" becomes

ti   me is tard   y late in tim

e[67]

One works to determine which fragments relate to which, where one thought or sentence ends or begins. And when one is done synthesizing words and sentences, one must then begin the work of interpretation, requiring not just an account of this phrase but of the corresponding phrases, all rendered in like manner. The spatial arrangement, further, makes it possible, even likely, that one's eyes will not scan correctly from left to right or that one will locate semiautonomous groupings of words in stanzas abstracted from a conventional left-right reading. Vertical reading of clusters may substitute for horizontal ones, as in the following passage:

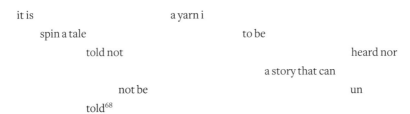

To read this is to translate: "It is a yarn I spin, a tale to be told, not heard nor a story that cannot be untold." The telling is emphasized over its reception; it will linger, haunt, persist. It is an attempt to "recapture the past *for* the present," which entails "a reconceptualization of the present" and of "ourselves" in the present.[69] However, it is also possible to read the words differently: "spin a tale to be told not" could form an imperative or "a story that cannot be" or "cannot be untold" could be a lament, similar to "Zong! #4": "this | should | not | be | is," which could mean "this should not be 'is'" or "this should not be[, but] is."

The poem's spatial arrangements are indispensable to its effects, and the topic relates to the underlying realities of black life, the historicity of history, and ultimately the production of a new i-mage, new theories for thinking our present's relation to the past. *Zong!* constantly unsays itself, insists on its not-saying by saying multiple things at once. Its "grammar of distraction," borrowing Jay Wright's phrase, gives itself to fragmentation and exhibits a "disposition for punning," with a faith that a pun "raises the dead."[70] The primary difference between Pritchard's and Philip's grammar of distraction is not just their respective topics but their differing commitments to fragmentation. Philip's "poetics of fragmentation" implies a more expansive set of recombinatory possibilities. In *Zong!* this "grammar of distraction" yields an antirepresentational unsaying faithful both to the impossibility of telling this story and the injunction to tell. The event and the story of the event are constitutive of the existence—and nonexistence—of the "New World African." The story cannot be told because to do so threatens simply to make it symbolic of a history bigger than itself—the story of the Middle Passage—and because the event it wants to narrate cannot be contained by narrative conventions, which would have to have it end.

Philip's explicit concern with the *un*dead—neither living nor dead, neither present nor absent—marks her project as one of witness more than recovery or "giving voice," and witness requires fabrication. Hayes, Pritchard and Philip share a practice of generating nondialectical contradiction and undoing hierarchical binaries that Philip refers to as "hauntological[,] . . . a wake of sorts, where the specters of the undead make themselves present."[71] For Jacques Derrida, hauntology is a name for the "untimeliness of the present"—what is now and what appears in this now. Haunting notionally precludes the possibility of a "pure" facticity or a "pure" concrete poetry, since each concept is haunted by the need of some example to figure it. Haunting is also a figure of the unfinished event, for conceptualizing—bearing witness to—the noncontemporaneity of the present. In Derrida's words, to haunt "does not mean to be present, and it is necessary to introduce haunting into the very construction of a concept. Of every concept, beginning with the concepts of being and time. That is what we would be calling a hauntology. Ontology opposes it only in a movement of exorcism. Ontology is a conjuration."[72]

"Pure" ontology is a conjuration both because it would require discussion of Being "as such," with particular examples conjured away (a pure "facticity" of the word would require analysis only of the unwritten, unspoken word, or the transparent-to-itself word) and because it would have to conjure a fundamental "wordliness" uncontaminated by the specter of "worldliness." *Zong!* suggests a vision of time as accumulative and recursive and articulates a genealogical account of history—a narrative of "descent from ancestors by enumeration of intermediate persons"—that would account for those unknown ancestors around which the present shapes itself.[73] A figure of constitutive incompleteness, hauntology speaks to the resistance of those "intermediate persons" whom we risk instrumentalizing, again, if we understand them simply as those beings leading to us and our present. The serial poem "conjure[s] the infinite(ive) of to be of the 'negroes' on board the *Zong*" Philip declares, bringing "conjuration" close to "conjugation," marking that which does not appear in the name or concept of Negro.[74] Witness is an act of conjuration that calls into being what remains nonpresent in invocation or evocation. It is a fundamentally *poetic* gesture of witness, moving us beyond the ontopology of race, language, and culture and telling a truth that depends on the "artifice of the form" to tell the truth of that which would not make itself present in the impossible telling of the tale.

Philip's poetic witness testifies to the past that has not passed, bearing witness to the event of the *Zong* massacre in such a way that honors its persistence in the present. As she puts it in "Zong #4," "this is | not was"—the event is ongoing, not safely sequestered in the past.[75] The statement is emphatic: this *is*, has not passed, and this *is not was*—an overlap that, unlike slavery's logic of double negation (the slave is not not human), insists on the positive being of this event, even though now as then it remains not invisible. Ian Baucom states that challenge as "recalling to memory the violence of the imperial past" while refusing the "Hegelian and post-Hegelian model of historical time which views this past and its violence as, in fact, *past*."[76] Philip's unsaying—the method through which she does not tell the story that must be told—entails a reinterpretation of historical time. To "not tell" is to retain what is singular in the event of the *Zong* massacre—the drowning at sea of these 133 Africans—and what is exemplary but difficult to name about all those who survived and were enslaved. In practice, the poetry Philip produces is one of resistances, including the resistance to poetry. This paradox of the story that animates *Zong!*, that cannot be told but must be told, that is not told and "is" the not-telling, is a fitting development of her poetics and its play between presence and absence. Her poem is at once anticonclusion—until we have accounted for these "intermediate persons" in an important sense we are not fully what we are—and anteconclusion, always postponing any final word. Fittingly *Zong!* ends with a palimpsestic section where words are printed over each other, literally overwriting and crossing each other out, until the last word, a pun: "reason."

If the paradigmatic examples of concrete poetry work by creating a discursive context in which the sense (sensation) and sense (meaning) of the words combine and cancel each other out, Philip goes a step further by creating a palimpsest that is at once mimetic of words faded with time, washed away, whispering over each other in the dim echoes of history. The few clearly visible words and phrases—"then vedic," *"ave,"* "to ile ife," "sow the sea," "told cold," "sos," "os," *"ratio,"* "Ben," "reason"—do not give us enough to allow us to do much more than witness the unraveling of this tale. The conditions of conclusion, a story with clearly delineated beginning, middle, and end, especially that last requirement of all narrative, are not in place. By beginning with the assumption of the silence within language and living speech, with the assumption of something unspoken and unspeakable within testimony, the poem extends the structure of paralepsis—saying by claiming not to say—positing not only the right to nonresponse but explicit counterinterrogation. *Zong!* "makes space" for other questions, for reorientations of time within the reading process and the unfolding of the text. Through this, Philip tells an impossible story without yielding to the conditions of possibility for that story, which is oriented toward the anticipated time when the ancestors can appear as a future.

Zong! addresses witness as an ethical, ontological, and poetic problem, providing perspective from those aboard the ship who witness each other and the phantasmatic "women who wait" for letters they will not have received. Invoking Celan's famous aphorism "no one bears witness for the witness," I would argue that in addition to positing a legal framework,—where the poem bears witness (as testimony) in the place of those who cannot, corroborates their story, and usurps the story of another—the poem attests the necessity of invention, in the form of poetry or fictionalization. As Pritchard tends to leave matters unresolved, *Zong!* asks readers to bear witness to their sense making as a revolutionary act, acknowledging that despite its familiarity and historical documentation this is a story that in some ways one cannot know and speak at the same time. However, it is not enough to imagine oneself the ancestor of the unjustly enslaved or the hapless crew, both of whom lack the ability to master their historical situation. One must also see the ways the terms through which we receive the story effectively make present what is not there, in this case the pastness of a story that *Zong!* presents as our present inheritance, governing the sayable, thinkable, and calculable as possibility.

Concrete poetics articulates anew the link between the bones (*os*)—of language and of ancestrality—and the speaking mouth (*os*) of poetry associated by conventional metonymy with the presence of the speaker who uses a language as nonreflexive medium. If *Zong!* defines black life, it is not for the present; it is rather the "i-mage" of the future, the ancestor yet to return to us. The title page, inverting the conventions of the slave narrative and other writing where one must authenticate and bear witness to the truth of another's writing, says that

Zong! is "told to the author by Setaey Adamu Boateng," identified as "the voice of the ancestors revealing the submerged stories of all who were aboard the *Zong*." Rather than Philip presenting herself as the one who authorizes the speaking of this other, introducing and clearing the way for this voice to speak itself, she makes the ancestor responsible for her own textual performance, a constantly deauthorizing figure that, rather than bolstering her "voice" detracts from it. Like the names of the conjured ancestors in the footer of "Os" and at the end of "Ferrum" who cannot witness for themselves, whose *os*—whose bones and mouths—cannot be recovered, this persona at once marks an impossible speech and the only "authentic" speech that could be possible. The only possible witness here is that which remains open to its own fictionality as a counter to the legal fictions and norms that supported and emerged from the institution of slavery. The work of reconstruction begins with and returns to the work of deconstruction, in this way re-marking the violence entailed in the formation of identity or in a single and simplified timeline wherein no ghost could ever appear. Positing this ancestral voice, as authorizing and originary brings together the two senses of witness and concreteness with which this chapter begins—the testimony of one present on behalf of others who see themselves expressed and the disjunctive textual practices that make us return to the text to reread and rehear that voice. Together, they suggest the desire for—and impossibility of—"pure utterance," of innocent naming free of any implication.

The phrase "broken witness" resonates with the more familiar phrase "broken English," used to mark someone's habitual use of English in nonstandard ways. "Broken English"—in the active sense, *breaking* English—is applicable to all of the writers I consider in the chapters to come, particularly the second chapter. Experimental writing, imploding and transforming English by sight and sound, requires a high degree of proficiency with the language. It also requires a sense that mere proficiency is not enough, in much the same ways that conventional form seems to these writers inadequate to the task of balancing the legacy of concreteness in Madhubuti's understanding with Philip's apprehension of language's originary displacement of any black sensibility while avoiding the consolation of false transcendence. To "break" also describes the rupture the English language as an institution of colonialism and slavery has been, that place where English breaks and breaks off.

two

Establishing Synchronisms
Sycorax Video Style and the Plural Instant

Naming and defining the contours of an age, increasingly the project of Bajan scholar-poet Kamau Brathwaite's experimental practice, is one of the most urgent political and epistemological problems for any era. The answers one provides to "what time is now?" largely determine the ways a moment registers, or fails to register, and how we articulate the past historically. Naming an age—for example, "post-9/11"—predicates a time within which lives and geographies become hierarchically related to one another, and some crises fail to register, slipping into the fog of the quotidian, making even the language of "before" and "after" complicit in the tacit privileging of the west in the official graph of time. Thus, the meanings and allotments of time are always urgent political questions, even if it is not time itself that we discuss. Brathwaite, self-consciously writing from a Caribbean locale that was conceived in the metropole as peripheral to modernity, has proven throughout his career especially astute in his attention to these problems, occupying the position of poet as witness and chronicler, mixing personal and historical privations and triumphs to produce a poetry of and for our time.

Since the period of disaster he refers to as his Time of Salt—his wife's death and the dissolution of his immediate community, the destruction of his homes and archives of Caribbean writing by Hurricane Gilbert, and his near death at the hands of burglars in Kingston, Jamaica—Brathwaite has developed a new graphic poetics he calls (among other things) Sycorax Video Style (SVS). In contrast with the concrete poetics I discuss in the previous chapter, whose self-canceling texts call on readers to attend to the process of reading and the evocative capacity of language beyond representation, SVS ostentatiously repurposes older technology and poetic techniques to transform the poetic voice. More precisely, I argue that, revising and extending Brathwaite's arguments regarding nation language in his famous *The History of the Voice*, SVS draws out the processual nature of the poetic text in the service of the voice's retreat—its withdrawal and retracing. SVS's conjunction of shifting typefaces, indeterminate syntax, ambiguous, images and "calibanisms"—deliberate orthographic transformations of words that rely on their written or phonetic form—synthesizes techniques of orality and visuality in ways that upset the critical tendency to privilege the former in criticism of black writers. Rather than being a mode of expression that links the individual poet to an ideal collective, Brathwaite's reconfigured voice moves between registers, creating frequently dense syntactic and referential networks that suspend his poetry between testimony and artifact.

Part of SVS's strategy, then, is to thicken both the texture and textuality of writing, insisting on the social significance of the materiality of print and the mediality of language as a means to authorize different understandings of the relationship between personal and global time.[1] A politics of expression tends to neglect the materiality of print and print practice in favor of what Harryette Mullen has called "trope[s] of orality" or voice, despite the importance of print media to black writing in the typographically experimental work of, say, Pritchard, Russell Atkins, De Leon Harrison or Black Arts poets such as Sonia Sanchez.[2] SVS's radical typography makes those tropes of orality visible *as* tropes of orality. In this way, SVS both develops and departs from Brathwaite's celebrated notion of nation language to reconfigure the meanings of poetic expression, producing a poetics of the page that responds to the pressing demands of personal and geopolitical history. More than commenting on present conditions, SVS poetics underscore writing as a kind of technology through which to connect the individual and the collective and through that to imagine new ways to answer "when is now?" and "when is the nation"?

I develop this point through analysis of some of Brathwaite's post–Time of Salt poems, but it will be helpful to say a few words at the outset about SVS as revision and extension of his celebrated concept of nation language; later in the chapter, I demonstrate how his nation-language arguments inform his transformation of the technique of fragmentation associated with T. S. Eliot. One could argue that SVS achieves at the level of the page itself the fragmentation associated with modernism, analyzing and generating the pieces of a civilization to come rather than mourning the ruins of a civilization that has passed, but that would be only part of the story. SVS's ensemble of techniques undoes the hierarchy between orality and visuality while, in a different register, illustrating orality to be a function of visuality insofar as it serves as an aural racial marker. Nation language emerges in his *History of the Voice* as a catachresis for the "submerged" African aspect of the English language that traditional English prosody suppresses or distorts into the mask of dialect. Crucially, nation language emerges as part of a larger project of cultural interpretation that unseats European literature, metonymically invoked through iambic pentameter, as the standard against which the literature of the former colonies should be measured. Brathwaite's insistence on literary and aesthetic standards rooted in the Caribbean and the lives of the people who live there is perennially important, especially for the processes of decolonization that follow the end of formal colonization. From this perspective, the development of nation language and other aesthetic practices indexes the Caribbean as the site of confluent, creolizing cultures and the site of a contest over the definition of culture in a decolonizing world in a moment when the United States has emerged as a new center.

Further, and more salient to my analysis here, though Brathwaite's lecture title refers to "the voice," his object of analysis is literary technique, which "carries with it a certain kind of experience." Insofar as the history of the voice lecture emerges from his prior analysis of the overlapping, contradictory processes of creolization, "voice" is a metaphor for human signification that already includes print or the "voice" of the drum.[3] Nation language renders poetic techniques—prosody, tropes, rhythms, conventions of representation—as media of expression. "The hurricane does not roar in pentameters," he argues, so Caribbean writers need to develop the "syllables, the syllabic intelligence, to describe the hurricane, which is our own experience," and attend to "the actual rhythm and the syllables, the very software in a way, of the language."[4] Rhythms and software are neither part of the language nor external to it: they are the technologies, which take on different meanings at different times, through which we understand and apprehend language. In this statement, stressing representation as a process of abstraction and affinity, Brathwaite reverses roughly a century's worth of cultural interpretation, moving from representation as artifact to crafted language as a kind of testimony and, emphasizing his reference to "syllabic intelligence," to a sense of culture as inhering in transactions between people rather than objects.[5] I therefore argue that the "nation" of nation language is a catachresis: it is not a given structure of sociality and common orientation but holds the place for those common experiences and ways of being together through which a people might come to think of itself as one. This "we"-in-progress opposes the romance and distortion of dialect ("language used when you want to make fun of someone"), which determines a people from without by imputing to them an appropriable way of using language.[6]

Nation language, then, marks a critical and aesthetic attempt to stay alert to the media of language whose submerged "African aspect" awaits some future activation and valuation. Brathwaite's break with English prosodic traditions targets their limited repertoire of images and modes of experience and their ideological presuppositions, which frame the act of representation. Nation language's emphasis on the submerged "African aspect" of English orients it toward a poetics of the plural instant—the multiple, competing traditions operational in a given conjunction of space-time—rather than toward a unified, transhistorical voice or spirit. Dialect fails because it makes the other an object (of knowledge and derision) that, as object, can be contained by and interpreted in light of normative paradigms of acceptable difference that define the ruling order. The notion of the plural instant retains a sense of culture "in its otherness"; it is a living way of doing and knowing for which representation as a literary mode is poorly suited.[7]

As the title of his 1984 lecture indicates, Brathwaite is invested in the historical and generic norms that mediate the supposed unity of the poetic "voice"— the discourses and underlying concepts that make it legible and meaningful and by which it comes to represent persons, races or territories. SVS tropes that voice: rather than emphasizing a voice expressive of a self or a people, it uses fonts' ragged edges and extradiscursive materiality to highlight the production of that voice and its call out to others. Its spatial arrangements and graphic elements are not mimetic of some inner or outer state of fragmentation but instead stress language and poetry as media of expression. Where concrete poetry is concerned with "vivifying the facticity" of words to break habitual associations and formulas of commons sense, SVS seeks in the sensual form of written language what Elaine Savory calls a "pan-generic textuality," repurposing and re-presenting words to make different social relationships thinkable.[8] Its turned words emphasize the processes of poetic expression oriented toward new understandings of poetry's address to a collectivity it calls into being, often using apostrophe, the ur-trope of lyric expressivity. Through this, SVS's troped orality considers the ways we read and what kinds of experiences literature makes available, and, ultimately, opens up possibilities for imagining novel forms of community in a multivalent, contested present.

A VOICE MADE VISIBLE

Part of the theme of Brathwaite's Time of Salt trilogy (*Shar: Hurricane Poem* [1990]; *The Zea Mexican Diary: 7 Sept 1926–7 Sept 1986* [1993]; *Trench Town Rock* [1994]) is the breakdown of community and the failure of the nationalist project, which leads to the need for new, yet more radical poetics. Together, these events figure a conjunction of personal loss, vulnerability, bureaucratic indifference, and a loss of social cohesion registered as "a kind of RIFT VALLEY in my senscape."[9] Formally and conceptually, SVS poetics reimagine his earlier poetry, foregrounding the historical, printed specificity of the material letter and the mediality of any "Word [that] becomes | again a god and walks among us."[10] Even in these lines, from *The Arrivants*, his New World trilogy, the Word is not self-revealing but requires the mediation of human form for its effect. As a medium refers to a set of contingent social practices of transmission and making legible, of reception and interpretation, mediality refers to the medial specificity or "mediumness" of a given text, with SVS frequently playing off the norms of print media to make "voice" visible.

Rather than the voice being the vehicle of the word, the word becomes a vehicle for any voicing, a reversal that alters the possibilities and valences of expression. J. Michael Dash's exemplary argument that Brathwaite's early poetry expresses faith in some "original coherence," underpinned by a belief that "the poetic Word restores [and draws its power from] a time that is ahistorical, impervious to change," does not prepare us for the later SVS work, which emphasizes to a greater degree the meanings of form and language as medium.[11] Through Sycorax, Brathwaite articulates what he calls a genuine "alterNative," a notion of culture "in its otherness" predicated on difference and differentiation, and a poetic procedure linked to what he calls "trans-liminalness, trans-limitness erasure of xpectant boundar(ies)," emphasizing the "trans-" of transmission or transit.[12] SVS figuratively and, often literally, revises poetic and graphic lines between publications, stressing the "word that is our threshold to the world," he intimate relationship between "word" and "world."[13]

Brathwaite's influential nation-language concept turns on generating "a rhythm which approximates the *natural* experience" and on the historical fact that English itself has been "influenced by the underground language, the submerged language that the slaves had brought," which was itself "constantly transforming into new forms."[14] Nation language is a performative version of English that is "like a howl, or a shout, or a machine-gun or the wind or a wave."[15] It becomes the medium through which to "try to see the fragments/ whole," that is, articulate a submarine unity from among the scattered archipelago and across the black Atlantic.[16] SVS emphasizes the plurality and internal differentiation and historicity of language, poetry, and writing by drawing persistent attention to its concrete, situated particularity. The result is what I call a "plural instant": rather than a logic of time or modernity the plural instant is a graph of temporality that "establish[es] synchronisms, American, recurrent timeless | relating this to that, yesterday to toda | (y)" through "anticipatory, interlinked & contradictory images" irreducible to a single nation or history.[17] Significantly, this concept allows us to see England, Africa, and the Caribbean in both pre- and postcontact, pre- and postcolonial formations, preserving the temporal meanings associated with each. "Plural instant" marks a moment of transition, the culmination of one moment or epoch and the anticipation of another for which the term "new" or the concept of a "break" is mystifying: it is a way of attending to the overlap of moments—and political claims about their meanings—that seem to conclude without decisively ending. Concretely, it might refer to the moment of spiritual and physical wreckage following the hurricane, the transition from typewriting to "writing in light," or the ambiguous figure of Coleman Hawkins between swing and bebop, between personal and global memory. Something of the past, and the future it imagined itself on course toward, now interrupted, persists in this plural instant, but now its meaning and fulfillment will mean something else. Yesterday's dream of freedom fulfilled might look too narrow, or regressive, for present circumstances. This conception of internally differentiated time requires a reconceptualization of the relationship between experimental traditions that sees them as sharing a common historical frame.[18] Therefore, my reading figures "originary coherence," like nation, as a product rather than restored state and sees SVS's emphasis on the sensuality of print and daily experience as part of a project of changing the valences of words and poetry in light of interwoven personal and social concerns. In the face of history and the present conditions of life and writing, the question becomes "What kinds of new words are formable? become formidable? What form(s) become possible?"[19]

The function of the poetic text is not simply to validate group experience or speak for or represent the nation but to create the depth of the plural instant, linking writing practices across time, from the medieval dream vision to computer-processed writing, in an effort to capture "the heart of culture in its otherness." The "nation" of "nation language" becomes a future anterior construction rooted in a fundamentally temporal poetics. The "African aspect" of English is immanent but occluded, and the issue is not experiencing or knowing that aspect but imagining the experiences that aspect makes possible, which in turn forces us to reimagine the terms of everyday life. Though there has so far been little sustained critical analysis of SVS, Brathwaite's own commentary has been extensive.[20] SVS exploits "the notion/possibility/reality of diversity of the printed word in th | (e) 'age' of the mural/computer" likened to "handcraft. un- | mass-producing psychology and using modern (modem) technology more like needlewo | rk *embroidery* those who prepare shrouds & tapestries."[21] This account, blending histories and modes of production, which is related to Brathwaite's repeated and revised accounts of his method and to his serially revised and republished poems, constitutes another temporal level of these poetics: slightly outdated modern technology (a computer and printer he worries will soon break down) recovers and reproduces, ironically, older forms of not yet industrialized art making. The home computer, emblematic of contemporary consumer culture and the hyperconnectivity that blurs the lines between the spaces and practices of leisure and work, re-creates a mode of life and connectivity thought to be superseded. The technological "voice of the Stylewriter," a kind of printer "long since out of production," supplements and supplants the poet's "voice," "despite its non-Laser 'deficiencies' of 'clarity.'"[22]

I have stressed the trope of "voice" in my account of Brathwaite—and relied so much on his own account—for two reasons. The first is that I want to keep in focus the ways that Brathwaite's visual poetics modify dominant notions of poetic expression and the politics of expression. The graphic participates in the remediation of the self-reflexive "voice" of the modernist lyric (a document, in Eliot's conception, of "the voice of the poet talking to himself—or to nobody"), fashioning it as a more abstract, not quite representative and not quite expressive mode that anticipates a collectivity.[23] Brathwaite's SVS poetics deconstruct the lyric mode, insofar as the play of typography, allusion, and revision consistently prioritizes the "fragmentation" of the unitary voice, using some of the markers and structures of the lyric to different ends. The voice is a trope of orality—multiple, printed, and in transit—hence the importance of apostrophe and a generally conversational, digressive style in Brathwaite's recent work. Even more acutely for a Caribbean writer, apostrophe, drawing on an intertextual history of apostrophe and the prosodic traditions that uphold it, lends the speaker presence and is the medium of re-signifying historical differences.[24]

I also want to emphasize the extent to which Brathwaite accounts for his own work, making the production of a self seem to be part of the project, however ambiguously. His "postSalt" work increasingly takes up personal themes, and the journalistic memoir has increasingly become one of the genres his work articulates. Even as SVS amplifies the mediality of expression, the play of personal modes of expression blurring the line between singular and exemplary expression seems to align Brathwaite's poetry with the modernist lyric as practiced by T. S. Eliot, an exemplar of the English literary tradition from which Brathwaite announced his break. The lyric has been at the center of many debates surrounding poetry, and discourses disclaiming or reclaiming it have proliferated; at the same time, the accusation that some writers, especially writers of color, "believe" in lyric self-presence has helped justify the whiteness of the avant-garde. My aim is not to rehabilitate the lyric but to situate Brathwaite's comment that T. S. Eliot is the "only 'European influence' I can detect and will acknowledge" within his larger SVS project.[25] Eliot had become passé among many poets by the time Brathwaite published his first collection, at which point the lyric increasingly carried the stigma of complicity with what Nathaniel Mackey calls the Cartesian "separation of the ego from the rest of the world in order to achieve knowledge of and power over the rest of the world," taking the world as an object for its (intending) subjectivity to master.[26] While many black writers resist the "Cartesian" model of Western subjectivity and thus reject the traditional lyric, Brathwaite goes in a different direction, seeking a poetic "self without ego, without I, without arrogance."[27] This notion of selfhood superficially resembles Eliot's "impersonality," through which the individual poet expresses the genius or "mind of Europe," but for Brathwaite's larger intellectual and literary project, saying "I" inaugurates a question of the nation and one's name, or *nam*, a semiexpressivist concept-metaphor of social being whose full philosophical implications are beyond the scope of this project.[28] Conceiving language as medium, *nam* operates alongside the notion of a plural instant as a figure of heterotemporality.[29] Brathwaite defines "nam" variously as an "in-dwelling, man-inhabiting (not hibiting) organic force," "soul grit or kernel," "capsule, space capsule, seamless container, seed, egg, atom, atomic space within the atom space," or "grit sand pebble seed safe secret | – unquestioned not necessarily visible – | out of which strength comes, where the heart of the culture resides *in its otherness*."[30] It is a figure for culture in progress, the heart of culture's unplanned, undisciplined transformations that reflect processes of creolization rather than the unfolding of national or racial spirit.[31] *Nam*, as the source of expression, is what withholds itself from expression.

The relationship between Brathwaite and Eliot, a topic of perennial debate, turns on the term "fragmentation," which I relate to Brathwaite's project of "establishing synchronisms" within the postcolonial world by reconfiguring subjective relations. SVS deploys an apostrophic structure of address as a primary means of reconfiguring those relations, but the "speaker" becomes simply another kind of object, allowing the poem's subject to be *nam* as an ineffaceable trace of the process of differentiation that overturns simple unidirectional narratives of influence and power. Whereas for Eliot "fragmentation" names a sense of disorientation in the face of the waning institutions of culture and value that threaten the subject's sense of coherence and self-sufficiency in the modern era, for Brathwaite "fragmentation" is one name for social disintegration and discontinuity between the different sites of the Caribbean archipelago connected by slavery, colonialism, and the ongoing projects of decolonization.

Crucially, the historical root of fragmentation in either case is imperialism and the creolized cultures that result in the colony and the metropole alike. For the British-identified Eliot, recourse to the expressivist "mind of Europe" resolves the issue by silently synthesizing (or co-opting) elements of cultures introduced through colonial contact into a transcendent, putatively mono-cultural tradition that remains intact. By contrast, Brathwaite identifies two competing, simultaneous forms of synthesis: "inter/culturation, which is an unplanned, unstructured but osmotic relationship" and "ac/culturation, which is the yoking (by force and example, on the part of those with power and prestige) of one culture to another."[32] "Inter/culturation" is the name for the structural incompleteness and internal breakdowns of the "ac/culturation" process, nam-ing that mechanism whereby each culture is changed in the encounter with the other. To emphasize a "submerged," "African aspect" of English, which met-onymically invokes the trace of the colonial relation more generally, Brathwaite offers the concept-metaphor nation language, which imaginatively and ana-lytically uses the historical processes of inter/culturation as a lever against the relations of power and force implied by ac/culturation. Nation language empha-sizes the plurality and internal differentiation of Western imperial cultures, tradition as Eliot imagines it and the fictionality of any pure "mind of Europe." The colonial relation cuts both ways, and in the "inter/culturated" postcolonial present, colonizer and colonized share a common temporal horizon. Ac/cultura-tion is not merely the imposition of one culture onto another but also the process by which one culture changes itself to secure its dominance over another culture and maintain legitimacy. In this reading, nation language does not refer to accu-rate imitations of popular speech in literature but to a use of language to capture the emergent spirit(s) of a palimpsestic place. In the terms of my introduction, the "nation" is textual: it refers less to an idealized national spirit than to the fact that no one spirit precedes any example of culture. *The History of the Voice* devel-ops the implicit argument in Brathwaite's much-cited aphorism "the unity is sub-marine."[33] For the "symbols[s] of leadership" that undergird the idea of a salutary "wholeness" in "nation" as conventionally conceived to be recognized as such, immediate sense perceptions have to be intuitively linked with reflexive sense and categories of knowledge; Brathwaite's "voice," by contrast, requires breaking links that connect immediate sense perceptions with reflexive concepts.[34]

Brathwaite is also responding to the same historical predicament as his gen-eration of white European and American avant-garde poets and African Ameri-can poets (he cofounded the Caribbean Arts Movement in 1966, a year after the formation of the Black Arts Repertory Theater/School), who similarly rejected or reworked the notion of "voice," albeit in different ways.[35] Thus, it is important to ask what Brathwaite means by "Eliot" when he says Eliot "is the only 'European influence' I can detect and will acknowledge." More than aesthetic possibilities, Eliot figures institutions of "ac/culturation." If I persist, with Brathwaite, in referring to the "voice" of poetry, it is only because it should be clear enough that Brathwaite's interest is less in problems of "poetic communication" than the notion of the "assumed voice" of the colonizer (and the colonizer's own "assumed voice" of authority).[36]

While a certain reified voice—the dialect of racial and working class Others—helped Eliot early on achieve that sense of overlapping voices "overheard" in his early work, Brathwaite stresses the importance of "Eliot's actual voice—or rather his recorded voice, property of the British Council" to his development of a concretely located poetic "voice." Brathwaite underscores both Eliot's "dry deadpan delivery," and "the riddims of St. Louis (though we didn't know the source then)," which were "stark and clear for those of us who at the same time were listening to the dislocations of Bird, Dizzy and Klook [drummer Kenny Clarke]."[37] In the same passage, Brathwaite stresses the value of "the conversational tone" and the "*riddmic* and image-laden tropes" of Eliot and John Arlott, a famous BBC cricket commentator understood to "[subvert] the Establishment with the way and where he spoke: like Eliot, like jazz." Against Eliot's own accounts of his poetry, then, Brathwaite implicitly insists on the prevalence of this local, personal, concrete history in Eliot's work, which is in turn legible—or audible—through bebop, relocating Eliot from a cosmopolitan European tradition to an American one, from white modernism to an American popular culture meaningfully informed by African American modernism.

Moreover, Brathwaite stresses the *idea* of Eliot and his place in establishing norms that have the effect of making Caribbean poets always seem belated rather than synchronous with Eliot. In the context of modern poetry, "riddim" pluralizes "voice" and gives it communal rather than personal functions. It takes the place of fixed forms, describing a harder to quantify process that forms the basis of formal invention and reinvention.[38] I would argue, therefore, that the value of Eliot is not, as Charles W. Pollard has it, in the resources Eliot's poetics might provide for a more adequate representation—techniques of depiction and "speaking for"—of the Caribbean as an ideal "unified cultural community."[39] The idea that Eliotic modernism becomes both a "point of reference" that helps Brathwaite (and Derek Walcott) "to understand and to represent better their postcolonial experience of modernity" lends itself to the patronizing and false view that writers in the postcolonial periphery adapt established metropolitan forms to local materials, which retains Europe or the United States as the centers of culture and innovation.[40] Eliot, whose recordings were disseminated by the imperialist British Council, was *part* of Brathwaite's experience of colonial modernity, not external to it, and the decline of British imperialism is part of both poets' experience of modernity.

Rather than adding to a transforming tradition, Brathwaite's nation-language poetics draws on the culture that will have resulted from inter/culturation, refiguring the ethnocentric binaries that support the processes ac/culturation. The most fundamental difference between Eliot and Brathwaite, as poets, lies in their different understandings of the status of the "voice" of the poem, the former addressing a more or less stable audience and the latter, like Philip, attempting to use English toward different ideological (or ontological) ends. In Philip's perspective, the imposition of language is violent and negating, and the transition from formal colonialism to neocolonialism does not significantly change matters. Brathwaite's notion of the nation-language voice emphasizes the specific underground histories and rhythms of Caribbean life that somehow "speak" through the poem, without representation being the poem's primary function. Brathwaite rejects the objectifying conventions of modernist dialect on the grounds that they fix too firmly the positions of the standard and the nonstandard, a binary opposition in which the latter is regarded as merely a corrupt— and illegitimate—version of the former. Dialect, in other words, is a mode of self-referential vernacular invention that purports to record language as it is used, from the vantage point of (and for) those who do not use language that way; nation language affirms itself as an act of invention. Practically speaking, nation language is a participatory, "synthetic" language less rooted in a romance of the folk or the poet as speaking for others than in the poet's attempt to address the nonsynchronism, or heterotemporality, of the postcolonial present.[41]

Lacking a single narrative history or "mind" to express, the "nation" of nation language is not a positivity or origin to be recovered or forged *outside* the relations of colonial or neocolonial domination but names the site-specific forms that any language, any culture takes, an internal fragmentation that is a language's way of being. SVS blends apparently outmoded but still recognizably modern technology with the sites of postcolonial history thought to receive modernity secondhand and with an idealized history of English literature— increasingly, as we will see, generating a "pangeneric textuality" informed by metaphors of medieval print culture and genres such as illuminated manuscripts and dream visions. With SVS, the "voice" of "a simple MAC SE30 and an almost xhausted Stylewriter printer" supplements the poet's "voice," in order to "mak[e] possible the revolutionary return of speak-voice-bo- | dy cinema-performance riddim in what we can now truly say is MODERN poetry."[42] With it, Brathwaite imaginatively "revitalizes" ancestors as diverse as Amiri Baraka, Sterling Brown, Aimé Césaire, Nicolas Guillén, "the Yoruba-Bantu continuation poetry of *vodoun*," and "the Black Church generally." Brathwaite's mixture of genres and republication of revised earlier material brings thematic and formal attention to the underlying principles of organization—of inclusion and exclusion—that genre *and* publication entail, putting his work "into ?conVERsation w/ established 9–5 (9"X5") publishing. where all our kinetic & hieroglyphic word-ideas as BOXed up into these neat 'library-shelf' formats."[43]

SVS allows Brathwaite to develop a multiply voiced poetics with which to hail an emergent community or nation. He describes it as a process of "holding a broken mirror up to broken nature"— using the printed word to affirm and mobilize the political possibilities inherent in nonsynchronism of the postcolonial world.[44] Similar to concrete poetry, the graphic component of script is not supplemental or secondary but is the medium and the content. SVS deconstructs the hierarchy that privileges a politics of expression over the written text by making the form of the text central to its "content." Brathwaite's experimental graphic poetics is a material poetics, invested in what cannot be immediately subsumed to meaning. Though his "postSalt" work, like his earlier New World trilogy (collected as *The Arrivants*), thematically emphasizes the historical migrations and continuity of life on both sides of the black Atlantic, SVS challenges readers to attend to the space of the page—the arrangement of spatial and syntactic elements—without subordinating spatial poetics to an experiential, expressive voice.

Into the Image of Sycorax

The hinge between genres—for example, verse, prose diary, chronicle, academic prose—in the syncretic SVS work is apostrophe, an ur-trope of the lyric voice through which objects, by being addressed, are contingently elevated to the plane of subjectivity. The inverse is also true: the subject, relating to those objects, becomes analogous to them. Apostrophe traditionally guarantees the solidity of the poem's imagined speaking subject to the extent that although the invoked, absent other does not—and is not expected to—speak back, the structure of address confers being to both. In other words, apostrophe's calling out gives the poem's voice its solidity: for it to call out to something absent, the voice must be in some sense *there*. Apostrophe, which Jonathan Culler has called a "sign of fiction which knows its own fictive nature," displaces subjectivity onto the surface of the poem itself.[45] The time of apostrophe is "a special temporality which is the set of all moments at which writing can say 'now.'"[46] In the heterotemporal, intercultural Caribbean, "saying 'now'" is not a neutral act but an argument that charts the fractures of the incomplete processes of inter/culturation and ac/culturation. Brathwaite's use of apostrophe becomes, in this way, a political act once one asks who is being called and to what "now."

Apostrophic interjections help to "invent" the nation of nation language as the discovery or production of what may have been there in another form. As Jacques Derrida has argued, invention relates the new, "that is, something quite other that can also be quite ancient," to a present set of possibilities and to a possibility of a reconceived present: "The very movement of this fabulous repetition can, through a crossing of chance and necessity, produce the new of an event."[47] The sense of the new as also quite ancient, as a return to what may not have been there the "first time," makes it possible to see Sycorax as an advance on the much older Ariel-Caliban debates among Caribbean and Latin American intellectuals. Briefly recapitulated, taking Shakespeare's *The Tempest* as an allegory for the New World and its politics, Uruguayan essayist José Enrique Rodó argued in *Ariel* (1900) that Ariel should be a model for the Latin American intellectual's relationship to Europe and to culture. For Rodó, Caliban, who learned the master's language only to curse, is a figure of sensuality and depravity (*torpeza*), a figure of the leaderless mass or mob unconstrained by higher ideals, while Ariel represents a nobility of spirit that at once elevates culture and is expressed by that culture. Taking up the question in 1971, Cuban poet Roberto Fernández Retamar rejected the idea of a unitary Latin American culture and privileged Caliban, "the rude and unconquerable master of the island," as a model for the intellectual, although both Ariel and Caliban remain "slaves in the hands of Prospero, the foreign magician." Retamar stressed the importance of critique and resistance, even to the point of romanticizing Caliban.[48] Both arguments ultimately turn on twin problems of masks (Ariel or Caliban) and reconstituting lost origins; as such they risk mistaking what are only, in the end, names in a play for something substantial.

Published prior to Retamar's essay, Brathwaite's poem "Caliban," from *Masks*, the third part of *The Arrivants* trilogy, takes up these concerns. The poem's first section, complaining that "you have heard it all before O Leviticus O Jeremiah O Jean-Paul Sartre," concludes by collapsing modern history—from Castro and the Cuban revolution back to the emancipation of slaves in the West Indies and Columbus's "discovery" of the New World—into a single unfolding time:

It was December second, nineteen fifty-six.

It was the first of August eighteen thirty-eight.

It was the twelfth of October fourteen ninety-two.

How many bangs how many revolutions?[49]

The poem introduces Caliban through an adaptation of his freedom song from *The Tempest*, rewritten into Carnival time, and finally into the performance of the limbo—"*limbo | limbo like me*"—that concludes with a "hot | slow | step | on the burning ground."[50] Insofar as the dance is linked to a "long dark deck," presumably of the slave ship, and the practice of ensuring "the god won't drown," here too is a desire to recover origins and to recover alternate forms of ancestrality. This recovery would avoid the easy reassurances of the law—God's law, the law of the prophet, or the law of the dialectic—by turning to the "submerged culture," "where the music hides," that Brathwaite comes to associate with Sycorax.[51]

Turning to Sycorax, Caliban's "submerged" mother who appears only as a name in *The Tempest*, Brathwaite tropes the Ariel-Caliban debate; through her he stresses the textual nature of that debate. She is also textual in the sense that, in the introduction, I argue the figure of the veil is textual: neither fully an "ontopological" object nor simply an ideal or fantasy but both.[52] She is not recovered but conjured, making her a complicated figure of invention that repeats as origin, collocating Shakespeare, those mothers lost at sea during the Middle Passage, all those childless mothers produced by slavery, and the gods that did not drown en route to the New World as literary ancestors. A silent character is thus playfully situated as the figure of the "mother tongue," and she is also an ideal figure for the poet, who makes him- or herself present through the image of a voice, in this case by imagining the withheld voice and absent speaker. Where *The Arrivants* makes extensive use of languages other than English (especially Akan and Haitian Kreyòl), Brathwaite's SVS primarily reworks English, producing foreignness through words phonologically or orthographically turned into other words. However, the invocation of Sycorax merits additional elaboration, especially in light of the long history of slippage between concepts of materiality, maternity, and the matrix or womb taken to "birth" invention. While the abstract, deraced figure of the *maternal* figures prominently in theories of creativity, the figure of the *mother* is always already racialized. As Laura Doyle argues, the mother "harbors a knowledge and a history rooted in the senses of a racially and sexually specific body" making her "the point of access to a group history and bodily grounded identity" and "the cultural vehicle for fixing, ranking, and subduing groups and bodies."[53]

To the extent that Sycorax figures origin for Brathwaite, one must under-stand an originary exile rather than originary plenitude or home. Sycorax is a figure of natality, of the historically situated fact of birth; nonnative, she appears where she does not necessarily belong and has no "proper" place. Sycorax may signify a bodily past but also signifies the desire to bring her nearer, to re-member her as an act of invention, lessening the distance between her as object and the subject of the poem. Her uneasy positioning is clearest in one of the few poems where she "appears" as a cospeaker: "Letter SycoraX" (fig. 1), a revision of the earlier "X/Self's Xth Letters from the Thirteen Provinces" from *X/Self* (again revised and reprinted as "X self xth letter | from the thirteen colonies" in *Ancestors* [fig. 2]).[54] Here are the opening lines:

Dear mamma

*i writin yu dis letter/***wha?**
guess what! pun a computer o/kay?
like i jine de mercantilists!

Dear mumma
uh writin yu dis letter
wha?

O

i mean de same way dem tief/in gun
power from sheena & taken we blues &

guess what! pun a computer
kay?

like a jine de mercantilists?

well not quite!

gone
. . .

well not quit!

uh mean de same way dem tief/in gun
-power from sheena & taken we blues &
gone

say
wha? get on wid de same ole

story?

say
wha? get on wid de same ole
story?

okay
okay
okay
okay

okay
okay
okay
okay

if yu cyaan beat prospero
whistle

if yu cyaan beat prospero
whistle?

no
mumma!

No mamma!

Fig. 1. "Letter Sycorax"

Fig. 2. "X self xth letter | from the thirteen colonies"

Though the poem is nominally a letter, the second revision makes its dialogic structure (between X/Self and his mother, whom Brathwaite occasionally identifies as Caliban and Sycorax) clearer. Lineation along with typography now offset the mother's replies. The poem enacts a series of dilations and contractions of time, starting with its startling interpolation of the letter recipient's reply, breaking up and redistributing the effects of the voice understood as a singular consciousness. The delay between the epistle's being sent and received, for example, is annulled, making the title a pun: the letter invoked is both alphabetic character and missive. "Letter" also refers to the mark of education (i.e., "person of letters"), as X/Self suggests that his use of the computer co-opts the "mercantilist" culture, mirroring that culture's own practice, for which his mother rebukes him: "*say | wha? get on wid de* same ole *| story?*" Her criticism has several facets. On the one hand, his rehearsal of the mercantilist's history of exploitation and appropriation, however accurate, is pat. Merely knowing of and restating past ills, even if they shape present conditions, is inadequate to the task of justifying or explaining the present, much less changing it. On the other hand, the rest of the poem (and in retrospect, the fact that there are a number of versions of this poem) calls into question the idea that one's actions merely repeat some actions in the past. "You have heard it all before," as the poem "Caliban" laments, literally, in this case: "taken we blues and gone" alludes to Langston Hughes's "Note on Commercial Theater," revising the earlier poet's pronoun to the plural "we" that Hughes's "my" could always be taken to stand for.[55]

The vacillation between the senses of "letter"—alphabetic mark, education, missive—is drawn out in the title "Letter Sycorax" and in "X self xth letter" by the enlarged, capital "O" that ends the fourth line, dividing the word "okay." The graphic separation of "o" from "kay" makes the "o" polysemous. The effects of this fragmentation or mobilization of the word are complex, being both semantic and rhythmic. In one register, the isolated, extra-large capital "O" recalls lyric apostrophe and thus a tradition of intelligibility with and against which the drama of the poem works. The enlarged "O" recurs, set apart in the word "okay" ("but is one a de *bess* tings since cicero O | kay?") and again in the middle of a word (e.g., "& a whole rash a de so-call creole econOmiss").[56] Each subsequent revision amplifies X/Self's uncertainty regarding his link to society, whether he is breaking away or repeating ("like a jine the mercantilists?"), and the first-person pronoun ("I") is replaced with an indefinite article ("a") or rhyming syllable ("uh"), suggesting at phonic fidelity and a shift away the sign of the speaking/perceiving subject.[57] Subjectivity in the poem becomes an effect of the figured synchronism between writing and reading rather than a precondition.

Because of the poem's dialogic nature, which emphasizes the instantaneous relation between sender and recipient, I read the phrase "i writin" or "uh writin" as a nation-language rendering of the present progressive "I am writing." In all versions of this poem, Brathwaite omits the auxiliary verb "to be," thereby connecting the grammatical subject directly to the participle. The effect of this collapse is to make synchronous, figuratively, the times of writing and of reception. Because the time becomes aporetic (I am writing? I was writing? I will be writing? I will have been writing?), the time of the action moves from a definite, though blank *now*, to an indefinite time, as in the simple present or future tense (*now* I write, I will write) or as with modals (I can write) or aspectuals (I tend to write). Through this expansion—pluralization—of the times of writing, the poem draws attention to the time's formal presentation, suggesting an "externally" static time and an "internally" dynamic time—that is, within the poems' use of those norms, new temporal relationships proliferate. This plural instant marks a departure from the historical sweep of *The Arrivants* and its focus on epic time and recovered origins.[58]

The rest of the poem's strategies turn on a series of puns and lists. X/Self says his computer is not "one a dem pensive tings like ibm or bang & ovid | nor anyting glo. rious like dat," conflating thought with price (*ex*pensive), conflating brand names (IBM, Remington, and perhaps home technology manufacturer Bang and Olufsen) and the names of the writers of antiquity (Ovid, Cicero), and emphasizing the physicality of typing with a typewriter, which eventually gives way to "chipp/in dis poem onta dis tab- | let || chiss- | ellin dark- | ness || writin in lite."[59] SVS, from this perspective, transfers the physical labor of writing to the page. The poem moves symbolically from typewriter to chiseling poetry in stone to the computer and vacillates between the biblical Moses, his brother Aaron who made the Golden Calf, and "one a dem dyaaam isra- || light."[60] The context of reading remains unclear throughout the poem, following a punning logic that allows many phrases and even words to rest between two different discourses, as in an especially rich passage where X/Self marvels at modernity:

> a doan really know how pascal & co
> balt & apple & cogito ergo sum
> come to h/invent all these tings
>
> since de rice & fall a de roman empire
> & how capitalism & slavely like it putt christianity
> on ice[61]

The passage is masterful in its array of optional puns that articulate brand names and historical figures. Pascal is both mathematician Blaise Pascal and the computer language; Cobalt is the CAD program and the mineral mined from central Africa; Apple is the computer company and the putative inspiration for Isaac Newton's discovery of gravity; "cogito ergo sum" is Descartes' paradigmatic expression of subjective experience; *The Decline and Fall of the Roman Empire* is Edward Gibbon's epochal text. Fittingly, the list ends with *Capitalism and Slavery*, Eric Williams's epochal study of the centrality of slavery to the development of capitalism (and the centrality of falling rate of profit to the abolition of slavery), implicating X/Self's use of the computer within a much larger history and more complicated geopolitical present. What seems to begin with an effort to resituate an origin through the figure of Sycorax instead becomes a broader meditation on the entanglement of origins and an uncanny doubling where one's words always come from and depend on an earlier discourse—*The Tempest*, for example. "Letter SycoraX" ends with an open-ended, ecstatic apostrophe—"& | mamma!"—but "X/Self Xth Letter" ends with an allusion to one of Brathwaite's most celebrated poems, "The Dust" (on left) from the earlier *Arrivants* trilogy:

you crops start to die	&
you can't even see the sun in the sky;	*mumma!*
an' suddenly so, without rhyme,	
without reason, all you hope gone	*why is dis*
ev'rything look like it comin' out wrong.	*what it mean?*[62]
Why is that? What it mean?	

Whereas in "The Dust," Brathwaite's famous poem constructed around the discourse of women at market, this exasperation about disorder is made ironic by the metrical regularity of the lines that precede it, in "X/Self xth letter" it is ironic at a deeper level. Seemingly unmotivated, it breaks the frame of the imagined dialogue, introducing a question—"what it mean?"—that departs sharply from what had seemed to be the poem's central question—"what is the bess way to seh." "Suddenly so," the two tracks of the poem—the possibilities of "writin in lite" and the synchronism of histories that seem to exclude each other—collapse into a common disorder. Readers who catch the references to Hughes, Pound, and Bunting would not be able to answer the question within the terms of the poem that precedes the concluding question. In this final gesture, Sycorax's cited question deconstructs the dyadic structure of the dialogue between Sycorax and X/Self,

implicating readers as well in the structure. Sycorax is a figure not only of ances-
trality, of a citation that repeats as origin, but also of responsibility to the *arriv-
ant* whose unruly demand requires answer, a break with and return to the past.

Saving the Word

Given Brathwaite's concerns with loss and erasure, one might expect the com-
puter to figure as a more permanent mode of preservation and transmission,
but its function is more complicated. If in his earlier argument, rhythm and syl-
lables, the syntagmatic arrangements of language that shape expressivity, are
"the very *software*, in a way, of the language," the hardware must be the associa-
tive or paradigmatic level, which makes the puns seem so excessive, extended
to the conventions of printing.[63] This, then, would underscore the "video"—
literally, "to look or see"—of SVS as documentary, preservative, and, as I argue,
a mechanically facilitated means of arranging time. At one level, video is an
elaboration of one of Brathwaite's other major concerns: a sense of the word as
always "coming into being."[64] Through video, Brathwaite conjoins the Timehri,
Amerindian petroglyphs ("glimpses of a language, glitters of a vision of a world,
scattered utterals of a remote Gestalt; but still there, near, potentially commu-
nicative"), and the "obeah blox" of the computer itself.[65] However, Brathwaite
also claims that SVS is part of an attempt to return to the "world of **ILLUMI-
NATED MANUSCRIPTS** when the written word could still hear itself speak,
as it were."[66] I understand this "hearing" to emphasize a poetic "voice alight
with echo . w/ the birth of sound," a testimony rather than an artifact, imagin-
ing a predisciplinary literature, saving the word from ideological and concep-
tual enclosure.[67] In different terms, Brathwaite's comments about SVS suggest
an effort to locate subjectivity in the words themselves, giving priority to the
"writing in light" rather than particular topics. Similar to medieval illuminated
manuscripts, this mode of writing does not take for granted the word's trans-
parency. Unlike those medieval manuscripts, however, SVS incorporates what
would have been didactic, marginal drawings into the writing itself, making
typeface an ambiguous element of prosody, or style, rather than explanatory
illustration. SVS marks a threshold separating the experience *of* poetry—the
"performance" of words on the page—and the experience *in* poetry—the sys-
tem of *references* and presumed relations between historically determined peo-
ples discussed or implied.

Video as documentation, extradiscursive "illuminations," and the obscur-
ing effects of narrative convention come together in an appeal to poetry at the
end of "Heartbreak Hotel," added to his revision of *Mother Poem* in *Ancestors*, his

second trilogy, which was among the first works published in SVS. Like its companion poem "Pixie," "Heartbreak Hotel" mixes verse and journalistic prose (supposed to have been transcribed from a radio broadcast) to tell the familiar story of a child who has run away from home and come back to a society that has not done enough to protect her, while trying to transcend the limitations of that familiarity. The poem's speaker—occasionally interrupted by the voice of the child or the mother pleading for "someone to help me and my chill-|dren"—addresses the "howling city needing|love" and then bemoans "the lives so broken|w/ inglorious/sounds o broken & incongorous||woods." The shift from addressing the city—a metonym for the people in it—to the woods is surprising and unresolved: the poem immediately addresses "words" as if correcting itself: "o words so shoved about so worn & coil we cannot slip|yr sandals on and wear them comfortable out into the|bleeding streets of chance."[68] The poem has turned back on itself, addressing the failure of imagination that can do no more for girls like Pixie than to recite their fate in sensationalized ways. Further, the phrase "lives so broken" retrospectively leads one to anticipate "so broken" to repeat, making "sounds o broken" seem like a typo. That momentary hesitation and sudden shift in mode of address is one of Brathwaite's central strategies: the sounds are broken, as are the incongruous woods/words. In that double take, the terrain of the poem opens up, allowing it to address a larger set of interrelated problems by setting the conditions, including the italicized, bold font, that encourage us to glimpse "submerged" words and worlds just beneath the printed ones. The poem concludes with a long apostrophe that extends and complicates these questions without offering definitive resolution, save making a case, through apostrophe, for poetry against narrative:

> *o homeless daughters needing love yr utterances erupting interrupting*
> *in/to this place w/in this poem. trampelling the mothers you becoming*
> *battering yr wooden palings down and tumbelling*
>
> *these imaging enjambments scraggeling across the yard across the sands*
> *unto the very edges of this poem*
> *w/out its midday angelus its black lip iron ritual of bells*
>
> *where very words need love. need you. love too*
> *o nicolas guillén. o sapphire. o belov:ed. rita dove*
> *my brother martin carter butler yeats . how can we tell*
>
> *these dancers from they dance?*

[69]

These lines, to borrow John Hollander's phrase, "trope their scheme," identifying "imaging"—envisioning and making images—with enjambment, a word that in French literally means "striding across or straddling, enfolding the margin."[70] The very edges of this poem fold into the poem itself and inform its final calling out to the ancestors, or at least the ancestral. If apostrophe always threatens to become merely an invocation of invocation, this layering of apostrophes, alluding to W. B. Yeats's famous apostrophe from "Among School-children," initially reads as an ironic demystification of lyric and, through that allusion, as a reactivation of the question regarding retrospection and the forms that commemoration or elegy can take. As with the allusion to Langston Hughes in "Letter SycoraX," Brathwaite changes perspective, this time from the abstract "how can we tell the dancer from the dance" to the particular: these dancers, their dance.[71] The invocation of Yeats after a list of writers implicated in decolonization broadly conceived juxtaposes the idea of a progressive decline dictated by the narrative with the atemporal inventiveness of words, of style as the possibility of an event of rupture with the possible.

In slightly different terms, this specific allusion makes an argument for poetry as a medium of the word. The written, apostrophic word effects a "revitalization of origins" as an act of invention: to *revitalize* what has neither died nor existed as such, to make a place for the *arrivant*, the unknown and not-yet-named.[72] What initially seems to be a typo ("sounds o broken") becomes instead another moment of apostrophe or another instance of a repeated "o" that informs much of the passage. The emphasis on language as medium, through invocation of other media and through the active morphing of language tropes, calls into question the capacities of language and literature. Analogizing (through allusion) the task of the poet to that of the dancer, the practice indistinguishable from the work, Brathwaite offers the means by which to change the units of analysis to other units of sense making, such as the paralinguistic "@." That symbol, thought to go back to early modern mercantilism, at once designates a particular location and the dematerialization of place in a world connected by information technology. Ending here, it functions as another submerged apostrophic address, another submerged "o," left suspended like the final "& | mamma!" in "Letter SycoraX." The list of names of poets functions as an apostrophic gesture calling together a community of those who love the "very words."

Troping literature and literary conventions informs much SVS work, especially *Shar: Hurricane Poem* and "Nam(e)tracks," which similarly deploy graphic marks that visually approximate an apostrophic "O." In the case of the "Nam(e) tracks," these marks serve an ambiguous function of introducing space between two competing voices without fully separating them, again with Caliban being instructed by his mother and O'Grady, a Prospero figure whose name comes from a children's game similar to "Simon Says."[73] Their function is somewhat less ambiguous in *Shar*, whose refrain "what can I tell you" explicitly marks the insufficiency of literature understood as representation. Yet, like many of Brathwaite's post–Time of Salt publications (e.g., *Barabajan Poems, ConVERSations with Nathaniel Mackey, Golokwati 2000, MR/*), *Shar: Hurricane Poem* begins with a text that at the very least holds open a place for the literary word. This text, entitled "Saving the Word," coauthored by Carolivia Herron, largely (and uncharacteristically) reprinted without revision, is a transcript of Herron's introduction of Brathwaite at a conference on epic poetry 22 September 1988, after Hurricane Gilbert had destroyed his home and archives of Caribbean literature ("drafts unpublished manuscripts letters diaries artefacts books books books books thousands of miles of tapes LPs") in Jamaica and of Brathwaite's response to both the hurricane and Herron.[74] Herron (according to the transcript) breaks off from her prepared comments to invoke "lost words," the library of Alexandria, and "the long attempt to keep the words of a people from being destroyed." She then reads a note Brathwaite "wrote when he heard of the hurricane" wherein he repeats and responds to the question "what can I tell you?" Echoing Herron's concern over lost words, Brathwaite asserts, "You have to be concerned with the sources of a poet's life a people's | inspiration and try to protect care for as best you can those sourc- | es" especially "the archives— that written mem | orialized recorded record of his/her life/hope/history/art." He concludes by condemning "our Caribb culture" as "too much a reaction—if not reactionary—plantation culture," which in my reading is also the problem of the available media narratives for lost girls like Pixie.

The hurricane, however, has a larger claim on the imagination of the whole region, not through empathy but because its destruction was so widespread. Another way of understanding Brathwaite's criticism of Caribbean culture is that the hurricane reveals an underlying reactionary plantation culture that indifferently witnesses the loss not only of its words but the *sources* of its words. *Shar* does not document the hurricane, then, but the regeneration of the unincorporated word. Its verse opens by analogizing the hurricane to a bomber, moving to a partial catalog of the destruction ("wood | has become so useless. stripped. wet. | fragile. broken. totally uninhabitable | with what we must still build"), alternating such repetitive, staccato lines as "wasted wasted all

all all wasted wasted wasted" or "And what. what. what .   what more.   what more can I tell you" that transition from despair to defiance, from the indicative to the imperative mood (figs. 3–5):[75]

 o

sing
sing

clatter of ashes
collapses of coal

Fig. 3. From *Shar: Hurricane Poem*

into flame
shatter of leaves

sing
sing
sing

.ular clink
of the chains & the

Fig. 4. From *Shar: Hurricane Poem*

Fig. 5. From *Shar: Hurricane Poem*

The imperative mood here functions as apostrophe, calling out to any reader, any implied "you" interpellated by its demand, but also calling back to the poet as a kind of justification of poetry in the wake of a disaster. The imperative and other direct appeals to an audience that serve to justify the practice of writing will become common uses of apostrophe in Brathwaite's work of this period. *Shar*, the word itself historically linked through orthography to both "share" and "shear," tends to accompany these calls with magnification of text and negative space, which "amplify" the function of words *as* words. One page, for example, simply has a repetition of the phrase "& | sing. | ing" printed large enough that the period used in the place of a hyphen to break up "singing" appears as a large, filled-in, apostrophic "O," or singing mouth:

Fig. 6. From *Shar: Hurricane Poem*

Corresponding to this change of typeface is a change in the leading (space between lines) and kerning (space between letters), which, as tense does, pluralizes the readings of the poem by changing the means through which words are encountered. The reader who proceeds too rapidly, for example, will miss the transition from the imperative "sing" to the adjective "singular" (fig. 4). Brathwaite creates a situation where the reading must begin and return to letters, both as signs within a signifying chain that produce reading and as sensible signs in their own right. If the enlarged capital "O" is part of a set of elements that act on a center (the technologically mediated scene of writing) and vary in relation to it by deemphasizing temporal specificity (a single *now*) in order to produce a saturated moment, here the recurrent closed "●" designates the differential power or force of the mark. That mark is the somewhat paradoxical sign of an unvoiced apostrophe that underscores the video element of SVS, but this graphic apostrophe emphasizes that the word is saved through its use, through being worn down and reconstituted, through being shared.

Trying to Ghost Words

With video, Brathwaite has chosen an especially apt metaphor for his use of the graphic texture of writing. An iconic instance of modernity and surveillance culture that "has a powerful claim for being the art form par excellence of late capital," video is a sign of transmission or imparting itself.[76] It makes possible a magnification of the everyday, memorializes the quotidian and the insignificant, and in the same gesture produces an anxiety that *this* time, *these* moments, will be erased, lost from the more general flows of space-time or modernity. It also captures moments that might otherwise be lost or displaced from narrative histories of nation-states. Capturing and making return moments that other-

wise could disappear is another way the idea of video helps situate Brath-
waite's poetics, which consistently point to what language obscures, "ghost-
ing" words—giving the impression that absent words have appeared—to draw
attention to what remains absent in available ways of writing and thinking. At
once an injunction to look and a reminder of what has not been seen, video
figures a broader formal means through which the work draws attention to its
own construction, further highlighted by Brathwaite's practice of revising and
republishing works. In its moment an emblem of anticipated repetition, of pri-
vate re-viewing, video forces us to ask about the plural time of an event and its
resonances.

The question of the event's time is most salient in the question of "time of
the Haitian refugees" posed by "Dream Haiti," one of his "DreamStories"—
prose writings in the general mode of medieval dream visions such as Dante's
Divine Comedy, which blend history, prophesy, current events and divergent
subjectivities. Breaking with the dream vision, however, the moment of falling
asleep is suppressed, and the narrator of the DreamStories (often identified
with Brathwaite himself, linking the medieval divinely inspired dream vision
to the psychoanalytic analysis of condensation and displacement in a subject's
dreams) typically does not have a guide through the dreamscape. The journey
sits between political or philosophical commentary and a text demanding inter-
pretation. These texts posit an *ontology of dream* rooted in video: time in these
DreamStories is not linearly organized but refracted so that moments antici-
pate and echo each other; time as circle *and* arrow both disrupted. As with many
of his SVS works, Brathwaite has published multiple versions of "Dream Haiti."
An earlier version of "Dream Haiti" begins at sea "where the US Coast Guard
cutter was patrolling / along the borders of the Mexicans & my brothers – / the
what was called 'the Haitian Refugees.'"[77] This "dream ontology" is rooted in
the materiality of video itself, whose frames are not single or discrete, as in film,
but mutually constituted or interlaced. Each video "frame," a catachrestic term
because video does not actually have frames, contains and is contained by part
of the frame before and after, which in part accounts for glitches during play-
back and makes video editing difficult. Video time is differential, moving from
A to A' rather than A to B.[78] In this way it refers both to the serial revisions of and
within poems. In addition to figuring documentation, video becomes a meta-
phor for invention—fabulous repetition—that exceeds the frames through
which the given world is given by insisting on an interrelation of things and
times.

Such differential transitions also register between versions, clarifying the degree to which the word is an active element in his poetics rather than a transcendent quality. The transformations of language in "DreamHaiti" lend themselves to a more fundamental question of naming and predication and the ways representation obscures the represented. A later version of "Dream Haiti" (fig. 7), subtitled "in a strange land," revises the beginning of the tale:[79]

> the blow & wet metal sides of my nerve
where the US naval Coast Guard cutter was patrollin
all along the borders of the Mexicans & my brothers –
in what was call in the dream . the Time of the

Fig. 7. From "Dream Haiti" (2007)

In both instances, brotherhood is emphasized alongside the intervention of the U.S. Coast Guard (which becomes typographically important later), but the addition of "in the dream" adds a layer of mediation to "what was call[ed]," and introduces a further deferral of the overdetermined designation "the Haitian Refugees." Again, this is an unvoiced apostrophe. Both instances that I consider here follow this identification with the immediate question rendered (figs. 8 and 9):[80]

//// I write Shante Chackmul & ask
WHAT NAME BAHAMAS GIVE TO
HAITIANS WHO COME TO YR OUSE

TO BEG WRUK ////

Fig. 8. From "Dream Haiti" (1994)

//// mi write
Shantí Chacmoul
. ask WHAT NAME BAHAMAS GIVE HAITIES WHO COME ADOBE
BEG WOROK ////

Fig. 9. from "Dream Haiti" (2007)

This question, which the narrator proposes to write to Shante Chakmul/ Shanté Chacmoul and which is set off by four unpronounceable slashes, ////, is an intrusion of the frame of the tale into the tale, setting the question aside in advance. The slashes also signal a very complex, compound reference that conjoins the name of a Bahamian resort (Club La Shanté) and a the name given to a pre-Columbian, Mesoamerican stone statue (Chac-Mool), which figures a man reclining with a tray over his midsection. The allegorical "Shanté Chacmoul" suggests that modern tourists in the Caribbean repeat an ancient posture, even as the Bahamian government works to keep the "Haitian Refugees" from interrupting their time, shielding those tourists from any implication in producing Haitian poverty or corruption. Here, then, Brathwaite establishes a synchronism between an ancient rite and a present one, pluralizing the time of the crisis, albeit ambiguously, introducing what later will become an explicit theme of refused kinship.

In *DS(2)*, the words "Haitian Refugees" (fig. 7) are nearly illegible, suggesting on the one hand a further refusal or deferral of the epithet and on the other the ways it obscures those it refers to. The graphic presentation recalls the epigraph, apostrophizing Haiti: "one day we turn our head | and look inside you."[81] Almost illegible, that call that "we" "look inside" seems mocked, since that looking still may not read correctly. Here one of the most salient features of SVS, the tendency to make reading always a rereading, takes on its most obviously political valence: this "look inside" is always a second look. "We" have not looked and cannot look at Haiti "as such"; "Haitian Refugees" mark that which we cannot or, due to the distortions of our apparatuses and norms of perception, of production and reproduction, can no longer "read." The category—the words—is "revitalized"; the refugees again become *arrivants*, unknown in their singularity. This is a literary event: in telling of those not yet known, those who do not correspond to their name, the poem moves to undo even the "we" that is the subject of this look, making them no longer calculable. This apostrophic "look inside" does not refer to a redeemed version of the past but is an affirmation of that past and this present. Like all apostrophe, though, it links the subjectivity of the speaker of the lines with its object, Haiti, bestowing on Haiti its own subjectivity. In light of the specification of the "[t]*ime* of the 'Haitian Refugees'" in the newer version, we are invited to ask—and implicated in the question —what *are* the times of the "Haitian Refugees"? In the continuing aftermath of the 2010 earthquake, what are the times of the dead?

These blended times generate a "plural instant." Through such devices as repetition and shifts of narrative perspective—from first-person singular to first-person plural—the poem acknowledges the differential frames necessary to think the times of the dead: the twenty-five on board the boat built to carry only "13 or 14 or 15." The dedication to "many more thousands gone" links these Haitians (via allusion to the Negro spiritual "No More Auction Block/ Many Thousands Gone") to the Africans who died during the Middle Passage. As with "Caliban," there is only one continually unfolding revolution—the plural instant establishes a synchronism between a historical event and those that follow it. Time doubles back on itself like the movement of a wave, which is also the movement of reading ("as if I was already turning the leaves of the | waves").[82] The journey itself, at sea for an unspecified period, reinscribes both Henri "Cristophe on La Ferrièrre walking that sloe corridor of water" and "Toussaint Legba all the way out on Napoleons joyless eyeless island of | torture on the glacial seas of the Jura," linking both to the slave "dungeons of guinée & gorée."[83] "Dream Haiti" insists on the implication of the spectator with the spectacle, both through self-reference (the repeated "as I say" or "as you can see") and a first person that links the author-narrator with the "Haitian Refugees," even onto death: "& there was so much goin on all above us | what w/ the ferrymen shoutin for survivors tho we was all quite dead & | bloated by this time."[84]

The deictic "this time" rather than designating a particular moment becomes another suspended moment, one located as much in the preventable future as in the preventable past but pointedly in the present of the telling rather than the past of the event narrated (that time). At this moment the narrative shifts the time to an unnarrativizable time: that of one's own death, a moment that, as the annihilation of any possible subjectivity, cannot properly be called traumatic but marks the "possibility of establishing certain synchronisms." Beyond memorializing or speaking for those who, invoking Marx, "cannot represent themselves," beyond "giving voice" to the suffering of others, prosopopoeia draws attention to an absent or broken link. This is aided by SVS, which centers the announcement along the vertical but not horizontal axis, printing the words in a smaller size than the "cul-de-sac" that describes the movement of the waves, which is another figure of restrained or proscribed movement: "'endless purgatorial passages'—if you can call it that—."[85]

The death of a "likkle bwoy" one has seen on television—"juss this glimpse juss this shot dripping w/history – | clear out the water *for all our howls to see*"— generates a sustained apostrophe, apparently to the reader (figs. 10–12):[86]

- let me say it -

that e nvr deserve

**back into the water
that e nvr deserve that e nvr nvr nvr
deserve**

that e nvr deserve

Fig. 10. From "Dream Haiti" (2007)

& yu chide me fe
chantin like
this? fe lament
=ing this seem
=ing perpetu
=al pogrom & pro
=gram like this?
this
season on
season persist

Fig. 11. From "Dream Haiti" (2007)

=uant anomie?
for tryin to ghost
words to
holla
this tale?

1234567890

Fig. 12. From "Dream Haiti" (2007)

To "ghost words" aligns Brathwaite with Philip's hauntological poetics of un-saying, here disarticulating words from the speaking (hollering) voice so as to enable it to speak from a position of something other than sympathy, which would put the focus on Brathwaite's pain rather than that of the Haitians. It also invokes video's differentiation of time and functions similarly to the doubled scene of reading I discussed in the context of "Heartbreak Hotel." Making the words "live off the page" has the effect of splitting their meaning between now, the time they echo, and some future time when they may re-sound. Only those elements considered secondary to meaning—that is, sound, rhythm, the form on the page, the graphic form of the letters—remain relatively constant. Rhe-torically, this direct address to the reader, from a right-justified textual margin, punctures and punctuates the narrative unfolding. We are reminded that one speaks only of the ones called "the Haitian Refugees," and that such reference is overdetermined by other discourses, a "perpetual pogrom" that informs their existence, as well as, by implication, ours. The perspective shifts between first-person singular and plural, an address to a "you" that is once "readers" and a particular critic, making the subjectivity of the poem unstable—it encompasses at once the empirical author and the poem itself, as well as the Haitian refugees and the Coast Guard.

The use of the present continuous, underscored by enjambment that separates the "-ing" ending from the verb stem, using an equal sign rather than a hyphen, underscores the *ongoing* nature of this scene, juxtaposing the timelessness of lyric with the nontimeless present time of reading. Simultaneously, the equal signs, like the number line that concludes the passage I have referenced, simply invoke mathematics as another system of representation, indicating the ways the Haitians are, in a sense, "not counted" in discussions of modernity save as aberration, even as Brathwaite's poetics tries to make a space for them. The referenced chant itself, punctuated again by an unpronounceable symbol that recurs throughout "Dream Haiti," inscribes this telling within an aspirant community much as the invocation of television does, insisting on the distance between the call and the longed-for response.

"Dream Haiti" in particular and the DreamStories more generally demand attention to the liminal spaces and crossed boundaries—between life and death, between nations in the ambiguous terrain of international water and after the would-be refugees land, between a praise song and an elegy, between would-be savior and would-be saved. However, "Dream Haiti" makes a deeper ontological claim through one of its moments of apparent error, linking the hands that grasp and the ropes and lifebuoys themselves. "[T]he railings / or stations & stanchions [. . .] was like *mode* of the same material or metal as our | fingers & the palms of our hands" and "we were trying to reach the lifelines that were made of the same material as | the thongs of our fingers & the webs of our skin."[87] As with "sounds o broken" above, the slippage between "mode" and "made" is no mere typo but an indication of the political valence of the "ontology of dream," indexing the permeability and changeability of identities within the dream and a common *substance* within the dream's theater. To say the railings were "*mode* of the same material" suggests, that is, a single underlying substance, as well as a possibility within the "senscape" of the dream space of reimagining connections between people and objects in the waking world by dissolving the frames through which objects are apprehended or ordered, including the singular ego as the locus of possible experience. This points toward a sense of interindividuation, of differentiation rooted in a common substance suspending the atomistic division and allowing us to think of community or "Relation" in Édouard Glissant's sense, despite there being no adequate frame through which such community as a political project can be thought. We imagine community because of—not despite—difference.

From the perspective of *nam*, the term "Haitian Refugees" does not get to the real *nam*, the place from which the time they name emerges and within which another future is still possible. It misrecognizes the "Haitian Refugees" as a historically new phenomenon rather than as part of a recurrent struggle. It is not the words but something not yet sounded in the words of a community or nation to be realized. The poems make something happen through adherence to the notion that "the heart of the culture resides in its otherness." *Nam* then, is a concept with a false bottom that seems to be kernel of unchanging "national" culture defined against official institutions, but culture is a churning self-differentiation. Apostrophe's call, rather than creating the self through the relay of the other, marks an essential foreignness at the core of existence, the open space of the *arrivant*, the unknown but anticipated. The emphasis, thus, is on the graphic act of calling, the insufficiency of the ways we are called, and the gaps in experience covered over by our schemas and ways of organizing knowledge.

The Only Word We Have

The word, along with the small typographical and orthographic distinctions between words and characters, holds a privileged position in Brathwaite's SVS poetics not just in its meaning but in its sensuous appearance, creating a new "senscape," a new aesthetics rooted in the experience of time and language. Within poetry, to emphasize the sensuality of written words and letters in this way is to privilege style, the word in the label "Sycorax Video Style" that is most easily overlooked. Privileging style deemphasizes the indexical or symbolic uses of language—related to the historically specific conditions under which a sign signifies (and thus those conditions under which literature "expresses," "reflects" or "responds to" social contradictions)—in favor of those sensual qualities of language and novel usages through which language changes or evolves. Style, the *medium* of authorship—the sense of the presence of a particular author or group of authors at a particular historical juncture—is the possibility of the new in language. Style marks and exploits gaps in signifying structures whereby meaning can be unfixed, in this case articulating the premodern with the modern and insisting on words' capacities to "live off—away from—the page so you can see . . . like see their sound," the result being a style "you really have to *see* rather than read aloud."[88] Already, this 'living' suggests an orientation to the literary text that apprehends it apart from the level of its language, understood as so many references and connotative or denotative meanings, and that sees a role for reading apart from the mechanical reassembly of the author's, or language's, intention. If this living is possible, it is only thinkable by imagining writing as oriented toward a future, or better, a future anterior audience rather than a given audience, and imagining a constitutively unfinished text as a challenge or corrective to notions of the literary work as whole or sufficient onto itself.

Voice, as stylized word, is the effect of the material letter and its spacing, at once "taking us back" to textual practices of the Middle Ages and integrating those practices with the new possibilities. We should place equal critical emphasis on questions of writing as a physical act that articulates chiseling into stone in a plural instant that also includes "writing in light." SVS's insistence on the processes of writing, alongside its incorporation of other texts through allusion and apostrophe, further emphasize writing as medium, from which follows a revived notion of reading and deemphasis on the unity of the artwork. Brathwaite's post–Time of Salt poems mark an increased interest in the construction of the poems' contemporary world, situating the voice of the author among those events in the complex role of witness, using the idea video to achieve broader literary effects and to ask us about the constitution of the everyday, the now.

Thus, I return to the issue I raised at the beginning of this chapter: the determination of an age and the question of the ways events register or do not. What would happen were one to declare all of modernity to have been the age of Haiti and to understand history on its basis? How would such a framing of time shape our sense of the present, our shared obligations, and our definitions of freedom? The attempt to relocate the axes of history as a political project regarding the meaning of time recurs throughout Brathwaite's poetry and prose projects. Among the most immediate, and most enigmatic, versions of this is *Ark: A 9/11 Continuation Poem*, that I close this chapter by considering. This poem most literally—and audaciously—establishes a synchronism: between a Coleman Hawkins performance in 1967 or 1968 and the attacks on the World Trade Center and Pentagon in the United States on 11 September 2001.

In the wake of the 2001 attacks on the World Trade Center and Pentagon and crashing of the plane in western Pennsylvania, some scholars and historians have stressed the relation between that September morning and "the other 9/11," 11 September 1973, when a U.S.-backed Augusto Pinochet led a coup that overthrew Salvador Allende's socialist Popular Unity government.[89] Observing that echo marks an attempt to claim a counterinterpretation of the time, placing the shock and mourning of that moment in a less familiar context of similar shock and mourning beyond the country's borders. To ask how, if at all, those two events, separated by nearly three decades, are related is to challenge 9/11 as a definitive break, to see recent historical events as part of a larger, global historical continuum. The politics of claiming the later event as part of continuum that included the earlier one are not about time per se but about its meanings and the futures imaginable in what was, in the moment, a "post-9/11" world. To insist on the continued resonance of 11 September 1973 is to question before the fact what a "post-9/11" world is, even as leaders in the frightened West framed the 2001 event as an attack by "regressive" or "backward" people whose religion prevented them from participating in modernity. The 2001 attack on an emblem of modernity was the confirmation that neoliberal modernity, initiated in part by the 1973 coup, was the horizon of desirable possibility.

Brathwaite, insisting on a personal narrative prior to 1973, rewrites the 2001 attack in terms of a longer history of globalism and inter/culturation. *Ark*, like most of the SVS poems, has appeared more than once: versions have appeared under the name "Hawk" in a special issue of the *Literature Review* on global New York and in his 2003 collection *Born to Slow Horses*. Those versions list the date of Hawkins's performance as 1967, but *Ark* revises it to 1968, a year before Hawkins's death. An explanatory note in *Ark* explains that "the first revise & xtending 'Hawk' (now **Ark**) appears in my forthcoming **Born to slow horses** [. . .] but what yu have here [i.e., *Ark*] is even further along along." All versions begin with initial text whose function as subtitle or invocation is unclear (fig. 13):[90]

Fig. 13. From "Hawk" (duplicated in *Ark*)

The text does not appear to be a title or heading so much as a legend such as one might find beneath a photograph. The rectangles where apostrophes ought to be may be familiar to anyone who has had the experience of attempting to view or print characters that, for one reason or another, are unavailable. They suggest the idea of reading as an act of deciphering codes. Almost all the references are double references, like the ones in eleven and the two dates—1968 (or 1967) and 2001. "Hawk" is both the bird and Coleman Hawkins (nicknamed Hawk). The Library of Congress has preserved his celebrated 11 October 1939 recording, some twenty-eight years before the London performance, of the jazz standard (composed by Johnny Green, Frank Eyton, Edward Heyman, and Robert Sour) "Body and Soul." The number of jazz albums entitled *Live at Ronnie Scott's* is practically innumerable, with artists such as Nina Simone, Ben Webster, and Johnny Griffin all recording there at different points. In a poem about the politics of memory and memorialization, the name of the club is itself a mnemonic device that recalls any number of records and like experiences. Thirty-three or thirty-four years apart, the two moments seem to call to each other, inform and animate each other, a reperformance of "Body and Soul" speaking to so much destruction and death, both in 1939 and 1967.

In the prefatory text, the Brathwaite pairs the World Trade Center's twin towers with "the marassa of the Twin (*marassa*)" in "the performance or audioglyph version," linking this event to larger New World myth systems and a more capacious history of modernity that includes the second free republic in the Western hemisphere. Like the numerals in eleven, the moment is twinned—the instant made plural—so that two events become simultaneous for the purposes of literature. However, that "audioglyph version" Brathwaite refers to appears to be the presentation of the poem on the page more than any future reading, despite his performance instructions. SVS meshes both signifying and conventionally nonsignifying elements into a common weave, a temporal-spatial double take that expresses "our native Caribbean aesthetic." To that end, "marassa" refers to *loa* of Haitian vodou, which represents humanity's twinned nature. The Divine Twins are "half matter, half metaphysical; half-human, half-divine."[91] Likewise, the poem is half image, half text; half sensory experience, half organization of intelligible signs.

Because I read revision as part of a poem that moves "along along," the first level of this politics is the changed year itself, which constitutes the direct insertion of historiography—and the danger of rewriting the past in the terms of the present—into the larger act of extending the meanings of 11 September. Letting the instant remain plural resists a reading that would incorporate a past moment into a generalizable narrative, instead relating each moment without reducing them to a simple explanatory matrix. Beyond the coincidence of dates, stressing Coleman Hawkins's performance of "Body and Soul" as a balm for the many dead and soon to die silently expands the explicit injunction "never forget" that marks the day's continued political valence. Moreover, it conjoins two qualitatively different international events, one of which seems to inaugurate a new era, the other of which is apparently only a personal memory: "my fall | -ing failing fading | leaves o love / o you this golden time in lon | -don early autumn of the first spill | -ing burn | -ing time."[92] Time spills and burns; an event that marks the disruption of Western sovereignty comes to be aligned with a history both much larger (imperialism and its aftermath) and smaller (that of a particular

Bajan man in London on an otherwise unremarkable date). Laying a claim to "9/11" and the "post-9/11" world as a time still meaningfully connected to an earlier, apparently innocent moment of globalization marks Brathwaite's experimental poem as an attempt to redefine our understandings of modernity, writing, and the place of race through a reconsideration of time and of moments as multiple or, better, extended. The earlier moment anticipates and offers a balm for the later; the later still contains the earlier moment as an unresolved kernel distantly related to the present crisis.

Simultaneously, the poem insists on the correspondence between these two moments, which are made to *reflect* each other. The initial lines read "Hawk | shrouded in mirrors. showers. haunted by twins," a dual reference to the Twin Towers and the reduplicated date—11 September—brought together in a plural instant such that each anticipates and echoes the other (fig. 14):[93]

but some day certain in the future of New
York. his magic enigmatic majesty now flow-
ering the room . his body glow-

ing *the only word we have* for what is now this glow-
ering around these future towers of his solo masterpiece
rising himself again in sound towards the silver cross

of an approaching jet. dissecting in the blue
the full white mosque and omen of the moon
just afternoons ago. high over Berkeley Square. over

Heroes Square. over Washington Square. Wall Street
Canal. the graveyards of the negroes. the body body body bod-
ies pour-

ing from this dark Manhattan strom-
boli into dim catacombs of dis-
appearing love & grace & pain & smouldering wound .

Fig. 14. From *Ark*

The attacks in Manhattan and Washington, D.C., become the dream or nightmare already inscribed in Hawkins's performance, his signature song literalizing in "the body body body bod- | ies pour- || ing from this dark Manhattan strom- | boli into dim catacombs of dis-."[94] The poem inscribes the world historical event within a personal memory that refers back to an earlier moment (the 1939 recording). The event becomes iterable, although on different terms, not matching events of similar kind but events that make an impression on the psyche in ways that cannot be known in advance. There is additionally a generalization of the process of inscription, yielding a graphic "voice" linked not only to speech but also to sound and light, to the airplane that inscribes a cross, and so on, all of which are brought together by the coalescence of these moments into one moment.

The idea of jazz improvisation, which Brathwaite identifies as a mode "expressive . . . of the problems of the whole civilized complex of living in the post-Faustian, post-Freudian world," transects the discontinuous time of Coleman Hawkins's performance and the attacks in New York and Washington, D.C., making the former grammatically predict the latter. Like the command to sing in *Shar*, the invocation of improvisation reintroduces a vigorous conception of freedom, a leap or opening to the future. *Ark* features the transcript of a woman who lost her firefighter husband, a plea ("so let me | my belovèd | love you love you love you love you"), and reiterates the scene of the performance of "Body and Soul" that sees "the volution of HAWK into HARK (vibration of sound into song) into ARK." Brathwaite labels the performance a cadenza—an unaccompanied flourish or break that often marks the end of a movement or of the song: it is a figure of prolonged ending or resolution, refigured as a figure of conjunction, rendered through the printed word. The poem concludes with a prayer for deliverance, revealing the poem to be a psalm, and ends with a call to "think think think of the space & peace of tomorrow."[95]

The figure of Coleman Hawkins, of course, may be a metonym of black cultural expression, especially improvisation, which Brathwaite has defined as a "force, a flow of power, an impetus that carries with it word, image, and consciousness."[96] However, Brathwaite also links Hawkins to his printer: "I've made the decision to present this poem in the voice of the Stylewriter. despite its non-Laser 'deficiencies' of 'clarity' for nothing can replace the blues of these ragged font edges and the call&response dread contralto tenorsax delivery."[97] The "blues" rests in the ragged font edges as what remains unexpressed in expression—the printed mediation of the word rather than the words themselves, with the thought of musical performance—and "call&response," adding an implicit question regarding the shaping of time, the orientation toward an uncertain future. If the poem dramatizes "time out of joint," temporality as itself in crisis—literally divided—improvisation becomes a force of vitality, the breaking through of the future insofar as it offers the thought of an utterance or inscription not yet made. Hence the pun "the axe + àxé saxophone" early in the poem, crossing African American slang for "instrument" and Afro-diasporic spirituality.[98] Brathwaite inscribes in his work figures or signs of the ever receding figure of origin, the image of Sycorax.

SVS locates agency in the words themselves as they form and deform poetry and articulate new possibilities of poetic time, reconfiguring the link in the imagination between the past and the present in order to welcome the coming of the new. The formidable, formable word, disseminated through apostrophe locates the primary source and destination of the rearticulated, re-formed formidable word in the recursive poetic acts themselves. Brathwaite's pursuit of "the heart of the culture . . . in its otherness" makes the core of culture difference rather than identity. The plural instant, not yet resolved into particular narratives or located in existing regimes of knowledge, is the moment of culture's development and transformation. The emphasis throughout much of Brathwaite's work on tropes of orality and calling addresses itself to the still unknown—the still submerged—in everyday experience. SVS's foregrounded mediality, a precondition of the sharing of experience, develops what is already implicit in the notion of nation language: the fluctuating moment of the *arrivant*, the unknown and not-yet-named.

three

[S]he sees herself, recalls a self extinguished of person, in excess.
Claudia Rankine, *PLOT*

The ideology of the stable voice, typified by a certain critical hermeneutics of "the" lyric, is one backdrop against which black experimental writing works, seeking to break the common sense link between poetry as personal and group expression without claiming some reified notion of the "universal." In different ways, the writers in this section of the book exemplify what I see as a broader trend of using the visual arrangements of words and other graphic elements to rework ideas of personal testimony or witness into more supple concepts and to introduce forms of address that intend audiences and communities in process. Where Kamau Brathwaite's work deconstructs lyric utterance, Claudia Rankine's and Douglas Kearney's postlyric poetics represent a dialectical interruption of the lyric mode, presenting a voice suspended between "I" and "we," centered and diffuse at once. I draw the phrase "dialectical interruption" from Virginia Jackson's work on lyricization, using it to advance my own argument that Rankine, Kearney, and other black experimental writers have developed a "postlyric" poetics to break the hermeneutic circle of lyricized and racialized reading.[1] On slightly different terms from Jackson's, I seek to recover practices and "material historical referents," obscured by the enclosure of the lyric and the hermeneutic of black genius, *as* historical.[2] In the case of these contemporary black experimental works, this analysis in part requires retracing the position of the racialized subject, whose speaking "I" features an extra layer of mystification. On the one hand, I refer to the preemptively "objective" situatedness in concrete affairs to which the black subject presumably speaks, which marks its voice as one of protest to victimization or injury; on the other, I mean to invoke the abstractness of the black subject read against the racializing project of speaking for and as the human in general. I do not wish to question the solidity of the phenomenological subject on which the fiction of the lyric rests (Rankine and Kearney address this concern by, in different ways, pluralizing the subject or emphasizing the obscure moment of expression) but want to put pressure on the presumed "objectivity" of lyric's subjective presence as a mediation of the general and the particular as it is usually read. Rankine and Kearney present a "voice" embedded in the languages of popular culture and the social languages of difference that is at once unitary and so multiply fractured and contradictory that it demands reconception of the singularity and integrity of the poetic "voice." They present what Clarence Major calls a "lyricism of [black] consciousness," "the *beat* as opposed to anything melodic."[3] Attention to that beat, the relation of different temporal patterns in their respective writing, can effect a dialectical interruption of the modes of social thought that condition the idea of the black voice, confronting readers with a subject that does not easily reduce to an appropriable object of knowledge. Returning to the terms of the introduction, it suspends the presumption of speaking *for* by making visible the literary production of "speech."

The notion of voice, like the lyric, has a long, contested history in discussions of experimental poetics. Anxieties over (the often polemically imputed) belief in transparent self-expression has led critics to neglect black writers in histories of avant-garde poetics because of those writers' putative fealty to "the self-presence of the expressive subject" or to argue that black experimental writing simply "opposes itself to the artifactuality of the lyric" and its voice.[4] That neglects too much writing, leaves unchallenged what it is about *the* lyric that is so objectionable, and takes for granted that there is only one way of using *the* voice (I emphasize the definite article to indicate the heterogeneity that underpins my conception of postlyric poetics).[5] Postlyric poetics uses certain recognizable lyric strategies in ways that disrupt the genre's hermeneutic enclosure, which figures the expressions and experiences of a singular intending consciousness that is in turn metonymic for race. This chapter argues that Rankine and Kearney use techniques associated with the mass media—a dimensionless present, abrupt transitions, recontextualization of older texts, graphic and pictorial elements—within a dense network of détourned poetic techniques to trouble and reconceive ideas of voice and identity, emphasizing the moment self-expression as a moment of self-othering. Doing so, their work highlights the moment of expression as articulation: a constellation of significations leading us not to the poem as document of mental processes but to the disruption of the epistemological presuppositions that allow for the metonymic reduction of writing to expression.

"Postlyric" does not refer to a new genre but to the use of received understandings of the lyric as a horizon of hermeneutic expectation, only to disrupt the very basis of that mode: the assumed solidity of the speaking, universal "I." The postlyric in this chapter, then, is less a modal distinction than a name for the poetic production of an "I" situated within vectors of power and history whose expression is always already in a certain sense public and intersubjective rather than private. As Claudia Rankine has put it, "When I use the first person, my wish is to expose the implications of what it means to speak from the seeming coherency of that position."[6] Kearney's *The Black Automaton*, meanwhile, returns us to a Du Boisian question of speaking in a socially stratified context where what one says is always already mediated by a set of racial scripts and norms, where one's speech is always at once singular and exemplary. Both writers' work exemplify a form of black experimental writing that puts the "I" under pressure from within the hermeneutic enclosure of the lyric, retaining the organizational and emotional effects of the lyric mode without presenting a stable, locatable speaker. Unlike in the lyric as generally understood, the "I" in Rankine's work, especially *PLOT* and *Don't Let Me Be Lonely: An American Lyric*, is merely a formal element among others, a citation—"the self extinguished of person" or the "'I'-less 'I' of narrative voice."[7] It is a mechanism for getting from one sentence to the next, rather than a representation of a "me." Using bracketed [IT] as the grammatical subject and analytical object throughout, Kearney explores the moment of individuation as one of alienating isolation. Their respective poetics mark the unavailability of—and continued desire for—established modes of personal and racial representation and norms of poetic expression in the postsegregation era, understood as a new stage in the struggle against an increasingly globalized antiblackness. Similar to a previous generation's hipsterism, people who live in racially segregated communities readily co-opt and enthusiastically consume black vernacular culture as a sign of coolness, remaining indifferent to the lives of the people who produce that culture. I discuss Rankine and Kearney together because their respective poetics, informed by the contradictions of a postsegregation media environment in which increased visibility of black people obscures the continuation of discriminatory practices, formally put the relationship between an "I" and a "we" at issue, from, as it were, the interior and the exterior of the "I." In the process, each gives the lyric voice to those whose mundane experiences do not register as worthy: the materializing "I" is given to those whose lives "can not matter."[8]

Visual effects extend the possibilities of meaning while simultaneously troubling generic boundaries, but they are not the primary concern of this chapter, which takes up the ways these poets reconfigure poetry's expressive possibilities. Those effects are part of that project insofar as they, along with direct allusion, continually remind readers of the media environment within which this work appears, without being commentary on that media environment. This exploits another characteristic associated with the lyric: its strange relationship to a past "now" that is made present again. The postlyric matches a mode that seems always to say "now" with a dimensionless, insistent mediatized "now." Making that "now" a question, both poets challenge readers to take the measure of the present and to see that present as structured by racialized and gendered knowledge and narratives.

Though Kearney's typographical experiments seem more integral to his poetics, both he and Rankine use spatial arrangements and extralinguistic signifiers to abrade the surface of those everyday moments. Their respective textual strategies differ from and defer those familiar stories that "everyone knows" about race and that therefore dissipate either into a triumphant narrative of overcoming or into the vague despair of our time. In this way, they draw attention to the plurality of our shared present and the history that has led to it and to the pliability of our ways of knowing and being together. Kearney and Rankine have distinct styles and strategies, but they both command a broad range of allusions to "high" and "low" cultural sources while experimenting with visual elements, as they approach the new expressive possibilities available to the black poet rather than seek the "strange meaning" of being African American at the dawn of a neoliberal twenty-first century. At its most ambitious, this experimental writing shows what is awry in the present and awakens us to the possibility of another possibility—alternate ways of valuing lives and imagining an inhabitable world together.

A SELF EXTINGUISHED OF PERSON

The links between Rankine and Kearney that I am most interested center on the ways both bind poetic subjectivity to contemporary events and media through allusion (Rankine reproduces the staticky image of George W. Bush on a television screen in *Don't Let Me Be Lonely*) and themes of black vulnerability. Kearney's work, like Brathwaite's Sycorax Video Style, is integrative; it presents words at unusual angles and in different font sizes, using brackets in ways that recall sentence diagramming. Rankine's work (using John Lucas's photography) more closely resembles collaborations such as John Keene and Christopher Stackhouse's *Seismosis*, or Erica Hunt and Alison Saar's *Arcade*, works in which the images resonate with and complicate the text without illustrating it and without the text being caption for the images. The relationship between the visual and spatial elements of the work I consider here is more ambiguous than in the poetry I discuss in chapters 1 and 2. Rankine's and Kearney's respective use of the visual hybridizes not only poetic genres and modes but, as with some instances of concrete poetry, pushes the poem into the world of visual arts. Simultaneously, both poets attune us to the vulnerability that informs many black lives in the present and to the anxieties that tend to accompany black presence irrespective of class status.[9] Part of this chapter's ambition, then, is to account for the intersection of a thematic and formal visual surplus. A central component of Rankine's and Kearney's respective experiments, I argue, is manipulating the "artifactuality of the lyric" to advance a "postlyric" poetics that retains the lyric's organizing effects without a unitary speaker.

The lyric mode and "lyricization"—the hermeneutic that produces at once the lyric and the theory of the lyric by reading all poems as the expression of a single consciousness—have come under criticism in recent poetry scholarship.[10] I have touched on some of the attitudes toward the modernist lyric in previous chapters. The long history of lyric reading, critics' gradual consolidation of all genres of poetry into the lyric, aided by modernist and nationalist debates at the turn of the twentieth century, has played an important role in what kinds of things we say about poetry, what kinds of things we think poetry says (especially when it says "I"), which techniques we consider significant and worth study, and ultimately which poems are worth serious attention. It forms the basis of the common sense of professional criticism. Poets and critics invested in the continuum of Language poetry have stigmatized the very idea of (lyric) expression and sought other functions for poetry. Poets who are part of what I am terming the "postlyric" continuum have developed poetics that anticipate and play off of ingrained reading habits, producing a kind of expression that effaces the imagined expresser. My aim is not to designate a new genre but simply to suggest that since a unified lyric tradition is a fiction, attention to the ways people deploy the devices associated with it can reveal an ultimately subversive poetics, especially in the work of black experimental writers attempting to unsettle the racialized hermeneutics that govern black expressive acts.

The diffuse (or absent) "I" in Rankine's and Kearney's work—an ostentatiously fictional "self extinguished of person"—is set apart from the "personal."[11] The first person never quite designates a persona but a "redirect[ed], juxtapose[d], or interrupt[ed]" self-in-progress that approximates the process of a person denied the opacity of isolated personhood.[12] This fractured, "decentered" poetic subject, a grammatical fiction, articulates a broader range of perspectives, incorporating the words of many others, without fully coalescing into a conventional narrative voice. In Rankine's and Kearney's respective poetry, this partially evacuated conventional locus of enunciation tends to be occupied by subjects whose race and gender position in U.S. society make them vulnerable to premature death.[13] Kearney and Rankine exploit the conventions of lyricization *as fictions*, investing the techniques of self-presentation with the pathos that one might customarily attach to the presented self. In other words, the techniques of self-presentation function autonomously from the idea of a stable self, encouraging readers to identify with the expressive act rather than the expressing subject. The poems become documents, rather than expressions, of their respective social locations. In their work, strategies of impersonality and citation are deployed to play with the norms governing black authorship as an institution governing permissible speech.

The poetry I term "postlyric" responds to the same problem that Craig Dworkin names in his discussion of "unoriginal," "conceptual" writing (e.g., Kenneth Goldsmith transcribing the September 1, 2000, issue of the *New York Times*) as a vanguard position for poetry in the introduction to *Against Expression*, an anthology edited by him and Goldsmsith. Dworkin argues that such "conceptual" writing "shows up the rhetorical, ideological force of our cultural sense of creativity, which clings so tenaciously to a gold standard of one's own words rather than to one's own idea or the integrity of the idea's execution."[14] The anthology—which includes work by Rankine, M. NourbeSe Philip, and Harryette Mullen (whom I consider in the next chapter)—dramatizes the absence of a shared, single "cultural sense of creativity." Much African American vernacular culture, often cited without attribution as someone else's "words," has been famously open to citation and to revising others' words, but the accusation of being derivative or "merely" conventional (following the norms of the white literary establishment) within black literary cultures has historically carried the charge of mimicry, mere imitation, or the sacrificing of cultural specificity.[15] Though one can certainly read Kearney and Rankine through the terms of Dworkin's polemic, "originality" has a different meaning vis-à-vis African American critical and poetic practice, often tacitly rooted in a quasiethical sense of obligation (or assumption that one has been faithful) to one's own experience that one expresses, which any analysis of originality must account for.

As I argue in the introduction, the term "expression" is polysemous in black literary culture, "self-expression" often carrying with it the sense that one expresses black genius. That basic proposition has become complicated in an era in which "Oprah has trained Americans to say anything anywhere," making self-expression more ubiquitous, while at the same time putting African American–identified phrases like "don't go there" in the mouths of white suburban-ites.[16] Blackness and black culture become abstract and alienable—mere signs or commodity—separate from black people. This situation is critical for all of the writers in this book, but these two writers make it a particular theme of their work, so I would like to develop it further here. How does one imagine black po-etry to be "one's own words" in this postsegregation moment, when race still deindividuates and the benefits of individual genius are no longer extended to one's race? The conditions of authorship are such that, on the one hand, one's expression can become another commodified sign of racial difference and that, on the other, one's skill can make one "exceptional," tacitly justifying the im-miseration and incarceration of the "unexceptional" black population whose supposed failures tend to be explained away by invocations of a vague cultural deficiency. The desire for some unifying term—what Elizabeth Alexander calls a "bottom-line blackness"—to square race as a quasiontological category with political and ethical obligation grows stronger, even as the terms of such unity become more elusive.[17]

The problem of black writers being at once singular (exceptional) and exem-plary (typical) has changed from the time when critics grappled with the place of blackness in black writing around discussions of the new black poetry a gen-eration ago. Those discussions, I would argue, continue to influence poets who wish to be both black and experimental, as well as their critics. One of that era's important African American poetry scholars, Stephen E. Henderson, is paradig-matic of a critic who recognized the newness of the poetry he saw but was also at pains to frame its originality as a larger established pattern of black expres-sive culture. His solution to the need for some term of unity was the concept of "fidelity." In "The Forms of Things Unknown," his preface to *Understanding the New Black Poetry*, Henderson imagines a continually unfolding tradition of Afri-can American poetry from the "secular folk rhymes" of the Georgia Sea Islands to the emerging experimental writing of the 1960s, making the original writ-ing relevant to the extent that it was faithful to (i.e., expressed) black genius.[18] However, there remains in his thinking a radical kernel that precisely diagnoses the conundrum of black experimental writing in the postsegregation era. Con-fronting the need to articulate the factors that would account for the particu-larity of black writing, Henderson settles on three broad categories: theme, structure (i.e., such racially marked categories as diction, rhythm, and the use of figurative language), and "saturation"—"the communication of 'Blackness'" and fidelity "to the observed or intuited truth of the Black Experience in the United States."[19] As an attempt to see blackness as an in-itself, saturation in principle makes the black writer's work at once original and a repetition, an invention of what already in some sense exists.

In Henderson's schema, "saturation" operates alongside theme and structure: "One must not consider the poem in isolation but in relationship to the reader/audience, and the reader [in relation] to the wider context of the phenomenon which we call, *for the sake of convenience*, the Black Experience."[20] Henderson's qualification is telling. It aligns his own writing with an experience too complex to be named by the slogan "the black experience" while lending that experience a contingent objectivity that he grapples with later in his essay. As an objective entity, saturation functions analogously to the veil in my discussion of *The Souls of Black Folk*, the terms of the (ever unasked) question's authorization of speech conditioning the reply. It obscures in both directions. Saturation is thus a condition of im/possibility for unmediated black expression due to the mediating function of the mass media and the larger fact that blackness is the process of an incomplete inter/culturation. The possibilities of black expression are not wholly under black control, which becomes especially troubling in a moment when black genius separates people from their race as exceptions, or when the absence of black genius normalizes paternalistic relations of power, violence, and discipline upheld by repeated public invocations of black pathology. Silence is one singular-plural movement of textual subjectivity and structure of address. The other, adapted by Rankine, Kearney, and other authors, is to deploy the conditions of writing as a black person—where commodity culture functions as a presumptive mask—as material historic referents with which to begin imagining a more communal voice.

Saturation, an indicator of fidelity to racialized experience, does not render the poem merely, to invoke Theodor Adorno's phrase, a "subjective expression of a social antagonism." Rather, social antagonism (for example, race understood as one method through which poets position themselves within larger contests over the meaning of history) is the starting point of a hermeneutic that must rescue something that seems like subjective expression from the confines of that antagonism.[21] However, the dialectical sense of saturation—a previousness that overdetermines the meanings of black texts and black bodies—has taken on a different cast in the moment of what Jodi Melamed has called "neoliberal multiculturalism," a regime of producing and managing racial difference in accordance with neoliberal policy and the dictates of global capital.[22] In this moment, images of blackness proliferate, often reductively evaluated as good or bad, with the bad marked as illegitimate, undeserving of the rights and privileges of citizenship. Postlyric poetry, with its decentered expression, must also capture some of the ambivalence of speaking as and for black in this moment. Fidelity is Henderson's explicit attempt to square the relationship between race and ethico-political obligation. Linking saturation to literary techniques, the "black experience" names something like an aesthetic community posited by, or that sees itself in, a literary text.

What for Henderson is a defining feature has by now become something of a shackle: if the black writer uses a word like "master," saturation means critics may assume she or he refers to slavery. The conditions of speech are also the conditions of partial silencing. However, the invocation of fidelity—an ethical stance toward some determinate truth—does not fully resolve matters. Indeed, I turn to Henderson's discussion in order to get at the ways contemporary discourses of multiculturalism and cultural nationalism alike render blackness textual—existing in advance of any example—and thus to ask what self postlyric poetry expresses. Henderson's caution through his essay opens up its more radical analysis, justifying the dialectical reversal of "saturation" I have described. He remains cautious about the sense of blackness he wants to use, reminding his readers of the implications of double consciousness and the multiple, not quite simultaneous frames within which blackness operates. The most peculiar example of this comes when he refers to blackness as a commodity: "Since poetry is the most concentrated and the most allusive of the verbal arts, *if* there is such a commodity as 'blackness' in literature (and I assume that there is), it should *somehow* be found in concentrated or in residual form in the poetry."[23] "Blackness" itself becomes a commodity, a form of value rather than a solid object, perhaps as a direct result of the objectification required to understand it as something other than the outcome of historical and political processes. For capitalism makes of objects fungible commodities with astonishing efficiency. Henderson, watching the growing popularity of black mass entertainment, seems to call out deliberately the threat of commercialization. To be faithful to a commodified culture entails a much more complicated operation of self-alienation, an operation that informs the postlyric.

As Michael North argues in *The Dialect of Modernism*, and as Henderson would have been aware, white writers of the "Americanist avant-garde" used a version of black dialect to articulate for themselves freedom from the nationalist protocols of language standardization. Drawing on an analysis of Zora Neale Hurston, North argues that in this context, "black performers are original because they can produce the best imitation of . . . themselves. Black performers *are* original not because they possess originality as a quality but because they produce originality as a *commodity*."[24] As commodity, a social relation that appears in mystified form as a relationship between things, "originality" of this kind is a market value (and a marketing term) subtended by its "exchange value," the ability of another to possess it for him- or herself, as an "authentic" expression of him- or herself that is external to the linguistic markers of black genius. One need think here only of the enthusiasm with which the white (and black middle-class) hipster adapts—or co-opts—the newest inner city slang, filtered through rap music, but condemns the "culture" of the inner city in the next breath. The point is not to fall back into familiar claims of inauthenticity but to observe the problems of co-optation, which in Erica Hunt's succinct phrase, allows the "dominant culture [to] transfer its own partiality onto the opposition it tries to suppress. It will always maintain that it holds the complete worldview, despite its fissures." The opposition that nonmainstream cultures seem to offer "is alternately demonized or accommodated through partial concessions without a meaningful alteration of dominant culture's own terms."[25] Put in somewhat schematic terms, relations of consumption transform and reify difference into "opposition," and opposition into a portable emblem of sanitized rebellion or tolerable subversion for those subjects who "consume" cultures to which they nominally do not belong and a sign of pathology for those who "produce" those cultures. The act of acquisition is also an act of selection: that she or he does not belong to the same class as those who produce the culture gives this mode of expression its heft and political value, making it, as it were, an unfaithful fidelity, a copy whose point is shoring up an identity ultimately acceptable to dominant norms. In other words, it is a fidelity to a set of significations with no political obligations beyond that mode of self-fashioning.

My purpose in sketching this basic situation, which manifests, for example, in the perennial popularity of blackface and racist theme parties, is to say something about the context of racial expression within which the postlyric emerges. What self, finally, expresses itself in an instance of self-expression, when self-expression belongs to a hermeneutic of racialized reading? When the expression itself can be "appropriated" as a mask of rebellion and self-difference for a disaffected bourgeoisie?[26] The commodity of "originality," like all commodities, is a fetish object that invests value in the object, thereby occluding the social relations the object represents. In this case, fetishism implies that the extent to which the producers (and the conditions and relations of production) remain out of sight secures a certain social relation and self-understanding. One wants access to the "soul" and is either indifferent to or anxious about the fate of the body. For race is also a technique of objectification and alienation through which one never quite owns one's own voice: the meaning of that voice is an external standard against which literary production is measured, often through the faithfulness of its representation or the felicity of its performance of what is "authentically" black. This, then, is the historical backdrop against which Kearney and Rankine have developed a postlyric voice that is real and ideal, material and immaterial, and ultimately a value—use value and exchange value—that depends on the degree to which whatever is imagined as nonblack is standardized, mechanized, or in need of revision.

The allusive postlyric voice flaunts its artificiality through allusion and other extradiscursive elements, participating in a racial discourse without reproducing race as a co-optable mask or insisting on originality—that is, on the expression of a unique racial interior. Originality, like black genius, is a social relation that masquerades as an object or quality in its own right, which explains the overrepresentation of black people in the field of entertainment (social reproduction) relative to other domains where the very notion of black life as "original" makes the presence of black bodies a threatening surplus (as did the institution of slavery, whose desired commodities were abstract labor power, and the reproduction of the labor force). That surplus, the appearance of black bodies where they are not expected, produces a kind of vertigo. The postlyric, as I develop it, is a modality of that vertigo, seeking in destabilized modes of expression other ways of naming and working through social antagonisms. It holds on to the emotional effects of what we have been trained to read as lyric subjectivity and racial specificity but plays the idea of a coherent self as fantasy, stressing that the raced, language-enmeshed self is always both public and private. The condition of blackness's legibility is that it be the raw material from which originality "spontaneously" derives, as well as a name for that spontaneity. So, in addition to destabilizing the lyric "now," the postlyric deforms by accretion that in the lyric that makes it available for a future hermeneutic, presenting something ultimately unrecognizable, strange: it is faithful to the textual nature of blackness as a social encoding of difference.

BECAUSE "HERE" EXISTS

The postlyric, as Rankine develops it, must pass through the saturated social languages of race and gender, which overdetermine poetic expression. In her earlier work, she uses "ruptured syntax and the fragmented text . . . to suggest, and perhaps reflect, the process by which existence (being in time) is enacted—which is to say, the text engages irruption, interruptions, and discontinuities in order to approach the initial silence of being."[27] Her later comments suggest that the interruptions, discontinuities, and "grammar of distraction" *cite* genre without participating in it, allowing her to "write the poem from the moment of expression" of some feeling "rather than having to lead the reader [via the narration of events] there through events" and to "make language represent without being representational."[28] The emphasis, then, is on shaping the languages of representation and the attendant questions of what counts as representational —in short, on shaping the set of techniques that guarantee the realness of the represented. To make language represent without being representational makes problematic "the *initial* silence of being," which is only a nonoriginal, represented moment that secures a certain way of knowing being.

Postlyric poetics generally rely on exposing and undomesticating the underlying assumptions of being and knowledge on which the fiction of the lyric's expressive subject relies, including its singularity. Rankine's work turns on the interaction between genre and its etymological cognates—gender, *genre humain*, generate, and engender. All genres are abstract, formalizing grids that take historically heterogeneous forms and naturalize them—they have in common a way of attributing intention and of locating works in time. Practically, this means that all genres are sites of contestation: this contestation amounts to the conflict of the general and the particular instance that exceeds or overturns the rule but requires the rule of genre for its legibility. *Don't Let Me Be Lonely*, Rankine's most recent, book-length poem, draws attention to something she calls "an American lyric" in its subtitle, insisting on a claim to "lyric" that is nonuniversal and, insofar as America is a historical construction, nontranscendental —ergo "postlyric." Perhaps because its conception of utterance is ultimately at odds with that tranquil "silence of being," critics have shied away from Rankine's subtitle, referring to the work either as "poetic prose," neither lyric nor even poetry, or, owing to its strategy of textual and visual citation, as a "multigenre text" somewhere between verse and essay, punctuated and augmented by images.[29] The text is "multigenre" to the extent that the postlyric simultaneously belongs to and rejects the lyric mode, undermining its own conditions of legibility to the extent that those conditions are bound up with a stable speaking subject.

While a whole, healed, nonfragmented subject often seems a political ideal, especially for those whose historical experience is defined by disruption and discontinuity, Rankine's emphasis on pharmaceuticals selectively patching up vulnerable bodies for profit throughout *Don't Let Me Be Lonely*—and her earlier collections *The End of the Alphabet* (which begins in the wake of a miscarriage), *PLOT* (concerned with a couple expecting their first child)—raises an unsettling question about health, where one may be healing oneself for a capitalist racial order that wants to figure itself as without gaps and devour you whole.[30] The fragmentary, the partial, the wounded, and the reticent emerge as alternative, still ambiguous modes of politics, magnified by *Lonely*'s multiple speakers. Like Philip, Rankine voices the silenced, nonmonumental, ordinary experiences that fall below the threshold of the universal in her postlyric poetics. Their fragmented particularity makes it difficult to admit the degree to which they may speak for "everyone" rather than those constitutively excluded from that universal experience.

Rankine's use of the fictionality of the first-person pronoun—the assumption that the "I" conflates autobiographical and authorial presence to represent "the movements of her mind"— makes the text itself function as an open, internally differentiated "maximal self" without the burden of representation, which is exemplary of postlyric poetics.[31] Simultaneously, the interpretation that the varied voices in *Don't Let Me Be Lonely* in particular reflect a single consciousness reveals both investments in the lyric and rejection of that poems claims to representativeness. In her two most recent collections, Rankine's strategies ground poetic subjectivity less in contemporary mediatized experience than in the media that communicate that experience. Her use of pictorial images and pervasive references to personae watching television or reading newspapers represents at one level the composite, fragmentary nature of mass culture and everyday experience as a metacommentary on the historical processes, like emplotment, through which the subject as monad emerges. The net effect is the sense of a common or kindred feeling imagined on different terms. Rankine's work achieves a shared sense of separateness rather than identification, emphasizing an unlocalizable distance through her play with deixis by which a discourse orients itself in space and time. In *PLOT*, for instance, the phrase "Here. I am here." becomes a floating refrain, repeating as expectant Liv's address to the unborn Ersatz, ambiguously attached to both Liv and Earland (the expectant father), and finally to the baby itself: "And I am | because 'here' exists."[32] The floating "here" generates a peculiar sense of feeling without subject, rather like anxiety understood as a generalized fear that does not precisely come from particular situations but from the *fact* of situations, from plots.

Simultaneously, Rankine's poetics touch on those historical processes that produce the self as preeminently a subject to be disciplined through the exclusionary formal politics of law and personhood. *Don't Let Me Be Lonely* mobilizes the artificiality of the lyric genre alongside other generic intertexts and allusions—especially allusions to historical events and a historicized lyric "now" —to emphasize the telling rather than the told and to posit alternative forms of community. At issue is less experience—made present through mimesis or intertextual lyric and narrative conventions—than the connections that remain unthinkable between events and people and the ways literary conventions shape in advance and thus distort and overwrite the lives confession brings forward and makes matter. The concerns of *Don't Let Me Be Lonely* are thematically consonant with those of *PLOT*: in both a tendency to value romantic relationships—and women's lives—to the extent that they conform to certain narrative conventions informs anxieties about parenthood and the narrow possibilities of imagining selfhood.

I trace these general observations about Rankine's poetics through readings of *PLOT* and *Don't Let Me Be Lonely*, Rankine's last two collections and my primary concern in this chapter. Both are prose sequences: the first is a third-person quasinarrative recounting of expectant first-time mother Liv's thoughts and experiences, while the second is a series of first-person reflections on contemporary life, especially issues of mental health, black vulnerability, and forgiveness of historical violence. These texts are invested in the act of positing an "I" and are concerned with the ways such saying of "I" marks at once the precondition for belonging—it must be spoken in a necessarily shared language—and the impossibility of that belonging because belonging individuates, separates the speaker from the "we." In Rankine's poetry, so invested in the body's pain, confession of pain cannot escape the words used for confession. *PLOT* is primarily concerned with this problem, with the forms given to the unformed and nameless, the need for a definite form to make a life and to cope with the alienating effects of individuation:

> Oh, Ersatz, my own, birth is the limiting of the soul, what is
> trapped with it already owns. I could quadruple my intent
> toward you, be your first protection; but I could not wish a self
> on any self as yet unformed, though named and craved.[33]

Birth, the introduction of the other into time, and into narrative, marks an end of possibility or pure matter uncontained by any form (the self). An initial reading of this apostrophe suggests that the imagined child remains ersatz—a substitute, compensation, artificial. Apostrophe simply does what it tends to do: bestow subjectivity on inanimate objects as a means of demonstrating the subjectivity of the speaker, so that ultimately the drama is her thinking. However, there is a temporal catch in the phrasing: "I could not wish a self | on any self *as yet* unformed." The adverb "yet" points to an indefinite, but anticipated, time to come. It indicates the impossibility of the speaker's wish to shield the other from the burdens of selfhood, even as such selfhood is the condition for it hearing or responding. Though the self does not at the time of the utterance have any being separate from the speaker's imagining, it inevitably will. The "unformed" self that can be named is already formed, already has a position within discourse by merit of being "named and craved." Plot marks an inevitable "birth" of the other, a relation of the other to a novel set of circumstances, at once familiar and strange and once known and unknowable, formed but "as yet unformed." One is always already bound up in the plot of language.

Form in Rankine's *PLOT* is both noun and verb, a process as much as a quality, which extends even to a play on the history of language and orthography. The text is punctuated by a series of sections whose titles alert us to the "proximity" of words: "clock" to "lock," "inner" to "in her," "opens" to "person," "stuck" to "tuck," "weary" to "wary," "posed" to "exposed." A similar play informs the following lines' linkage of "streams," "dream," "reams," and "seam":

bitterly, sinkholes to underground streams . . .

In the dream waist deep, retrieving a fossilized pattern forming
in attempt to prevent whispers. or poisoned regrets. reaching into
reams and reams. to needle-seam a cord in the stream. as if
a wish borne out of rah-rah's rude protrusion to follow the rest
was sporded. split. and now hard pressed to enter the birth.[34]

The transposition of "dream" and "stream" depends on two different senses of immersion: one that can be read as literal ("in the stream waist deep") and one that figures a quality of intensity or engagement ("in the dream waist deep"), extending the possible senses of location. Such verbal play, relying on both phonology and script, enacts a parody of subtext, the writing beneath or encoded within writing. Each word apparently hides or obscures a word more fundamental ("clock," a metonym for the temporal mechanisms on which plots depend, stills or "locks" life in place) or gives way to a hidden lineage ("Lineage means | to step here on the likelihood of involution"), a play in language that, as it were, goes on behind speakers' backs.

"[S]hatter[ing] the surface that is the self," unforming the imagined coherence of the self and escaping the closure of plots, Rankine puts forward a postlyric sense of literary time that emphasizes the mediality of the letter against the materiality of the phenomenal world it is supposed to represent and that draws out the as yet unformed in language.[35] Part of what the poem represents is language's own structure, and poetry's role in the construction of social space. Asking what happens in the poem—not in its plot but in the act of expression—emphasizes the force of the event, suspending the referential or representational aspects of literature in favor of the performative aspects. Here, the value of feeling comes from recognition that "a life can not matter," can be unformed, can be uncounted and that, formed, will be counted in ways it cannot account for.[36] Attention to the time of inscription brings us to the recognition that to give a self to a self unformed makes it vulnerable, close to almost living, as "Liv" is only proximate to "live."

PLOT's play of deixis anticipates a speaker near the end of Don't Let Me Be Lonely who says "the poem is that—Here. I am here. This conflation of the solidity of presence with the offering of this same presence perhaps has everything to do with being alive."[37] The first part of the statement is the paradigmatic gesture of the lyric mode: claiming the solidity of presence through the act of offering it to another. The subject, though, is the poem itself rather than some entity of whose presence the poem is evidence. The gift is the moment of expression rather than the expression itself, which here remains nearly blank. Through a play of times that supplements the play of proximity and distance allowed by apostrophe and orthography, the poem offers a cure for the loneliness of the monadic subject attempting to know itself in the absence of other or exclusively in reference to the other. In this articulation, the poem moves us to another sense of expression and introduces a new complication of that time of lyric's conventional, timeless now, which allows us to understand lines like "you awake, justly terrified of this world" or "Sundays too my father got up early" as literary utterances rather than descriptions of past (or ongoing) events.[38] Saying "here," insisting on the location of utterance, complicates matters by yoking that lyric time to terrestrial or historical time as something other than the representation of a saying, in Rankine's terms "determined by indeterminacy."[39]

One concrete way the poem-as-saying-"here" manifests itself in PLOT and in a different way in Don't Let Me Be Lonely is through allusion. On that basis, we could read PLOT as a long engagement with Virginia Woolf's To the Lighthouse.

If the poem is saying "here" and bestowing solidity to the other, reading be-
comes a means through which one can "shatter the surface that is the self":

<blockquote>

             the conceived "we" a   bruised a purple
                                                  surface

erupting into

hush she hush she

hush

shush rushed   Within

            to shatter the surface that is the self

</blockquote>

(a surface, within itself triangulated, blocking the self until
pulled back tautly, until bits of hue and cry thrust)[40]

The parenthesis remains open, as does the relationship between the text in the
box and that outside, which is more elaboration than caption. This passage, part
of a section of "Eight Sketches: After Lily Briscoe's Purple Triangle" alludes to
Woolf's character painting a postimpressionist landscape in which James and
Mrs. Ramsay appear as a purple triangle, a figure "no one could tell . . . for a
human shape," a figure that avoids likeness.[41] Rankine's paratactic engagement
with Woolf here, save the word "purple" and common words like "surface" or
"hush," is not at the level of language but concept, the idea that "Mother and
child then—objects of universal veneration . . . —might be reduced . . . to a pur-
ple shadow without irreverence."[42] The allusion transforms Mr. Ramsay's con-
cern with adequate representation (and shifting representational norms) into
a broader meditation on the relationship between an "I" and a "we," between
the self-fashioning and the law and community ("hue and cry") that arrests the
process. Woolf's novel reflects on a generational shift of sensibility, especially
toward motherhood, wrought by history; Rankine's text tropes Woolf or, better,
cites "Virginia Woolf" the author. This section of "sketches" concludes with di-
alogue, Earland asking Liv whether the baby will be the only "customer" for her

breast milk, then excusing himself through allusion to Augustine's *Confessions*: "the lowliness of my tongue confesses." As N. H. Pritchard's poetry witnesses its own undoing, Rankine's speakers confess the priority of others—especially other texts—for the solidity of their selves. *Don't Let Me Lonely* "confesses" the failure of words alone to capture the truth—the noncorrespondence of the true and the real—in much the same way that the repeated adjective "sad" seems at once a necessary statement of care and pointedly inadequate to reckon with lives simply not mattering.[43] Quite apart from rejecting the idea of representation as mimesis, through which the work follows a more fundamental truth to be reconstituted in the contemplative mind, the graphic poetry discussed in this chapter aspires to the primacy of the event. The graphic then, in addition to "confessing" the inadequacy of language alone makes a claim for the force of the event of encounter, of primary experience.

Though Rankine's work is not serial, she returns to the postlyric self as a surface and the play of deixis. I read *PLOT*'s allusions and emphasis on deixis as consonant with *Don't Let Me Be Lonely*'s statement of poetics that the "poem is that". It continues: "Here both recognizes and demands recognition. . . . In order for something to be handed over a hand must extend and a hand must receive."[44] If we take this to be a genuine statement of poetics, a hand stretched between Paul Celan and John Keats's "The Living Hand" ("see here it is— | I hold it towards you"), saying "here" complicates traditional lyric temporality by emphasizing the act of saying—of extending the hand—over the experience expressed. Saying "here" in this case is a citation, producing a postlyric voice that is neither here nor there: the effects of personhood are distributed across the surface of the poem—and they are quotidian. Being here, saying "here," however, is not a cure for loneliness, nor does it address the central thematic of waiting that marks *PLOT* and *Don't Let Me Be Lonely*:

> Or maybe hoping is the same as waiting.
> It can be futile.
>
> Waiting for what?
>
> For a life to begin.
>
> I am here.
>
> And I am still lonely.[45]

Don't Let Me Be Lonely presents a fugue of voices speaking in the first person, weaving together discussions of depression and the pharmaceuticals meant to treat it, death, television, racial violence, everyday anxieties, and the geopoliti-cal uncertainty following the terrorist attacks in New York City and Washing-ton, D.C., in 2001. The speakers have trouble sleeping, research a book on the liver, and reflect on American optimism, forgiveness, legal and extralegal vio-lence, among other topics. The concerns are related but not identical, largely presented through one speaker addressing another rather than relying on the convention of speech to an implied audience. The text, consisting largely of passages that read like scenes without any plot to fix them, uses as many nar-rative conventions as poetic ones. The effect is a restrained, not fully locatable emotional gestalt that is typified by repeated phrases like "I feel . . ." or "it makes me sad": "Sad is one of those words that has given up its life for its country, it's been a martyr for the American dream. . . . It meant dark in color, to darken. It meant me. I felt sad."[46] *Don't Let Me Be Lonely* aspires to capture a story of the nation and its people, now, in this moment, but the moment of its telling is dis-continuous. The poem does not look at the nation's founding but its present, presenting its collage-form voices like a series of snapshots. The voices are not unified by a common experience but by a common historical horizon that de-fines their speech as confession, disclosure of the truth of the self and of the predicament of the self. It is an "American Lyric"—and postlyric—to the ex-tent that the collective voice is marked as belonging to a certain class and racial strata of America.

Don't Let Me Be Lonely remains alert to the differences that inform the experi-ence of "common experience." The particular ways that Rankine's poem upsets some of the conventional underpinnings of the lyric genre, presenting both re-ality and its representation as deformed, creates a demand for an attention not exhausted in the kinds of identification associated with the lyric. Without flat-tening the several voices in *Don't Let Me Be Lonely* to a single "I" we can identify as "Claudia Rankine," we can observe that much of the poem's emotional reso-nance comes from references to contemporary culture. The pharmaceutical in-dustry, the tech bubble of the late 1990s, the racially charged murders of James Byrd Jr. (by private citizens) and Amadou Diallo (by NYPD officers), the assault of Abner Louima (by NYPD officers), and the terrorist attacks of 11 September 2001 all feature prominently in the text. Its range of references is impressive, but its range of photographic images—from pill bottles to the Auschwitz's in-famous gate, from Byrd, Louima, and Diallo to Nelson Mandela—further set it apart. Some of these—including those of Byrd, Louima and Diallo, scenes from westerns, images from Princess Diana's memorial, and Paxil's slogan "Your life is waiting"—appear interspersed with the text on twenty-eight image of televisions, eighteen of which are on pages by themselves, featuring an image of then president George W. Bush's face, distorted with static.

Although pressing the issue of this experimental work's relationship to lyric threatens to devolve into ahistorically or uncritically "reading lyric," the work's subtitle, "An American Lyric," raises the question of its generic investments. What statement of longing or belonging comes available in that identification, that claim to resemblance to other works called "lyric" or "poetry," for a poet for whom resemblance is singled out as a cause of "loneliness" ("the foundations for loneliness begin in the | dreamscapes you create. Their resemblance to reality | reflects disappointment first")?[47] Might we think the resemblance in similar terms to the "proximities" I referred to in my discussion of *PLOT* or to *Lonely*'s play with anagrams (e.g., "what alerts, alters")?[48] Does the subtitle simply invoke a compromise between being and resemblance, as in an episode in which a speaker's friend relates the story of encounter a woman she identifies as an Auschwitz survivor:

I was in Auschwitz, but how did you know?

Because of the A [tattooed on her arm along with an identification number].

It turns out the A's collision with Auschwitz is pure co-incidence. The A in the identification number stands for the German word for worker—*arbeiter*.

An image of Auschwitz's gate follows. The episode is in many ways exemplary of the strategies of *Lonely*. It offers a complex example of citation, one of many in the work, which serve as one means through which the text suspends representation in favor of something more complex but harder to name. The speaker of this section recounts a friend's account of an encounter with a woman to make the point that "Frieda Berger and I had defied history in order to have it," by having lived and been born, respectively, despite the Holocaust. The "detail of the letter A" allows the friend "to be true to her life as precisely as it is lived," which is to say through symbols that always offer to resonate in other contexts than those intended.[49] The speaker recounts her friend's recounting of the Holocaust survivor. Histories, local and global, intertwine here into a mundane retelling sapped of any personal interest, except for the "being between" that inspires people to share such stories.

All of this, however, points to a larger question of the function of the image of the gates at Auschwitz and of the other images in the text. In a text that features confession without identifiable confessing subjects, the images become another example of interest and of citation. In this, they resemble references to the writings of G. W. F. Hegel, Jacques Derrida, and Cornel West and to such poets as William Ernest Henley (by way of domestic terrorist Timothy McVeigh), Joseph Brodsky, Paul Celan, Czeslaw Milosz, César Vallejo, and Aimé Césaire. Citations from those famous figures appear alongside miscellaneous text from ad copy and a message from a friend who develops Alzheimer's: "THIS IS THE MOST MISERABLE IN MY LIFE." They do not stand for location—the value is not in the identity of those cited—but for function: the disparate bearers of sharable thought. The image of the iconic gate to Auschwitz here does not obviously illustrate anything significant about the reported conversation, nor does the conversation serve as a caption to the image. If anything, the image mocks the lyric ideal that, since Wordsworth, has stressed poetry's ability to reanimate past experience in the present or to speak for survivors. Their conversation may be somehow proximate to death, but the emphasis is on their respectively having missed death.

I have been developing a reading the relationship between the images and text through saturation in the era of neoliberal multiculturalism, where the very ubiquity of these images and slogans form a kind of prepossessing schema for any expression. My reading is in broad sympathy with Christopher Nealon, who makes an argument about "the historical imagination that gets attached to the idea of textuality in poetry in English" in the period of late capital and the waning "American century."[50] Late- or global capital, for him, marks an historical shift in the history of textuality. In that context, Rankine's self-conscious use of citation becomes a means by which to create a textured, density of references that point to present historical conditions without representing them, as part of an attempt to articulate new configurations. However, I cannot justify opposing "European literary modernism" to "an American history of violence against black people" or calling that violence "history."[51] Nealon argues that Rankine "maintains a lyric attitude toward her materials" by "highlighting the movement of her mind," adding that "her practice of citation sets in motion a perpetual analogy *between* lyric . . . and the other textual and linguistic forms it records."[52] "Lyric" in his account remains distinct from other textual and linguistic forms, retaining its status as a means of recording some other experience or contemplation. The images, for him, are part of the mechanism that "establishes 'lyric' as a master category meant to be intellectually powerful enough to withstand the intrusions of the image stream, even to take energy from it, even to mock it."[53] My point, on the contrary, is that the images operate alongside the overall rhetorical strategies of the poem to refract the lyric "now" into a more capacious time rooted in language's mediality. They frustrate our habituated ways of reading poetry in part because they present the mundane, typically unmemorable texture—graphic and otherwise—of everyday life that literature typically edits out. Further, more than a master category, the lyric is complicit in *Lonely*'s sense of isolation, being a vehicle for the plots necessary to give life meaning. The images, then, are one aspect of a strategy of disrupting the will to narrative.

I would therefore nuance Nealon's second proposition—that the practice of citation creates a "perpetual analogy": rather than being opposed to citation, lyric itself is another of *Lonely*'s citations. After all, genres are intertextual; they function *as* genres through their tacit "citation" of the conventions of previous works, and lyric is a category of *interest* and prestige (or, depending on one's sensibilities, scorn). The desire for—and impossibility of—a noncomplicit lyric perspective is part of the issue *Don't Let Me Be Lonely* contends with: the speakers never quite achieve contemplative distance from their own particularized forms of experience. This is another sense in which I read the work as postlyric and as another mode of temporal revision of the lyric: instead of speaking from the place of the safety implied by contemplation, the speakers in *Don't Let Me Be Lonely* speak from the present of the crisis. The medicated, depressed, suicidal, misrecognized and above all precarious selves are both subjects and objects of their experience, impressed on by the images and borrowed phrases that seem to arrive of their own volition. This is another way of explaining the poignancy and inadequacy of feeling "sad." The American lyric of the subtitle, I would argue, is not just a generic designation but also a question rooted in the precarious space and time—the ambiguous "here"—with which the poem ends.

Drawing on television appeals to a sense of time *and* space, a delocalized "here" of lyric expression, upsetting one of the lyric's chief genre markers: we may not know where the speaker is supposed to be, but we know she or he is *somewhere.* Therefore, indicative though they may be of late capital's "image stream," or objective renderings of the current conditions of making meaning and poetry, the televisual images are another feint at immediacy, undercut by the groundless play of deixis in Rankine's poetics that continually ask readers to consider spatial and other relations between sender and recipient. Recalling the concerns of *PLOT* and *Lonely*'s deployment of narrative and lyric effects, which are not fully recognizable as either, we might ask whether the images mark an attempt to get to the idealized "moment of expression," a moment that participates in previous moments without emplotting itself on a timeline with those moments. What if, in other words, they mark insubordinate moments that can recognize other personal or public pasts, other personal or public futures? To regard the images in this way would be to start to think together the various layers of precarity presented in the text, such as the observation near the beginning that some lives "can not count." We could then see this poem as continuous with poems by others poets who engage the visual, including Rankine's own *PLOT*, which makes similar use of citation, the theme of loneliness, and the idea of photography:

> [. . .] Either way, and yet . . . there had been a
> beginning . . . *The pregnancy has made me feel less lonely.* The start had
> startled her. She held her found thought like a photograph
> before her. A beautiful photograph? A true photograph? Real?
> Was it a real photograph? The "true real." She recalled the
> phrase from college, the phrase but not its meaning.[54]

The reference is to Julia Kristeva's concept of the true-real ("le vréel" in French, a portmanteau of "the true"—"le vrai"—and "the real"—"le réel"), which similarly seeks a more immediate relationship between the true according to positive science and the real in the psychoanalytic sense. Recalling the phrase but not its meaning can serve as an analogue for these images, signs whose signification—and function—is ambiguous. There is a familiar gap between recalled knowledge ("any kind of knowledge can be a prescription against despair") and the ability to reactivate what was once known and correctly apply it to a situation.[55] The photographs do something other than mimic our present immersion in an omnipresent, reified image stream. They still the "image stream" but offer only partial recall, which participates in the larger strategy of citation and semiautonomous affect, as with the smiling image of Amadou Diallo. The stilled moment can then lay claim to being the origin of a new series of thoughts, images, or experiences. If *Don't Let Me Be Lonely* is in part a critique of the present and of the idea of the present as already belonging to a plot of the self as a character, then it matters that the memory of pain, like the memory of a phrase out of context, can simply become mere data, beyond any power to comfort.

Rankine's references, however, are not all allusions to the media. *Don't Let Me Be Lonely* also cites and revises another of *PLOT*'s statements of exhaustion, drawn from one of its paralinguistic text boxes whose function seem analogous to frames. The effect is a playful recollection of Claudia Rankine as author, which may or may not be connected to her as person. As with the images, her text becomes just another ambiguous marker of partial recall, which lends itself to resignification:

> and still dimming, easily as any sunlit patter, with this
> difference: the low ceiling compresses, harbors bands and
> sheets, plates of bone: gasps, occupy, occupy the hurt
> articulation cross-hatched into this shallow space: murmuring
> face, facing: a banked stamina called: I, I, I
>
> undiminished and the beached floral, the ochre—[56]

In *Don't Let Me Be Lonely*, the line becomes the more commercially saturated "[a]gain and again these were Kodak moments, full of individuation; we were all on our way to our personal best. America was seemingly a meritocracy. I, I, I am Tiger Woods."[57] This paratactic list links those moments recorded, remembered, cherished, held on to as signs of who we are, and the commercial forms that underwrite "us." "I am Tiger Woods" is the tagline to Woods's first commercial for Nike offering Woods as another in a line of vanguard models of spurious racial transcendence. Individuation and identity become commodities, similar to the ways an earlier moment, through allusion, conflates financial well-being with being in general—"To roll over or not to roll over that IRA."

Rankine's postlyric poetics permanently *suspend* the lyric and with it the principles of generality through which writing and life are perceived. The radically open, heterogeneous "I" becomes simply a "voice" calling us into new forms of association. The poem asks, with the international chorus of poets it cites, what "American" means, for example. This is one sense of the poem's generalized apostrophe: saying "here," or perhaps "*still* here," expressing something other than "I am." It is not apostrophe such as one finds at the end of *PLOT* ("O father O mother this soul my own").[58] *Don't Let Me Be Lonely* is confessional without confessors, and postlyric subjectivity is one trope among others. This confession is not part of a process of subjection nor does it establish the temporal coherence of the subject: it is atemporal, achronological. It defers the logic of a time structured around an already, a now, and a not yet predicted as possible in favor of the unknown "yet" of the event. The poem marks the location of a "speaker" who is not "there" except as a speaking function. This makes for a radical formal innovation, turning the reception of the work itself into a kind of event. If we think of the images as something other than illustrations of the ideas of the text, consider them instead as integral to the text, as the subtitle of *Don't Let Me Be Lonely* explicitly challenges us to, then the challenge is to see form here as creating one composite, impure material. The same already contains difference. If at a thematic level the work issues a challenge to correct the "fundamental miscount" of the *demos*, the procedures through which a life can be made, structurally, insignificant, the images push this even further, forcing us to wonder about the forms in which the other can be counted correctly.[59] The graphic components, emblematic of oppressive immediacy, are also a renewable call for recognition, a durable reminder that we will have been misrecognized. The call to imagine new forms of democratic collectivity must also respect the historicity and complexity of the social field as it is imagined, as well as the ways that social field has been founded on necessary exclusions.

The images, like that which they imperfectly recall—recite and resituate— are sensible without necessarily being meaningful. They draw our attention to the threat of erasure. The sensible—the ability to make those faces, those lives, and those deaths deemed unfit to mourn—and the sense of community that has allowed Eleanor Bumpurs, Amadou Diallo, Abner Louima, Sean Bell, Troy Davis, Trayvon Martin, and too many others to be mere names whose significance we are constantly on the verge, collectively, of forgetting—is put on trial. The "we," hinted at in the phrase "American lyric," is put on trial. The poem does not call for expanding the sphere of public sympathy or redefining personhood but for rethinking the *demos* and those procedures through which some human lives can be made structurally insignificant and disposable, visible only in narrative as a reminder of some people's proximity to disappearance. The images push this even further, forcing "us" to wonder about the forms in which the other can be counted correctly. The graphic is a spur against generalization, a reminder of something that once "meant something real," something weighty; it is the index of a "me" not yet alienated from a "we." Yet the work stops short of prescribing the forms that any future community might take, while its floating affect makes it difficult to read it merely as critique. Rather, Rankine's work defines the moment expression "between now and yet" as a moment of precarity that, unbidden, may yet return to us with startling, ambiguous urgency. That return is a revision of this moment and the older one and an opening onto some yet unpredicted time.

THE WAY [IT] IS

Douglas Kearney's postlyric poetics repurpose a fictive lyric subjectivity rooted in echo, in a relay between levels of discourse that renders the text always in process and grounded in history, to ghost a communal feeling in an atmosphere that precludes tranquil recollection. In particular, he repurposes rap and other black-identified texts purported to be the "voice of the people" reworking them to speak to the present moment. Emphasizing the synthetic processes of reading, his stress is less on the reading subject who remembers and successfully reconstitutes all the references (although doing so is one part of the work's pleasure) than on that sense that something will have been remembered and on poetics as an ultimately communal project. His idiosyncratic graphic presentation emphasizes the interpolated lines. The lines themselves tend to belong already to an intertextual network of citation, involving readers in a constitutively incomplete project of synthesis—a reconfiguration of sources and echoes—that underscores the moment of expression as iterable. Hip-hop stands in his poetics as the latest preemptive mask for understanding (and pathologizing) black life even as it is praised for its fidelity to black culture. Think here of the repeated alibi for deplorable lyrics that they are "true to life." Kearney's strategy of allusion ultimately proves hauntological, marking the untimeliness of the present to make a place for unacknowledged forms of ancestrality: ways of "misremembering the present" so as to recover trajectories from the past to a different future.

My reading focuses on the three-poem sequence "The Black Automaton in de Despair of Existence," whose delocalized "here" turns on the implied temporality of sound recording and cultural circulation. Using a graphic and typographic presentation that recalls sentence diagrams (and with it both failing schools and assumptions of black intellectual deficiency) alongside an allusive strategy that coordinates lyrics from "high" and "low" culture, Kearney's work sits at the intersection of sight and (implied) sound. His general strategy in *The Black Automaton* involves polyvocal textual displacement, estrangement, and uncanny welcome. Take "The Black Automaton in de Despair ub Existence #3: How Can I Be Down?" (fig. 1):[60]

THE BLACK AUTOMATON IN DE DESPAIR UB EXISTENCE #3: HOW CAN I BE DOWN?

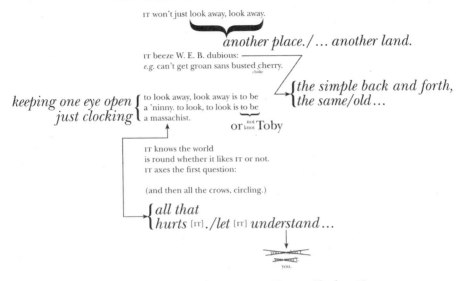

Fig. 1. "The Black Automaton in de Despair ub Existence #3: How can I be down?"

The enlarged, italicized segments are all allusions to popular rap songs (that in some instances themselves allude to other rap songs) and create a reading situation in which the voice of another may always intrude, despite the arrows' orchestrations. The entire surface of the poem is expressive, but it does not provide a sure sense of how to coordinate statements in time. Expression becomes a process without beginning or definite end. Beginning with the title, Kearney mixes genres, articulating serial drama ("The Black Automaton in"), plantation literature ("de Despair ub Existence"), and depending on where one places the accent—"I" or "down"—either an earnest confession of pain or a rap-inspired drama. The opening line cites "Dixie," which in turn yields to Arrested Development's 1992 hit "Tennessee" ("another place, |... another land"). "Tennessee"'s alternative memory overwrites, imperfectly, the racist nostalgia of Stephen Foster's "Dixie," which is invoked through allusion and the title's Negro dialect while also signaling the current regime of "neoliberal multiculturalism" more fully developed.

However, the poem shifts register (and discourse communities, or habitus) with the orthographic pun, reinvoking literary black dialect ("IT beeze W. E. B. dubious"), and references to the Roots' "Clones" ("the simple back and forth | the same"), Bell Biv Devoe's "Poison" ("keeping one eye open . . .") and (possibly) Run-D.M.C.'s "Mary, Mary" crossed with Toni Morrison's *Be-*

loved ("busted [choke] cherry").[61] I list these allusions to draw attention to the ways punning generates differential temporal frames—not a "simple back and forth"—of being and knowing. The invocation of Du Bois, I would argue, emphasizes double consciousness as a temporal concept as well as an epistemological one, underscoring the coexistent but incommensurate registers that inform the production and reception of the literary and historical text while denying any master narrative or code to arrest the play of significations. [IT] "beeze dubious" stresses the potentially immobilizing hesitation between, in Du Bois's vocabulary, being Negro or American, a contradiction whose resolution was a matter of politics rather than representation. All of the songs Kearney invokes (and *Beloved*) were commercial hits during an especially destructive moment in the "war on drugs," around the time of the Rodney King riots in Los Angeles, and when Bill Clinton and Republicans and members of Congress were issuing racially tinged calls for welfare "reform." The problem is familiar: blackness became symbolically valuable under the banner of "celebrating diversity," but the fates of African Americans did not materially improve. For the Du Bois who understood that the only way to resolve the contradictions inherent in the "strange meaning" of being black in the United States was to fundamentally change the United States, this embrace was indeed dubious. If the racial formation corresponding with the performance of "Dixie" was such that one could claim to like individual black people but to distrust blacks in the abstract, the moment of the late 1980s through the mid-1990s was such that one could "celebrate" black culture in the abstract while ignoring suffering black individuals, who were often abstract and spatially remote.

Like Rankine's speakers, Kearney's IT is unable to achieve contemplative distance from its immediate surroundings, leaving it to the structure of the poem to effect that distance. However, Kearney's poem, published after the election of the first black U.S. president, explicitly marks a torque in Du Boisian double consciousness. The black subject still experiences "itself" through differential frames of knowledge and experience in this particular moment of commodity circulation, but signs of racial difference have become increasingly disarticulated from material realities as racism advances under officially "color-blind" policies. The embrace of metonymic signs of black culture such as rap music emblematizes progressive racial attitudes even as the lives of those racial others worsen. The self—an objectified IT—is held between abstracting discourses: cultural forms taken to express the quintessence of exceptional, representative black genius (Toni Morrison, rap music), on the one hand, and the realities of "unexceptional" black life, on the other. The poem graphically links "mas-sachist," a neologism that simultaneously recalls conventions of Negro dialect and suggests erotic attachment to suffering at the hands of the "massa" (either the literal one or the metaphorical one that the conventions of representation of black speech may be said to figure), back to "Tennessee" and ends on a sus-pended question overtaken by "all that | hurts [it]. / let [IT] understand . . . ~~you wouldn't you won't~~ you," whatever of you or IT there is to understand. Histori-cal knowledge suggests pleasurable pain, a form of self-denial that tropes liberal claims that awareness or "tolerance" of the racial other will resolve broader, systemic structures of racial difference. "To look away, look away is to be a [pica] 'ninny," to accept Dixie and all of its continued legacy. "To look, to look is to be a | massachist | or {not | knot |} to be / Toby," referring to the famous scene in *Roots* where an overseer forces Kunta Kinte to accept the name his master gives him.[62] The vacillation between possibilities is the result of graphic form and the normative pretenses of sentence diagramming. To look is to be en-snared, to be too well assimilated, to be too tied with a race subject to lynching ("knot"). Pointedly, the unmarked "you" moves from grammatical subject in the struck lines to grammatical object of ITS own understanding. The poem is thus postlyric to the extent that it stresses the fictionality of the structure with-out privileging the intending consciousness or contemplative subject.

Like other poems in the series, this poem operates at the level of its enun-ciation, hailing a readership that will at once understand references to "Dixie," rap songs, and literary fiction that do not quite generate a unitary meaning. "IT knows the world is round | whether it likes IT or not." "Round" here is a pun for the overlapping, not quite synchronous meanings of the poem, and the pro-noun pun makes clear the despair of existence, being thrown into a world that extends beyond ITself spatially and temporally. As Greg Tate observes in the jacket blurb, "Kearney's poetry flows from a consideration of urban speech, negro spontaneity and book learning not easily parsed if you haven't fully di-gested every major hiphop [*sic*] lyric composed between 1979 and 1983 and spent a considerable amount of time backtracking the library stacks stuffed with Zora Neale Hurston and Ishmael Reed's neo-folkloric tales."[63] In Tate's characterization of Kearney's poetics, one senses already the emergence of new aesthetic criteria. "Every *major* hiphop lyric" implies a fixed and accepted set of standards, the unavailability of which is equally key to Kearney's poetics and his challenge to a larger regime of common sense. Kearney's overlapping frames of reference do not resolve into either a generic "universal" discourse or a modernist system of allusions to a greater tradition. No one frame seems adequate to explain or contextualize all the references one parses.

The reference to Du Bois is analytical insofar as the ability to recognize these disparate sources typifies the upwardly mobile black intelligentsia, doubly remote from the habitus of the worlds they leave and of those to which they seek to gain entrance. In Kearney's hands this "contradiction of double aims," as Du Bois refers to it, seems to index the paradox that becoming more "universal" as a result of succeeding in the field of cultural production means becoming less black and that the more one can operate in two different discourse communities the more alienated one feels from each. This is one sense of "the despair of existence": the disorienting experience—recognition, bemusement, the embarrassment of pleasure out of place—an African American person may feel hearing "Ridin' Dirty" in a commercial advertising the safety features of a Volkswagen to suburban white families in a neighborhood where the presence of Chamillionaire, the song's performer, would likely trigger a crisis.

How can I be down (depressed)? Black and brown are increasingly subject to premature death, treated as surplus population, a new kind of problem to be solved—it is hard to celebrate cultural advances when we have daily confirmation that for the black artist "all safety is an illusion."[64] How can I be down (affiliated)? My experiences and social aspirations have surreptitiously engendered a new class habitus, and with it new possible forms of community. The poem draws on these contradictions in order to make alienation into a token of welcome, redrawing the outlines of that experience of internal "code switching" and reminding readers that this is a shared habit of mind. Kearney's spatial organization implies a complex temporal and experiential experience, encouraging readers to focus on the adjective "black" rather than the noun "blackness" as a primary point of analysis. As much as it is tempting to imagine an ideal readership who would understand all the references, the act of synthesis will necessarily vary from reader to reader, and mere knowledge does not resolve the situations limned through these dense references.[65]

Kearney's postlyric textual strategies depend primarily on spatial arrangements that dialectically disrupt the norms of both lyric and racial reading, transforming prior statements into a form somewhere between collage and chorus. It is, again, a permanent suspension of the genre that problematizes the "we" the allusions imply. In "The Black Automaton in de Despair ub Existence #1: Up Ye Mighty Race!!!," which follows #3 in the collection, the strategy is less double take than near-simultaneous overlap (fig. 2):[66]

THE BLACK AUTOMATON IN DE DESPAIR UB EXISTENCE #1: UP YE MIGHTY RACE!!!

{ smack needle and wheedle
{ youngbleeds and biddies. *with everybody saying:*
swing down.../let me ride.

{ crack know shit—where TVs sit
{ and skeleton bricks. *who's that peeking in my window/pow!*
broken glass everywhere!

IT can't piss in a pot,

so the need is in a haystack.   /   so the lights have run off with the spoon.
looking for it is falling off a log.   /   coke is it and life is opening a can.

IT has a window to throw IT out of.

[IT] *can kiss the sky!*

up, up...

Fig. 2. The Black Automaton in de Despair ub Existence #1: Up ye mighty race!!!"

The tone of the poem does not correspond with the title's nominal despair or with its general emphasis on "black" as adjective rather than noun. As with #3, the poem is abstract, even playful, offering two ways of finishing the sentence that begins "IT can't piss in a pot": "so the need is in a haystack" or "so the lights have run off with the spoon," together suggesting ITS money has gone to pay for a heroin addiction ("the spoon") rather than the electric bill. Each of those lines, respectively, alludes to a cliché (needle in a haystack) and to a nursery rhyme ("the dish ran away with the spoon"). The interplay of graphic presentation and allusive strategies communicates this despair instead. "Up Ye Mighty Race" relates to lines about heroin and crack cocaine by the mock diagrammatic structure that, like the exclamation points, ironically resituates Marcus Garvey's famous exhortation. All of the allusions, however, are citations of citation. Garvey's call (later adapted by dancehall artist Buju Banton) operates alongside references to Dr. Dre's "Let Me Ride" (which interpolates Parliament's "Mothership Connection (Star Child)"), Grandmaster Flash and the Furious Five's "The Message" (referenced in Puff Daddy's "Can't Nobody Hold Me Down"), and Redman and Method Man's "How High?" (which recalls Jimi Hendrix's "Purple Haze.") This complex of overlapping allusions tropes the very idea of black genius as the unfolding of a unitary folk spirit, making its simultaneity of reference into a moment of expression that is not a unitary moment of lyric understanding but a fractured set of relays, revisions, recitations, and unstable exhortations. One thing captured is a shift in rap itself, from Melle Mel's despair at "people pissin' on the stairs, you know they just don't care" to Ma$e's non sequitur "it ain't about the money, Puff, I just don't care." The poem figures a similar gap in the transition from "IT can't piss in a pot" to "IT has a window to throw IT out of," reversing the colloquial "you / he ain't got a pot to piss in or a window to throw it out of," that is, you are or he is poor. Here, IT has a window but cannot—will not—"piss in a pot" because IT is no longer poor, though still not secure.

Taken together, the locus of despair seems to be nostalgia for the race politics and sense of racial solidarity of earlier moments. Puff Daddy's and Ma$e's "Can't Nobody Hold Me Down," in particular, is quite remote from Grandmaster's Flash and the Furious Five's "The Message," insisting on an isolated "I" even as it invokes Melle Mel's representative "I." The "despair" is of the unavailability of such an "I." To identify with the "The Message," ideally, to see oneself as part of a community and to seek communal responses to social problems. To identify with "Can't Nobody Hold Me Down" is to aspire to individual solutions to social problems—to transform oneself rather than one's neighborhood. "IT" figures that transition-in-process, showing that what appears to be contradiction between the two versions of lyric utterance is ultimately continuity. Neither version of lyrically mediated uplift is quite adequate to present historical conditions. The Goodie Mob reference—"who's that looking in my window? Pow!"—is the only one that does not obviously recall an earlier song. The enjambment that gives way to "broken glass" is dramatically satisfying in its insertion of an elision break between the "pow" and the consequences of a projectile, presumably a bullet, hitting the would-be intruder behind the window. The effect is to draw attention to the now absent figure, "nobody now," in "Cell Therapy." The possibility of sudden, complete disappearance structures the rest of the poem's depiction of slow death due to drug abuse (a narcotic high being substituted for the title's uplift). The subject becomes "IT" in a difference sense: a body rather than grammatical subject, required by a narrative that represents it but otherwise missing or unavailable. Ma$e's colloquial "I just don't care" takes on a nihilistic cast. Some have justified the ostentatious display of wealth as a necessary corrective to images of black immiseration. However, increasingly, such displays underscore the radical separation of one from another and the ways one's former neighbors become threats to be dispatched, as the ostentatious wealth that proves one has "made it" becomes an invitation for others "peeking in the window" to take it. More directly, to "make it" carries an implicit requirement that one be willing to make another into "nobody now." The fidelity that Kearney's work demands is ultimately similar to that which Rankine's demands: fidelity with one that can become an IT, whose "life can not matter."

While I have emphasized the allusions in my readings, the graphic presentation of the poems—with arrows and enlarged sections highlighting those allusions without explaining them and the mock-diagrammatic structure rearranging the reading experience—is central to their effect, at once orienting and disorienting the experience of reading in time. The nested allusions open the affective and referential possibilities of the poems, creating an effect that highlights the thing forgotten rather than its recall. Memory in these poems is not of something that has already happened or recollection of past experience; rather, it is of habituated things that we need to encounter again, extending again to the "proximity" of one word to another, as in the second poem of the "Despair ub Existence" series (fig. 3):

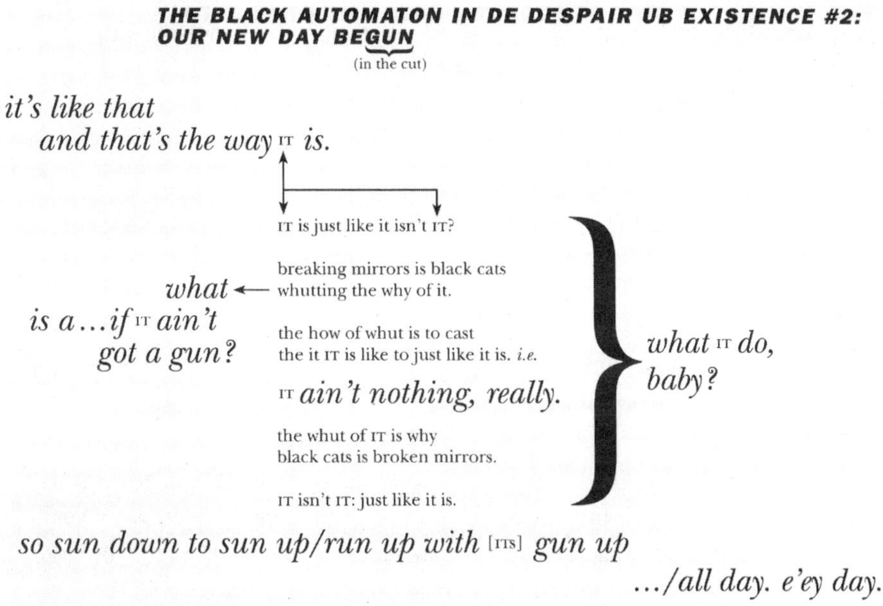

Fig. 3. "The Black Automaton in de despair ub existence #2: Our new day begun"

Between invocations of broken mirrors and black cats, Kearney stages a se-ries of ontological questions—most prominently "IT ain'st nothing, really"—that suggest both ITS contingency (ITS position is mere bad luck) and the concrete effects of its social location: "IT isn't IT: just like it is." Counterclock-wise from the top, the italicized references are to Run-D.M.C.'s "It's Like That," A Tribe Called Quest's "What?," Mack 10's "Westside Slaughterhouse," Ice Cube's "All Day Every Day," and an ubiquitous (now outdated) vernacular ex-pression, "what it do?" featured in too many songs to name, with the central "IT ain't nothing really" taken from Mobb Deep's "Shook Ones, Pt. II." Addressing the ontological question begged by the grammatical "it," this poem is more ab-stract than the others in the series. Inspired by Run-D.M.C.'s tautological con-struction ("it's like that, and that's the way it is"), this poem investigates ITS ontology, "the whut of IT," which the poem can only do through a mirror. More-over, as "breaking mirrors is black cats | whutting the why of it," the poem sug-gests that attempts to pin down ITS ontology neglects the historical processes that can make systemic disadvantage seem like mere bad luck. The corner-stones of Kearney's poetics in this series—allusions to vernacular culture and mock diagrammatic structure—converge here for a satisfying payoff that plays on the nonidentity of it and IT. As allusions in Kearney's work are part of an in-surgent practice of recontextualization marked by typography, repetition does not repeat the same thing. In other words, playing off the academic structures of address that sentence diagramming and allusion invoke, Kearney's improper citations deprioritize the idea of a original "proper" source. The line "IT is just like it isn't IT" wryly comments on the grammatical situation, pointing back to the "IT" in the second line. The reference to "breaking mirrors" and the roughly symmetrical structure turns on the phrase "it ain't nothing really," a context-dependent idiom that equally means "it is insignificant," "it is nothing," and "it is not nothing." The poem as a whole is a kind of mirror: "IT is just like it isn't IT" becomes "IT isn't IT: just like it is"; "breaking mirrors is black cats" becomes "black cats is broken mirrors"; "the how of whut is to cast" becomes "the whut of IT is why," and "whut" is a verb, an activity. In part, this poem responds to the previous poem where implied gun violence transforms ITS now to then, some-one to nobody, with IT on the run, figuratively and (within the implied diegesis) literally. The large curly bracket confirms a transition from the question of being to doing, defining IT by actions rather than attributes that tend to collapse into tautological babble. The noncorrespondence of the black subject with the icons of black culture is trope rather than theme; mirrored grammatical structures invoke the process of producing potentially new meanings and associations. In particular, "to be" proves untrustworthy: though the copula ("is") creates parity between "breaking/broken mirrors" and "black cats," semantically those are not fully compatible ideas, even if we ignore the difference in state between a breakage in process and a completed breakage. The subject—grammatical, historical, and phenomenological—becomes an open assemblage, realized in and through the negotiations of reading between discourses and the enclosure of language and received narratives.

The substitution of "it" for the first-person pronoun "I," like the temporal rearrangements engendered by the graphic presentation of allusion, makes Kearney's work, like Rankine's, at once lyric and not: "postlyric." As an analytic category, the "postlyric" invites us to attend to the noncontemporaneity of the poetic and historical present, what Nathaniel Mackey refers to as the "postexpectant" nature of the present (see chapter 5), which deviates from the present that was dreamed. Both poets assume a certain degree of interest in the objective situation of the biographical author but make that part of the structure of their texts, either through a persistent media sphere or through half-remembered and transformed songs that flow in and out of the work. The postlyric, then, is a way of analyzing the intergenericity of Rankine's and Kearney's poems in terms of traditional lyric effects and interrogating their avoidance of the closure, unitary voice, or perspective we have come to associate with the modernist lyric. Neither author uses poetry as an index of the poet's "thoughts" or "feelings," though each tempts that linkage, using lyrical techniques to extend writing's expressive possibilities.

Rankine and Kearney invest us in the "facticity" of generic norms, between "worldliness" and "wordliness" and, as with concrete poetry, in a temporalization of those forms that attempts to wrench both form and content from the unreflexive consumption of confession and to a new relationship with the text of confession. As ever, we are suspended between the retention of past racial associations and the anticipation or protension of new associations, and at that threshold, we may reimagine forms of community. Instead of fidelity to "genius" as the self-originating and clarifying expression of the sovereign subject or as the "expression" of "black genius," there is a fidelity to a modality of demystification that does not take the text itself as somehow beyond mystification either through its fiction of lyric presence or the surety of the lyric hermeneutic. Postlyric poetics emphasize the process of *poeisis* without reifying either the process or the product—the poetic subject or object. It is a process of art making that as a mode of social thought takes and reworks the shared techniques of inhabiting the present and pairs those with literary techniques to put

forward something at once familiar and strange. Thematically, through con-
cern with those modernity systemically renders most vulnerable, and formally,
through the evacuated subjective locus of expression, it shifts attention from
representation of lives lost or cultural authenticity bound to the vagaries of cap-
ital to those lives that might yet be saved, those people who may yet be loved,
that culture yet unformed. Social thought and its material limits are central
as part of the work's self-production. The interest of Rankine's and Kearney's
postlyric poetics lies in the arrangement of materials into contingent works be-
yond the mirror of representation, where we find the openness of new articula-
tions and articulations of the new.

part 2   above where sound leaves off

four

Sing It in My Voice
Blues, Irony, and a Politics of Affirmative Difference

A black play embraces the infinite.

Suzan-Lori Parks, "New Black Math"

Reference to music has become such a critical commonplace in discussions of black literature that to invoke it risks collapse into simple conformity to disciplinary consensus—the repetition of the "no-thought" in the discipline of black literary studies. It becomes necessary to refer to it, however, insofar as African American music fundamentally functions as both a sign of black genius and as a legitimating trope for black literary production.[1] Within some critical discourses, music's presence—the expression of a deeper impulse and tradition that persists relatively unchanged—functions as the sign of human freedom in an allegory of transformative resistance to the conditions of life, and for that reason exists in a hierarchical relationship to mute writing.[2] The writing I consider in this section uses a principle of musicality in order to transform the possibilities of print as print while drawing on some of the rhetorical and grammatical strategies music as creative principle makes available. Particularly in this chapter, which analyzes of an aspect of the blues in the work of Harryette Mullen and Suzan-Lori Parks, music is an extension of an idea of black literature as a transformation of the possibilities of black writing. Their respective invocations of music, in other words, don't make the music a model but a point of reference through which to extend literary concerns. Such a double gesture, in fact, is central to my elaboration of an abstracted blues irony in their work, which takes the blues to be a set of techniques to resolve specifically literary issues rather than a bearer of folk spirit. I do not invoke music simply to shore up the blackness of the writers here; each, in different ways, uses music—as practice and cultural form embedded in historical processes—to work out different conceptions of race in her writing.

In lieu of a metaphoric reading of blues qualities, my primary argument in this chapter is that an abstracted set of techniques most associated with the blues provides a platform from which to extend the expressive range of black writing.[3] Rather than treating the blues as a noun (and thus an appropriable sign of racial belonging), I consider the blues as an adjective—a set of techniques, including repetition and citation in addition to irony, that have no meaning on their own. On that basis, I develop a reading of a mode of blues irony—an irony that for these authors refuses to hierarchically privilege paradigmatic meaning over syntagmatic play. Repetition and citation are techniques of what I'm calling blues irony: the interruption of one discourse with a abrupt shift of register or unmotivated repetition that reorganizes the hermeneutic coordinates of a text. That reorganization changes the focus from the phenomenal given of experience to the found, opening up the text's expressive possibilities even as it destabilizes the idea of a text.

"Blues irony" participates in a larger project of affirmation, a play of non-dialectical contradiction that refuses reference to some transcendental signified to anchor or resolve the play of meanings. Affirmation in my argument has implications for thinking literature and culture more generally; it points to what can seem to be a self-undermining literary practice and also points to more supple and complex notions of identity and culture. In Mullen's and Parks's respective texts, the blues underscores what needs transformation. Affirmation provides the occasion to rethink the complexity of the historical text, allowing what has been misnamed to provide resources for a future instead of posing history as a set of inevitable occurrences to mourn or avenge. Rather than the dialectical development of differences or moments into a single timeline, affirmation names a horizontal play of heterogeneous differences. The effect of this affirmative blues irony often registers as disorienting humor, but it also questions the stable locus of meaning and the value of black expression by manipulating the materiality of literary language itself. Such abstracting procedures—the blues' modes of abstraction and a poetics that translates those modes to the domain of literature—allow Mullen and Parks to develop a literary practice aimed at "radical unlearning," a way of thinking that runs counter to disciplinary norms by duplicating and magnifying what in them is excessive, inscrutable, and absurd but no less effective for its absurdity. Blues irony undermines those readings that would render their respective experiments allegories of resistance related to a larger set of preconstituted political and historical struggles.

Both writers explicitly invoke the blues as a creative principle in accounts of their respective poetics. Parks identifies repetition and revision, or "Rep & Rev," a central element of her work, with the attempt to "create a dramatic text that departs from the traditional linear narrative style to look and sound more

like a musical score," while Mullen expresses interest in "the resources of po-
etry" beyond "communicating a specific message," resources that are related
to the "'music' of the language."[4] That "music," for both writers, figures a line
immanent to language that separates intelligible speech from mere pleasurable
noise, emphasizing the unruly sensuality of the former and the will to meaning
of the latter. One might think here of a blues moan, at once a sign of something
unsaid, a sign of some content that escapes words, a musical transition from
one phrase to another whose meaning is of a different order, and a way of sig-
naling belonging to a performance tradition. Or think of the twelve-bar blues'
A-A'-B lyrical and harmonic structure, which allows for a practically infinite
invention that derives from a stock of common musical and vernacular ges-
tures. That principle of generating and regenerating the vernacular unites Parks
and Mullen, albeit to different ends.

A blues irony is a modality of affirming at once the truth of two apparently
contradictory statements.[5] In this way, the blues affirms the ultimate ground-
lessness of community and the common, the absent centers of language and
"my people," but acknowledges that groundlessness as a means of disrupting
the apparent presence of historical fact or common language.[6] Referring to the
blues as a set of techniques and practices, associated with race as a historical
mode of elective affinity, I invoke the blues as a mode whose performative inter-
sectionality indexes a self subject to change and revision. Here, I mean to draw
out scholars' and musicians' claims for the blues' mode of address as at once
singular and plural. If we come on that singular-plural mode of address, ironic
juxtaposition, and repetition apart from its usual context, the blues' seemingly
unmotivated interruption of one discourse (or subject predication) can pro-
duce a startling disruption of the terms through which we understand texts and
identities. As my readings make clear, it is not just the use of these techniques
but also their use in unexpected contexts that informs my sense of blues irony
as affirmative. If, as Stuart Hall famously argued, "race is the modality in which
class is 'lived,'" that does not mean race is always primary: sometimes class is
the modality in which race is lived, and gender and sexuality inflect both. The
blues, owing to its practically groundless irony and its discursive promiscuity, is
especially well suited to capture and negotiate that flux.

A more general term for "performative intersectionality" is affirmative dif-
ference, which has applications beyond identity. "Affirmative difference" is
my term for that desire to think a historical difference—in its flux and its the-
oretical movement between cause and effect of political structures—"in itself"
without also abstracting that racial difference into an "as such." As Hortense

Spillers notes, there is often a strong temptation to thematize race as unitary so that "the cultures of the Diaspora and of the continent become, by negligible detour, a single project," and differences of historical experience become occluded by seemingly more urgent or fundamental questions of similarity.[7] To think difference as a precondition of conceiving the cultures of the diaspora and contingency as intrinsic to any common project beginning with the invention of "Africa" and "blackness" requires reference to a history that exceeds those diasporic cultures. Yet blackness is not nothing; it is the name of a site of historical struggle over competing articulations of difference whose meanings are embedded in the fabric of political processes. To affirm blackness in the absence of a transcendental "as such" requires thinking it historically, as a set of historically conditioned practices and responses to oppression, and as conditioning oppressive practices, without understanding race to be the condition rather than the outcome of modernity. Affirmation thinks in positive terms what is otherwise negative, a sign of a crisis and decision, despite the absence of a transcendental signified to which that difference refers.

The different abstracted blues that informs Mullen's and Parks's respective work figure engagement with the very creative core of the vernacular in its self-differentiation, the place where vernacular language and culture become almost incoherent. Those blues highlight an affirmative difference related to the insurgent thrust such rhetorical practices may have had in prior moments and the pleasure they allowed. Tracing the lines of an abstracted blues, I underscore a shared mode of irony in Mullen's and Parks's work that is most readily legible through blues traditions to which they both do and do not belong. I locate that irony between critical senses of the blues as "a web of intersecting, crisscrossing impulses always in productive transit," a "'coming home,' a gerund forever in motion, . . . a continuous happening," and as a mode that marks "a struggle within language itself to define the differing material conditions of black women and black men."[8] This latter sense—the blues as a struggle within language itself—is especially central to my conception here, though all underscore the conceptual opening the blues figures here. Abstracted into literature, the blues' affirmative irony becomes a challenge to the received truths about the nature of events, embedded in language and yoked to a tacit struggle over factuality, and reveals the complicity of facts with histories of violence and oppression that one counters with facts.

The affirmative character of blues irony—undermining the closure of concepts—performs the labor of desedimenting the conceptual bases of thought, for example, about the meaning and value of the vernacular. Affirmative difference shifts the locus of politics, figuring blackness and black culture as something people do, rather than something that *is*, and in the process shifts attention to what is to come, or to return. In that sense, affirmation also participates in a "politics of truth"—the conflicted truth about language, aesthetic techniques, or belonging abstracted from several true statements in a particular discourse—by unsettling the underlying tenets of ideology that appears to us as a set of unproblematic truths that "everyone knows." For example, Theodor Adorno argues that because "Negro spirituals, antecedents of the blues, were slave songs and as such combined the lament of unfreedom with its oppressed confirmation [...] everything unruly in it [jazz] was from the very beginning integrated into a strict scheme."[9] He uses a common-sense, patriarchal schema (the spirituals begat the blues begat jazz) to claim first that the blues and jazz have a conceptual solidity outside of practice and then that they ceaselessly recite the desire for a particular form of freedom as nonslavery. Allowing that African American performers may be up to something different, he concludes that white European promoters of jazz improvisation had mistaken the market-based freedom they already had as bourgeois subjects and consumers for genuine human freedom. His act of demystification rests on a mystification. Without engaging his historical argument regarding the European bourgeoisie's embrace of a certain "jazz," I would stress that Adorno's claim implicitly relies on a false assumption that emancipation was an adequate response to the spirituals' "lament of unfreedom." It was not. Further, his thumbnail folk-spirit sketch does not attend to the ways jazz revised the blues or the ways the blues revised its understanding of the unfreedom in the wake of emancipation, when blacks were effectively reenslaved. As Ann Douglas puts it, "The makers of the spirituals, a product of the antebellum, pre-Emancipation period, don't know what the blues man knows: the earthly liberation the spirituals look forward to has already happened and has proved a farce. The blues bore witness to a moment of immense and historic disillusion."[10] Adorno's statement of the dialectical "truth" of jazz as direct descendant of the spirituals treats emancipation as the only form of freedom the slaves could have dreamed of and ignores the difference between a decree of freedom and its realization. More surprisingly, and most germane to my discussion, he does not acknowledge that more than ideology the blues took and transformed the *techniques* of the spirituals.

Douglas's account gets at the blues as a recognition—and affirmation—of the groundlessness of a previous generation's dreams that I see in Mullen's and Parks's respective transformations of prior texts. Recognition of that groundlessness does not result in rejection or mockery but leads the new form to develop new techniques and to turn the older form's musical techniques and forms of expression to new ends. Indeed, Adorno's own sense of aesthetic techniques as fundamentally social might have committed him to a similar argument had his analysis not stopped at the presence of jazz or the blues as accomplished forms reflecting the culture industry in Weimar Germany. The blues functions in this chapter, then, as a token of affirmation in the senses I have been developing, including this last: turning old techniques to new ends. What may appear farcical or unintelligible in Mullen's and Parks' work is a sign of openness, of restless search and inclusion, a quest for an audience and a challenge to that audience to think otherwise.

Further, the "farcical" in the work of Mullen and Parks—the playfully affirmative reworking and ironic transformation of the spirituals' allegories into tropes—aims at the still unrealized "freedom dreams" of those who traded one form of enslavement for another, of those who complained "the country is celebrating one hundred years of freedom one hundred years too soon."[11] The blues dramatizes and insists on the yet-to-be-realized, at times invoking an almost cosmic sense of irony of life in a world where few meanings are stable, and nothing is fixed. One encounters an aporia—a void—here, similar to that one discovers with attempts to define with any precision or finality "the" blues or the "black" of Parks's "black play." Because "blackness" is not a transcendent signified, to affirm the "black" of a "black play" is to affirm the zero—not nothing, but also not definable as a simple presence. It is an embrace of the impossible, as when Mullen, in *Muse & Drudge*, seems to call for readers to "sing it in my voice," not in a contemplative act of mixing one's "I" with another's but in a more complicated one where a "we," for which there is, however, no sure basis, seems to precede an "I."[12] The blues, as a modality of bottomless irony and repetition—repetition as both a formal principle and as the more general principle of iterability—is affirmative to the extent that it remains open to the radically other. While it is sometimes "nothing but the blues," invoked for its own sake, Mullen's and Parks's abstracted blues is the openness to an unforeseeable future that will be something other than the continuation of a community as such.

HOW A BORDER ORDERS DISORDER

Throughout her work, Harryette Mullen engages the vernacular as medium, a kind of linguistic mask that makes sense of a more deep-rooted play with all of the signifying resources of language, from phonetics and anagrams to found and reworked texts (for example, her engagement with Gertrude Stein's *Tender But-*

tons in *Trimmings* and *S*PeRM**K*T*). In my reading of her work, irony as a mode of meaning's overturning explains an effect of the blues, and the blues explains irony.[13] Given that it names a reversal of other tropes and rhetorical devices, it is itself as notoriously difficult to define as trope as a zero is to define as a number. Zero is a number with no extension, being neither the sign of a definite quantity nor strictly belonging to any sequence; similarly, irony neither directly signifies nor operates as a unitary trope but disrupts tropes imagined to function within stable discursive situations. Thus, while I refer to "blues irony," I have in mind the blues' exploitation of the vernacular as a productive source of language in such a way that it pleasurably diverts, defers, or defaces all sense. Blues irony is neither the irony of vernacular signifying nor the "blank irony" of postmodern pastiche. While pastiche, as famously defined by Fredric Jameson, wears a "linguistic mask, speech in a dead language ... without any of parody's ulterior motives, amputated of the satiric impulse, devoid of laughter and of any conviction that ... some healthy linguistic normality still exists," blues irony wears its mask *as* a mask of living language.[14] It tropes the destabilizing performance of language without the performer's knowing, reassuring wink, allowing Mullen to vacillate between recognizable critique and affirmation. At the risk of reification, the figure of blues irony captures that rapid shift between sincerity and mockery as a specific technique rather than a general feature of African American vernacular culture.

Yet that risk is part of my point: both irony and affirmation are ways of describing two apparently incompatible alternatives, as in an expression like "if it wasn't for bad luck I'd have no luck at all." Such virtuosic verbal performance admits one into a community as much as it ostracizes one from it, even though, as John Coltrane is reported to have said, "the audience heard 'we' even if the singer said 'I.'"[15] That desire to hear a "we" in the singer's "I" can be as distorting, silently revising anything that doesn't fit a frame of received knowledge. *Muse & Drudge* turns to the blues as a vernacular form, buttressed by Clarence Major's and Geneva Smitherman's research into black vernacular English, to split the difference between her first collection, *Tree Tall Woman*, and her more experimental collections, *Trimmings* and *S*PeRM**K*T*, developing "a language to reach across the 'Black Atlantic.'"[16] Grounded in the idea of American English as a "miscegenated language," *Muse & Drudge* consists of quatrains theoretically readable in any sequence, many of them thematically concerned, as are Mullen's previous collections, with "the domestic space that is the woman's space and ... ideas of consumerist fetishism, our investment in objects."[17] Commodity fetishism, like irony, turns on the irreducibly double function of a given object, even as ironic citation of the everyday can reveal the limitations of the consumerist imaginary that, for example, transforms citizens into "taxpayers."

Reading Mullen's account of her work (she is referring specifically to her Stein-inflected works) in light of Stephen Henderson's observation that blackness is a commodity is instructive.[18] For Henderson, any such "commodity as 'blackness' in literature . . . should be found in concentrated or in residual form in the poetry."[19] To look for it, however, would be as fruitless as looking for some "residual value" in the dollar bill or the gold record. The relevant point of this chapter, however, is that the "counterfeit"—a constitutive possibility of any commodity exchange—works as well as the "real," that is, any "positive" appearance of racial difference. Blackness, like the cultural goods it modifies (e.g., performances, texts, and other markers of style), transforms from a differentiated existence into a difference as such, which then becomes the contested ground on which "authenticity" or "belonging" is contested.[20] Investment in the objects and signs that figure blackness occludes the social relations that produce and maintain blackness as a difference and that avoid considering its textual character, existing between onto-phenomenological object and mere abstraction. Mullen's use of the blues as a *signifier* of blackness, as a process within commodity culture and as a mark of significant difference within popular culture, rather than fixed referent makes it a marker of affirmative difference.

Muse & Drudge brings together a bracing blend of colloquial expression and vernacular forms, exploring, as it were, the "inner life" of those forms as they interface with experimental prosodic traditions. As Lorenzo Thomas put it, Mullen's work "not only presents the colloquial surface, but also demonstrates the process by which the colloquial language generates these phrases, which, in fact represent points of view, ways of seeing," deforming and reforming language.[21] Mullen transforms "the oral into something that draws together different allusive possibilities in one utterance, which is something that writing can do better than speech," and writing being "beyond the mimetic reproduction of speech or the oral tradition" (the oral tradition is, after all, a value within an economy of exchange).[22] Disenchanting mimesis by reminding readers that black lived experience is not outside of representation, on the one hand, and demonstrating the reifications and radical unlearning sometimes carried out through the vernacular, on the other, Mullen's work reenchants us with the unconstrained forms of expression and thought the vernacular often intends.

Mullen writes in a Stein-inflected "postlyric" mode, maintaining the focalizing function of an "I" without investing that "I" with the depth of character or the burden of representation. She abstracts even the use of the first person to "make it generic, so it actually fits into a blues conception of the individual, a subject that speaks, but not simply as itself."[23] This multiple speaking considered alongside the formal tendencies and tensions is part of the affirmative imperative to "hear two lines at once" and to think two things at once not with dialectical synthesis but irony's rapid oscillations of meaning.[24]

This multiple "hearing" starts with the very title of the collection, *Muse & Drudge*. Mullen says she "imagined a chorus of women singing verses that are sad and hilarious at the same time," among whom would be "Sappho, the lyric poet, and Sapphire, an iconic black woman who refuses to be silenced."[25] Sapphire is also one of the many names falsely given to the unruly, disruptive black woman Hortense Spillers cites in her litany of false names given to the black woman to figure the "meeting ground of investments and privations in the national treasury of rhetorical wealth."[26] Retaining the name Sapphire, which at once claims her refusal to be silenced as defiance and, potentially, unruly noise, is to affirm her, allowing Sapphire her complexity.[27] Mullen speaks of the work—written in mostly unrhymed, irregularly metered quatrains—as crossing two traditions, opening the long poem with following stanzas:

> Sapphire's lyre styles
> plucked eyebrows
> bow lips and legs
> whose lives are lonely too
>
> my last nerve's lucid music
> sure chewed up the juicy fruit
> you must don't like my peaches
> there's some left on the tree
>
> you've had my thrills
> a reefer and a tub of gin
> don't mess with me I'm evil
> I'm in your sin[28]

As is typical for the collection, there is no punctuation (save apostrophes), which greatly expands the semantic possibilities of any reading. These lines open with double vision of Sapphire rather than Sappho's lyre. As Marjorie Perloff has observed, "Each of the fourteen words [of the first stanza] functions paragrammatically" (that is, there are frequent breakdowns in semantic coherence, supplemented in this case by "drifts between intentional utterance and [seemingly] improvisational wordplay . . . [and] between meaning and sound");

the stanzas turn around a void of sense, invoking the very invention of mean-ing.[29] In many stanzas, at least some of the words are legible as multiple parts of speech. For example, "plucked" may be either adjective or verb, depending on how one parses the prior line. In structuralist terms, the paradigmatic (pos-sibilities of functional contrast that draw on intertextual contexts to establish a more general order) cannot fully govern the syntagmatic (possibilities of or-dering and combination that work intratextually), allotting the latter a relative freedom of invention. This is not to imply arbitrariness: the work's craft lies in the overlap of potential meanings—from both past and future—that some-how one must take into account at once. Like the blues, words and phrases here threaten to collapse into either the uncanny stutter of déjà vu or a void of mean-inglessness. It is not a "blank" irony but a groundless one: it seems designed to draw attention to the groundlessness of meaning and to affirm overlapping meanings. "Healthy linguistic normality still exists," but as a playful, disen-chanted vernacular.

Expanding Lorenzo Thomas's observation that Mullen's texts perform the surface of the colloquial, her irony reveals the real risks of the idea that there is a single black vernacular, a singular black "voice," to be inscribed within a white text. "Double voiced," as Henry Louis Gates Jr. developed the concept, may not fully capture the intensity of this play or its orientation toward a threateningly open futurity. Indeed, voice—the privilege of the oral over the written in under-standings of African American literature, is again at issue. Like "plucked," one can read "styles" and "bow" as different parts of speech, in this case, nouns or verbs. "Bow lips and legs" creates a parallel between "bowlegs" and the novel "bow lips," which at least initially appears to be a comment on the fragmenta-tion of the eroticized female body (assuming "bow" is not a verb). A novel ver-nacular utterance partially interrupts that sense: read as likening her lips to bow as a weapon, "bow lip" implies the woman's arrow-like, pointed tongue: the legs are "lonely too" because the pointed, sharp tongue marks Sapphire as an "evil" woman in the vernacular sense (invoking Bessie Smith a few lines later, the po-em's speaker lends credence to this reading, warning "don't mess with me I'm evil").

As Meta DuEwa Jones notes, "Sapphire's lyre" conjoins the stereotyped "rancorous black woman" with the lyre, an etymological cognate of the lyric, while her name orthographically evokes the ancient Greek lyric poet Sappho.[30] That pair, and the theoretical problem it encodes surrounding the limits of black women's speech, I would argue, is an act of claiming that name, making the poet a blues singer rather than vice versa. Hortense Spillers's ends her "Mama's Baby, Papa's Maybe" with a meditation on Sapphire and the promise that in *"claiming* the monstrosity (of a female with the potential to 'name')" and claiming her misnaming as insurgent ground, "'Sapphire' might rewrite after all a radically different text for a female empowerment."[31] *Muse & Drudge*, affirming the wrong name, gives a small hint what that kind of transformation might look like, and it involves changing the valences of all the terms involved. Irony, I claim, is a modality of that revision. The play of allusion turns (recall that "trope" means "to turn") and destabilizes all of the tropes of the opening set of quatrains again. "Whose lives are lonely too" alludes to Billy Strayhorn's "Lush Life," a jazz standard whose "I" commits to a life drinking with other broken-hearted people following the dissolution of a romance. That allusion anticipates the next stanza's "you must don't like my peaches | there's some left on the tree," which echoes a number of blues lyrics, including Bessie Smith's "Mama's Got the Blues." Allusions like these abound throughout the collection, drawn largely, though not exclusively, from an African American song tradition. The third stanza, for example, apparently revises "Blueberry Hill," Smith's "Gimme a Pigfoot (and a Bottle of Beer)," and the evil woman of the third stanza can be connected to any number of blues songs that complain about an "evil" woman (for example, Robert Johnson's "Kind-Hearted Woman"), which returns us to Sapphire in the first quatrain.

Though part of the pleasure of *Muse & Drudge* lies in mapping the allusions and their interaction with the poem's phonemic play and open structure, I would underscore the ways they operate alongside Mullen's "paragrammatic" arrangement of elements to create the sense that something is missing. Again, the title is an excellent case in point. As Mullen points out, traditionally "the muse is an exalted figure of inspiration, . . . a kind of spiritual, non-material being" who inspires an artist, typically figured as male, if not also white, to create.[32] The drudge is the one "cleaning the house, washing the dishes, and making the food" for the subject of the muse's inspiration.[33] There is an analogy, then, with muse linked to drudge as Sapphire is to Sappho—linking them shows that one requires the other. Mullen goes on to cite an old blues musician's double-edged allegory of the birth of the blues: "If it wasn't for women, we wouldn't have the blues." One level reminds us that the muse is always to be outside of the artwork (as inspiration) and inside the artwork as referent, while the drudge is inside and outside insofar as her labor enables the production of that art (and the forms of social reproduction that enable the consumption of art). This allegory turns on the catachrestic naming of "woman" as the origin of the blues, both the feeling and the music supposed to express it. That woman, however, is at once an empty category and one overdetermined by her place within a larger set of social antagonisms. Irony suspends—holds open—the allegory: "woman" is at once trope (a sign of unincorporated difference) and a simply posited other, unwilling romantic partner and the one who maintains the household so the music can be made, and the two senses rest uneasily side by side. To insist on all of these possible meanings is to affirm the groundlessness and necessity of "woman" as category and so reopen the project of reading as a transformative relationship with the grounds of the social.

Irony's political value in this context lies in its refusal to retain "woman" as a positivity, using it instead as an index of pleasure and social antagonism and of the bodies that do not exist as a stable "outside" to representation. Mullen's parataxis, which often omits the verb "to be" to force signification through juxtaposition, destabilizes the very work of reference. Mullen's use of irony opens up the systematicity—that which allows a signifying system to function as an internally coherent system—of this allegorical discourse of the blues by claiming this name *as* a name and spur to insurgent poetics. Her poetics interrupt allegories of value and meaning from within, taking culture and reference as processes that may not correspond with the stable unities they are supposed to represent in broader political struggles. From this perspective, the "surface" of the vernacular is also all there is to the vernacular. In Mullen's work, the vernacular has historical interest but no other solidity apart from its deployment as insurgent poetics.

Even as Mullen's work engages and reenlivens the vernacular, its irony can at times seem undirected, especially in her phonological play that reduces the vernacular to half-heard phrases that underscore it as a mode of playful affirmation rather than solid sign of belonging. A phonological similarity between "cirrus" and "serious" and between "attracts" and "attack" underwrites a line like "cirrus as a heart attracts," leading one to mishear "serious as a heart attack." Script and oral performance cross, allowing for the simultaneity of utterance she underscores.[34] Performed orally, the artificial—the aurally similar—will function as the real, but on the page the counterfeit is obvious. But there are also in her work a number of series that contain phrases that have a similar semantic content, which one can group together. For example, her play on the phrase "too poor to pay attention" seems to recur, for example, in "raised the cost of free expression" and at a stretch in "powers that be fighting | when there's no money to lighten."[35] This is more subtle than the phonological play of "cirrus as a heart attracts."

The reference to fighting when there is not enough money to suspend the associations of blackness (or to literally bleach the skin) shifts us from the familiar vernacular lament of poverty to a new series regarding the costs of things, what money buys, the ways work may pull us into a trap where we have to wonder for whom we are playing (i.e., performing), to the question what we are paying for, literally and figuratively. Thus it is unsettling, but not unpredictable, that the series opens onto, without incorporating, a set of references to skin whiteners: "hechizando con crema dermoblanqueadora (bewitched with skin-whitening cream) ǁ what we sell is enlightenment" to "history written with whitening | darkened reels and jigs."[36] These lines invoke the colorism (or, more plainly, the antiblack ideology that makes lighter skin a virtue) in the United States, Caribbean, and Latin America, and détourn Woodrow Wilson's infamous claim that D. W. Griffith's pro–Ku Klux Klan *The Birth of a Nation* was "history written with lightning." She extends the joke through the syllepsis "darkened reels and jigs" since Griffith's blackface performers "darken" the screen, and both African Americans ("jig" is both a slur against black people and a kind of dance) and white actors appear in blackface. In two vertiginous lines, she traces a nonlinear history of race, technology (the cinema), new approaches to knowledge and self-organization (the Enlightenment, commercialism), and racism. If "a border orders disorder," then Mullen's very deep, structural irony, renders borders porous and order temporary.[37]

Such punning typifies her more recent collection, *Sleeping with the Dictionary*, which hasn't received as much scholarly attention as has *Muse & Drudge* in part because it less obviously participates in a blues idiom. Yet I would argue that its rearrangement of vernacular forms, beginning with a table of contents that lists poems in alphabetical order, similarly involves a blues irony that affirms the groundlessness of the vernacular and those united by it. In this collection, she "not only presents the colloquial surface" but the standardized substrate against which colloquial difference is measured, crafting a poetics that invokes the vernacular as invention. Liberated from the quatrains and open series of *Muse & Drudge*, these poems abound in phonemic transformation ("Zen Acorn"), vernacular forms such as the toast ("She Swam on from Sea to Shine," which also rewrites Larry Neal's "And Shine Swam On"), and the "paragrammatic" ("Any Lit," "Wipe That Smile off Your Aphasia"). Deploying fewer allusions (save where they directly engage legal and other "found" texts), their focus on the processes of colloquial invention is sharper and yet more resistant to a narrativizing impulse that would save her poetics for more familiar forms of politics, and thus it is more radical—closer to the zero of meaning—as I read it. I read the poem "Between" as exemplary:

> My ass acts bad
> Devil your ears Charybdis
> Good engagements deep blue sea
> Heaven my eyes your elbow
> Last night jobs hard place
> Now his legs hell
> Rock the lines me
> Scylla her breasts shinola
> Shit the sheets then
> Yesterday my thighs this morning
> You your toes today[38]

At one level, this poem abstracts and distributes vernacular and idiomatic expressions that feature the word "between": "between the Devil and the deep blue sea," "between engagements," "between his legs," "between my thighs," "between last night and this morning," and so on. There is no obvious pattern governing the proximity of words commonly used in pairs (e.g., enjambment connects "shit" and "shinola," but "Charybdis" and "Scylla" are six lines apart, "my ass" and "your elbow" only four) or those phrases commonly preceded by "between": "the sheets," "my thighs." At this level, the effect of the poem depends on the pleasure of discovering all of the phrases arbitrarily connected through the preposition "between." A work of recombination, the poem thus makes a familiar point about the arbitrariness of signification, meditating on the ways the vernacular both joins and separates semantemes, joins and separates language users.

One can also read the poem as a short, impressionistic narrative of seduction, capturing the moment and its recollection for another (you). In the phrase "my ass acts bad," "my ass" can be a metonym for the sex drive, sex appeal, the body, or the personal pronoun in some instances of the African American vernacular—then seems to begin the tale with an excuse. "Devil your ears" speaks to the lie "you" will be told, "Scylla" and "Charybdis" names an irresistible situation. The movement between memory and narration, between one lover and another, is all inscribed in this space between, this time between the event and the narration, between lovers. The poem is not an allegory or puzzle, and choosing one or the other reading is unnecessary. The idiomatic expressions are all that explain and do not explain the affair, the affair comes to be remediated by existing phrases and the unthinking justifications they offer, and the vernacular as a mode of linguistic recombination continues to churn out new expression to express new thoughts for new, yet familiar, experiences.

The blues has historically been a space where women, in particular, could speak publically about intimate matters—lovers and domestic violence, for example—to an audience expected to understand. But if Mullen's poetry is "post-lyric," this poem's fragmentation of time and address seems to be in a certain sense "postblues," an attempt to make a public voice private again, connecting it to Parks's *Imperceptible Mutabilities in the Third Kingdom*, in which Mona expresses tragicomic longing for a private vernacular. "Between" lingers in that space between public and private, between real and counterfeit, between a process of differentiation and the circulation as a difference. The critical use of the vernacular asks readers to notice, as if for the first time, the groundlessness of the vernacular imagined to be the center of linguistic belonging in general and racial belonging in particular. Mullen's experiments mark something other than a straightforward political project of mastering the other's language or giving voice to others. Her work undoes hierarchies between the paradigmatic and the syntagmatic (and between black and experimental) and thereby challenges the limitations of allowable thought—enacting "a struggle between all of the things that engage us now and all of the things that we can't even imagine because they don't exist yet" or that exist but for which we lack proper names[39] Her critical orientation toward the processes by which people generate their vernacular frees her from concerns that readers may not know particular phrases. Like Parks's work, it points not just to the surface of the colloquial but to that which gives it force: a community that takes and reshapes it, which sees in the continuation of tradition not only the repetition of artifacts but of formal tendencies, and in that way it continually expands the sense of what the tradition is. To "sing it in my voice," to "put words in like I want them," to let a groundless performance of the vernacular open to the new, is to participate in a tradition by abstracting it as a gesture of affirmation.[40] In both Mullen's and Parks's work, there is a "blues conception" of the self, at once there and gone, on its way to and from somewhere else. Repetition sits with simultaneity, allowing for a more expansive sense of what has been thought and felt in this tradition and of what can be.

History and Dead Time

Though Suzan-Lori Parks acknowledges the influence of Samuel Beckett, Adrienne Kennedy, and August Wilson, her work is most legible in terms of the blues influence she also avows. It begins from the complexities of race in the present moment—the time of most of her plays is "now"—at times imagining the coming emancipation and at times lamenting that the desired moment has come as farce, even when it seems that her work is concerned with the past. To understand her work requires not just that we have knowledge of history but that we take "history" as itself historical, as carrying with it the capacity to reinscribe or naturalize the violence it reports. Irony in her work, as with Mullen's, worries the stability of categories, working out the social antagonisms inherent in the imperative to narrative. Refusing the obligation of "race relations," Parks has argued that "as there is no single 'Black Experience,' there is no single 'Black Aesthetic' and there is no one way to feel or dream or interpret or be interpreted."[41] Yet she also insists that her work is part of a project to expand the range of black writing while affirming the groundlessness of "blackness."

Staged or presented on the page as I consider it here, Parks's work plays on the boundary between the literary text and the historical texts and contested histories to which it refers and on the intimacy between the two modes of writing. Her plays invoke the past but reading them through the rubrics of a naturalist or mimetic theater obscures their radical character and their focus on the inscriptive act as an event in its own right. If we take seriously her claim to work "theatre like an incubator to create 'new' historical events," then the emphasis remains on the interval that Derrida refers to as the *"dead time* within the presence of the living present," the time between an event and knowledge of the event, irrecuperable as simple presence.[42] Reference to the past engenders new theatrical events, a new awareness of our present and sense of obligation to some future. Her theater becomes "haunted," so to speak, by "spectral" moments, moments that do not—or no longer—belong to time, moments between presence and inscription.

Thus, she explicitly rejects conventional theatrical time, narrative structure, and character, referring the figures on her stage not as characters but as, among other things, "ghosts":

ghost

A person from, say, time immemorial, from, say, PastLand, from somewhere back there, say, walks into my house. She or he is always alone and will almost always take up residence in a corner. Why they're alone, I don't know. Perhaps they're coming missionary style—there are always more to follow. Why they choose a corner to stand in I don't know either—maybe because it's the intersection of 2 directions—maybe because it's safe.

They are not *characters*. To call them so could be an injustice. They are *figures*, *figments*, *ghosts*, *roles*, *lovers* maybe, *speakers* maybe, *shadows*, *slips*, *players* maybe, maybe *someone else's pulse*.[43]

The conversational definition and staged process of revision, exemplifies her overall poetics and the ironic tone that informs her work. Narrative, naked assertion, speculation and marked uncertainty—for example, the repeated "say" and "maybe," the series of synonyms and metonymic substitutions—playfully form the open definition of the concept. Her gloss moves through registers of the visual and the tactile, the conceptually distant (figures, figments, players), and the intimate (lovers, another person's pulse), in one semicontinuous gesture that asks us to affirm all of these alternatives as simultaneously true. Following her definition of the figures in her plays as "ghosts," I consider the works' use of the not-present or not-yet-present. Her textual deployment of noncontemporaneity within an articulated "present" and *dis*continuity with the past avoids fatalistic readings of the present as the necessary outcome of some larger historical logic. Eschewing a representative logic within which race would operate as an allegorical sign, "blackness" in Parks's work marks an affirmative difference: a difference embraced in the absence of any external guarantee of community. As she puts it, "a black play *employs* the black not just as a subject, but *as a platform*, eye and telescope through which it intercourses with the cosmos."[44] Eye and telescope, "the black" is a means of intensification and sensual knowledge rather than an end; it is one element among others in a "black play" that "embraces the infinite." Neither present nor absent, blackness disrupts representation and, in Parks's work, often makes the work of representation and the unavailability of blackness outside of representation direct themes.

Parks's use of the blues-inspired "Rep & Rev," the black vernacular, ellipses, and especially her staging of historical context are part of the work of affirmation insofar as her staging disrupts their assumed, naturalist function. Her "playful" lingering in this unstable, predisciplinary space destabilizes the ground of interpretation, making writing seem to overturn and actively question its own customary procedures. In this way, her work is radically open, an illimitable affirmation that articulates references in a relatively free state, "without truth, and without origin," or, better, unfixed from disciplinary truth and origin.[45] That blues-inflected affirmation is the crucial political ground of her work.

Reading her abstraction as an active, primary locus of interest parts with much prior criticism that, with some exceptions, has tended to view its abstraction as secondary to the more fundamental requirements of race and racial politics—offering a better representation or challenging dominant views, critiquing stereotypes, and so on. A good case in point is theater scholar Robert Sanford Brustein, who argues that "*despite* her joyous encounter with language, it *cannot be denied* that Suzan-Lori is also writing plays *about* race."[46] Exclusive focus on themes of "black suffering, loss, and misrepresentation through history" or understanding formal experimentation to "operate specifically alongside an African American cultural experience" has the unfortunate—and unintended—consequence of locating that cultural experience as external to experimental form (and vice versa) while positing it as origin and truth beyond representation.[47] These analyses, valuable in their own right, point to the limits of "what we allow black people to do," even despite ourselves; limits that become clearer in the face of certain modes of abstraction.[48] Parks's plays obviously concern race, as blackness is as tied to a history of representation as it is to the violence of slavery and its aftermath. In trying to imagine a liberated future, her works are "about" race in the same way that "I Want a Little Sugar in My Bowl" is about table sugar: in both cases, one has to work through specific issues of metaphoricity, euphemism, and play, which open up larger concerns and avenues of meaning than simple decoding. Parks's work thinks *with* as much as *about* race as a preconstituted object (that is, something external to representation), with a blues-oriented awareness that often the only way out is deeper in. In less figurative terms, Parks's work, which aspires to "The-Drama-of-the-Black-Person-as-an-Integral-Facet-of-the-Universe," insists on blackness even as it affirms the dual sense of the Du Boisian veil, as enabling and disabling, and thus affirms the complicity of black genius in schemes of racial policing.[49] One cannot exist without the other. Her work thus draws attention to the boundaries of acceptable complexity that govern African American literature and shape the "strange meaning" of being black, interrogating from the other side questions of what black people are allowed to say or not. In pushing those boundaries, affirmative difference—proceeding from a specific historical situation where narrating history remains intimate with the violence it documents—marks out a hermeneutic with which to imagine other grounds on which to imagine race and literature.

History, then, is not a stable set of references but a contested hermeneutic that reduces contingency to an allegory of tropes—winners and losers, heroes and victims. To cite history as this text rather than a transcendent set of more or less neutral facts is to introduce the "work of dead time," ironically disrupting history's stable categories. This is one way of understanding Parks's use of staged footnotes, which turn the attention of the play to the coimplication of power and knowledge, calling the conditions of acceptability for a truth statement into question. *The America Play*'s "Great Hole of History"—the zero of history, both belonging and external to historiography as a condition of possibility—emblematizes a more general tendency in her work, which enjoins readers and audiences, in Saidiya Hartman's terms, to "think historically about matters still contested in the present and about life eradicated by the protocols of intellectual disciplines" without falling too easily into a romance of resistance.[50] There, the "intimacy" of historical document and the violence it narrates is literal, underwriting the very family structure that, for African Americans, has always been public and private, available and absent. Parks's account foregrounds the critical function of *poiesis*: because "so much of African-American history has been unrecorded, disremembered, washed out, one of my tasks is to . . . locate the ancestral burial ground, dig for bones, find bones, hear the bones sing, write it down. The bones tell us what was, is, will be."[51] The singing bones sing *as* bones, as artifacts that speak for themselves. They do not make the past present again as such; they re-mark and substantiate the void in and of history.

Staged as context, historical context ironically brings into the interior what would be excluded without one being able to resolve that play without imagining a different future. The "Great Hole of History" is a term, then, for what is constitutively absent in the present and in presence. It is neither nothing nor something, neither absent nor present; it is a zero, a nonreplaceable sign necessary to the mathematical operations invoked by such terms as "figure," "equation," "new black math," and so on. Deciphering, figuring out (in all the valences of "figure")—these require the constant returning of and returning to a zero. Rather than a sign of absence or plenitude, the zero persists, uncounted. The singing bones, like the Great Hole of History, refer the desire for history, the desire to be historical, and the challenges of capturing that. In Parks's work, reference to real world events is part of a deeper play, the illimitable opening onto other contexts and modalities of being.

A LANGUAGE OF CODES: *IMPERCEPTIBLE MUTABILITIES IN THE THIRD KINGDOM*

The historical text becomes one text among others in Parks's overall affirmative poetics, a text of contradictions whose truth remains unresolved. The irresolution of a historical text in which, for example, the same Jamestown that announced a Protestant version of freedom ("if any would not work, neither should he eat") was the first North American site to introduce African slaves turns on thinking two contradictory ideas at the same time, without fully resolving the contradiction dialectically. That irresolution marks those moments of saying "yes" to both (or more) alternatives, as with puns. As Parks puts it in *Imperceptible Mutabilities*, this irresolution "overlaps a gap"—that is, it is a gap as well as superimposes two gaps, leaving the text open. Her emphasis on history is part of a larger strategy to expand the range of permissible black writing and to complicate the ideas of black life. To this end, she often uses literature to define literature and insists on the dead time between phenomena and enregistration. A good initial case in point—and a good introduction to her textual strategies—is *The Bridge*, a short "black play" that interrupts the essay "New Black Math," again using literature to define literature. Two characters, Momma and her husband, Yo, sit on the roof of their New Orleans home, awaiting rescue after the levees break.[52] The names of these figures, of course, are the beginning of the dozens in African American vernacular. Their dialogue turns from a lament of the ironic timing of the hurricane, which strikes just after they have made their last house payment, to an ambiguous indictment of mortgages and banks. The play—one of two in the essay, introduced with the explanation that "a black play takes you to the bridge"—is ironic from the point of view of the aphoristic essay's larger structure and, appropriately, concludes ironically. The play in full:

The Bridge. A black play by Suzan-Lori Parks

Characters: MOMMA, an older woman, and YO, her husband.

Setting: they sit atop their house which is under 20 feet of water. Helicopters from the National Guard in the near distance are about to perform a heroic rescue of our characters, but first:

> YO: We just made the last payment on this house, too.
> MOMMA: Yo, sometimes it be's that way sometimes.
> YO: Everything we own is washed away.
> MOMMA: Bank owned the house, then us.
> YO: Now the flood owns everything, looks like.
> MOMMA: You know it, Yo.
> YO
> MOMMA
> (rest)

YO: How can you tell a nigger thats crazy from a nigger that aint crazy?

MOMMA: I don't know. How *can* you tell a nigger that's crazy from a nigger that aint crazy?

YO: The crazy nigger is the nigger that aint crazy.

Curtain.[53]

Parks defines a "(rest)" as follows: "Take a little time, a pause, a breather; make a transition."[54] The repetition of characters' names without dialogue is what Parks calls a "spell" (an elongated (rest) marked by the repetition of characters' names without specified dialogue or action), which Joseph Roach helpfully glosses as "a place in the performance for the expression of unspoken emotion, but also of transition from one feeling to another."[55] On the page, they are opaque moments during which "something happens" that is withheld. This play begins after the beginning of the disaster and ends before its end, turning on an irony that is also the structure of the world as imagined by its figures. The rhythm of their joke (which turns on a figure of antanaclasis where both repeated words change meanings) is vaudevillian but also A-A'-B blues-like: a blues for two voices. Here, the possibility of craziness as defining suspends the sense of the line.[56] The joke relies on a definition that is only apparently tautological—every nigger is either a crazy nigger or a nigger who is crazy—the repeated epithet at once naming the grounds of community and explaining the precarity of that community (for example, of those who are members of the middle class). To be a member of the vernacular community implied by the dozens is also to speak as a "nigger": crazy (the wild entertainer of the vaudeville stage), crazy (somehow accepting the absurdity of the world that undoes you), or crazy (unaware of the world's absurdity). One speaks from a position that determines in advance that one's voice will register as amusing or threatening noise rather than legitimate speech. Under such conditions, deploying a dual-voiced blues is instructive: to speak in one's own vernacular (which in this play is also one's *only* property), from the position of the other, is the condition of im/possibility for any speaking. The multivoiced blues-like joke reinscribes that marginal speech as choral, a suspension rather than a continuation of speech, as the play suspends "New Black Math" between essay and multigeneric experimental writing.

The play is an allegory of tropes depicting the vulnerability of the black middle class, with the flood, the final owner, itself being a trope for both Katrina and the mismanagement that followed it. The concluding joke at once affirms and suspends the allegory, shifting the question from immediate response to *this* crisis to another, ongoing crisis of the perennial vulnerability and precariousness of black lives (one wonders whether Yo and Mamma will be homeowners again or find a comparable community) and to a more general question of how to live on. Affirmation works on multiple levels: one accepts that the groundlessness of one's identity does not make it meaningless while also accepting scenes and phrases that have multiple meanings that one must try to read as multiple without resolving them to some primary, transcendent meaning. The joke's irresolution is the point, as it asks us to reconsider the drama it declines to conclude. Parks's improvisatory temporal innovations further suspend the scene: the (rest) and spell that precede this joke reflect the peculiar temporal situation of the play's action, between disaster and relief, before the end of the disaster but after the end of a particular way of life, in a particular time that's also part of the general stream of Momma's "sometimes." Being an allegory of definitions breaking down into ambiguous tropes whose voided authority is both threatening and liberating, the play takes place in an overlap of temporalities: Yo's and Momma's, the federal government's, the bank's, the flood's, and finally history's heterotemporality. The play marks a struggle within language to take possession of the elusive sources of language, only to discover the signifying structure open at both ends. The only way to negotiate this knot is to go through rather than seek some language or signifying structure outside of it.

Such a temporal-linguistic knot of language and power informs the first part of one of Parks's earliest plays, *Imperceptible Mutabilities in the Third Kingdom*. Most critics, as well as Parks herself, suggest that the play is in some way about the event of the Middle Passage, though like the institutions and practices of slavery the term "middle passage"—and the interstitial space it names but does not tend to refer to—takes on many meanings throughout the play. The play consists of three sections: "Snails," in which Molly/Mona, Charlene/Chona, and Veronica/Verona deal with infestation and surveillance; "Open House," in which Aretha Saxon confronts her bureaucratically dictated "expiration date"—at once her lease and her mortality, and "Greeks (or Slugs)," in which Mrs. Sergeant Smith and her children, Muffy, Buffy, and Duffy, await Mr. Sergeant Smith's return from war. Between these sections are two choral passages—"Third Kingdom" and "Third Kingdom (Reprise)"—that refer most directly to the historical Middle Passage and serve as choral sections, phrases from the play being repeated, transformed, or anticipated in them.[57] A housing project, verbally associated with the slave ships, spatially links the sections of the play, whose themes are the uses and meaning of history, observation and classification, the historical record, awaiting the absent or dead, generations, and the control of meaning. To a significant degree, the play is about the meanings of textual strategies. The choral sections, however, function like *The Bridge*: interrupting and redistributing meanings, suspending any straightforward allegorical reading.

The "Third Kingdom" sections and staged footnotes are my primary interest here, but I want to frame my analysis with a moment in "Snails" that typifies the textual strategy—and the thematization of textual strategy—of the play. Molly/Mona (her name changes in the course of the play) has just come home, depressed because her jobs training program has expelled her due to her failure to enunciate correctly. She's despondent and considers suicide: "What should I do Chona should I jump should I jump or what?"[58] Charlene/Chona does not directly answer but like many of Parks's characters offers Molly/Mona food. Then she announces, "Once there was uh robber who would come over and rob us regular. . . . Verona [the third roommate] she named him 'Mokus.' But Mokus whuhdunt his name."[59] Naming takes on an allegorical character when Molly/Mona responds, "Once there was uh me named Mona who wanted to jump ship but didnt."[60] In immediate context, the idiomatic "jump ship" refers to her contemplated suicide, but as the play progresses the phrase comes to invoke those Africans who jumped overboard to escape slavery, and the vernacular sense of abandoning or quitting. The phrase, pointing to the instability of a vernacular that can extend across so many incommensurate domains, is a rhetorical zero, a void where links between the history of slavery, social othering, language, and naming happen and do not happen.

The conventional opening phrase of narrative, "once there was," repeats throughout "Snails," for example, "Once there was uh little lamb who followed Mary good n put uh hex on Mary." The phrase comes to function as a mode of rhetorical displacement: "Once there was uh one name Verona who bit thuh hand that feeds her," "Once there was uh me named Mona who wondered what she'd be like if no one was watchin," "Once there was uh me named Mona who wondered what she'd talk like if no one was listenin."[61] The irony of the phrase "uh me" marks the overlap between subject and object in self-description, the impossibility of a self that talks without the possibility of someone listening. One reading of the play would be that the vernacular is a way of belonging to a community and is necessarily public, shareable, and alienable. On this interpretation, there is no speaking, and to some extent no subjectivity, imaginable that is not routed through the possibility of the other's hearing or response. But another reading—perhaps a better and more faithful one—would be that self-reference as at once a trope of self-knowledge and posited otherness exceeds ordinary rhetorical means, making the self simultaneously subject and object of its own understanding. The distancing enacted by the adverb "there" in the phrase "there was" introduces spacing even into the statement of identity, suspending the text between tropological and allegorical readings: Mona stands in for other black women stigmatized by their speech vs. Mona searches for identity against the objectifying tendencies of the school and the Naturalist who observes her.

The footnotes serve a similar function, suspending the play between an allegorical reading that could securely link slavery to contemporary forms of discipline and control and a tropological reading of the play's uses of the vernacular as a means of resistance. They follow the rhythm of Yo and Momma, both insofar as they disrupt another text and insofar as at a textual level they mark an affirmative difference, opening the play to new meanings without claiming mastery. They do not speak *to* or *for* the play's broader concerns but *alongside* the play as another complicating element, a statement of something new that is also a repetition, making the play into a "continuous happening," a continuous disruption of its own codes. First appearing in "Open House" as references to the Middle Passage, they ultimately function to extend the possibilities of the black play, enfolding a history that always seems to exist at the margins of black writing into the center.

At the beginning of this section, Aretha Saxon counts an unknown quantity, worrying that she must "know thuh size exact," worrying that she will have a "[h]ole house full," which she repeats as a "[w] hole hold full."[62] She goes from sounding as though she's going to be entertaining guests or family to making a calculation of human "cargo." Much of this turns on a series of written distinctions that are barely audible, if at all (e.g., "hole"/ "whole," or later "how many kin kin I hold"). Her dialogue tropes the use of African American dialect to make a pun, underscoring a relation between Aretha Saxon and the Africans transported across the Middle Passage, a short-circuited relationship whereby she moves from being like them to being descended from them, to being identical with them. In other words, the movement is one of metaphor—complementarity and correspondence, carrying over from one domain, from one time, to another to create a sense of simultaneity and identity. The presentation of another, incommensurate code disrupts that movement, making it a trope in a different discourse. Miss Faith provides an objective equivalent of the kind of work contiguity does in Aretha's dialogue, with a metatextual link:

> Miss Faith: Footnote #1: The human cargo capacity of the English slaver, the *Brookes*, was about 3,250 square feet. From James A. Rawley, *The Transatlantic Slave Trade*, G.J. McLeod Limited, 1981, page 283.[63]

When Aretha protests Miss Faith's calculation that "we'll fit six hundred people," Miss Faith follows with a second footnote—"600 slaves were transported on the *Brookes*, although it only had space for 451"—and the admonition "You give me the facts. I draw from them, Maam. I draw from them in accordance with the book."[64] These footnotes, whose relation to the "main text" is uncertain, cite the story behind the iconic illustration of the *Brookes*'s hold, which was a central part of the iconography English abolitionists deployed as part of their arguments for ending the transatlantic slave trade, now reduced to a semifree sign. That ship was already a heavily cited ship, having attained in its time the status, which it retains in our own time, of metonym for the Middle Passage. *Imperceptible Mutabilities'* abstracted scholarly apparatus shows how talking about the Middle Passage often leads one to discussing sources rather than events, leaves one with a ledger of places, dates, and numbers in the place of the history one wants to discover and reclaim.

Parks's textual practice recalls a characteristic tendency of blues performers to ambiguously recite lyrics from other songs, part of the point of such a technique being that listeners recognize the citation without being able to use the earlier text as a heuristic for the present one. For example, Ida Cox concludes her version of "How Long Blues" with an allusion to "Hesitation Blues." Likewise, Son House interpolates "Walking Blues" into his version of "Death Letter Blues." In both cases, the interpolated song is of a radically different emotional tenor but suggests a desire to extend the song by opening its semantic and affective terrain. Parks's citations similarly function as "uh speech in uh language of codes" that impede rather than aids the text, extending the range of referentiality without providing a textual key.[65] One recognizes that the footnotes come from another text, but their relation to the present text remains unclear. Like Mona's question, the footnotes are an instance of parabasis, "the interruption of a discourse by a shift in rhetorical register" that systematically hinders the text's momentum.[66]

The structure of the play—whose sections draw on common language but different generic and plot conventions—makes interruption seem the norm. In

broader terms, the play presents modernity as a set of interruptions—a "perma-
nent parabasis" or tug and pull between visions of and for the world—that, para-
phrasing Gayatri Spivak, allow false promise to continue to appear promising.[67]
The middle sections, "Third Kingdom" and "Third Kingdom (Reprise)," are the
most directly choral in their structure, however. These feature the five seers,
gnostic figures for whom no adequate narrative exists. They first come onto the
scene by announcing their names; their entrance is followed by a "spell" marked
by two repeated dashes rather than their names.[68]

> KIN-SEER: Kin-Seer
> US-SEER: Us-Seer
> SHARK-SEER: Shark-Seer
> SOUL-SEER: Soul-Seer
> OVER-SEER: Over-Seer
> ——.
> ——.[69]

Because this is the beginning of a section, it is not clear what transition—
physical or emotional—this spell designates. They repeat their names, which
this time is followed by a similar, three-line spell, the last of which is rendered
"—— . . ." The ellipsis makes clear the relation of the spell to "the work of dead
time," the gap between present phenomena and writing. If the spell is the time
when something unknown happens, depending on the interaction of actors and
director, the ellipsis extends this into an indefinite happening

After the ellipsis, Kin-Seer relates a dream:

> KIN-SEER: Last night I dreamed of where I comed from. But where I comed
> from diduhnt look like nowhere like I been.
> Soul-Seer: There were 2 cliffs?
> KIN-SEER: There were.
> US-SEER: Uh huhn.
> SHARK-SEER: 2 cliffs?
> KIN-SEER: 2 cliffs: one on each other side thuh world.
> SHARK-SEER: 2 cliffs?
> KIN-SEER: 2 cliffs where the world had cleaved intuh 2.
> OVER-SEER: The 2nd part comes apart in 2 parts.
> SHARK-SEER: But we are not in uh boat![70]

This dream of uncanny origin is apparently a repetition: either Kin-Seer has had
and has discussed this dream with Soul-Seer at some point in the past, or Soul-

Seer has had the same dream (or origin). As the dialogue proceeds, references to boats, "Bleached Bones Man," and, retrospectively (this interlude follows "Open House"), "how many kin kin I hold" suggest a rough allegory in which the two cliffs represent the shores of Africa and the Americas respectively and the interstitial space is the Atlantic Ocean as overwritten by memory. On such a reading, this is Kin-Seer's uncanny origin, and the transatlantic slave trade is the event that creates in one stroke "each other side thuh world." Simultaneously, this dialogue's position within the play, somewhere between recollection of previous lines and anticipation of lines to come, destabilizes that reading. It is the birth of a language rather than a historical origin.

Just as the footnotes seem to be an unmotivated repetition of some other text, the dialogue in this first section recalls the earlier scene (Kin-Seer echoes Mona/Molly with "Should I jump? Shouldijumporwhat?") and anticipates later scenes (Soul-Seer anticipates Muffy in the final section [whose mother suggests her name may belong to a secret code, making it unspeakable in Mr. Smith's correspondence with the family] with "Duhdunt-he-know-my-name?"). The potential simultaneity of references from the past and future within the context of this play reaches its apotheosis in "Third Kingdom (Reprise)," when four characters speak at once. Kin-Seer and Shark-Seer invoke dialogue from the first and last sections of the play, Soul-Seer invokes a pop song (the Hues Corporation's "Rock the Boat"), and Us-Seer speaks without apparent relation to other events in the play:

KIN-SEER	SOUL-SEER	SHARK-SEER	US-SEER
Wavin wavin wavin	Rock. Thuh Boat.	Shouldijump	Thuh sky was just
wavin wavin wavin	Rock. Thuh Boat.	shouldijump or	as blue!
wavin wavin wavin	Rock. Thuh Boat.	whut?	THUP!
wavin	Rock. Thuh Boat	Shouldijump	Thuh sky was just
		shouldijump or	as blue![71]
		whut?	

The overlap of lines reveals the limits of those allegorical readings that see the play as primarily concerned with the Middle Passage rather than a larger interrogation of the ongoing logics of familial separation and techno-rationalism that are continuous with slavery as the initiating institution of modernity. The choral sections disrupt even that reading, however, drawing our attention to those small, subterranean changes of register and context, unnoticed, that subtend our understanding of that history, insisting instead that there be no final word. My point is not to make form an allegory for content but to point out the ways that the Middle Passage becomes one referent among others, one optional citation in a play stitched from such citations.

The play's continuity is rhythmic, continually interrupting one code with another to locate a blackness both excluded from and inscribed in this history. Blackness becomes the "x" in Parks's tongue-in-cheek diagrammatic account of her play as an algebraic equation that calls on readers to "solve for 'x,'" the generative blank of the Middle Passage, an "algorithm for African American memory."[72] Blackness is at once the given and the unknown, that which constantly remakes itself. This chorus is "a dislocation of time in which the audience experiences time as memory but out of sync with [historical] chronology."[73] The obverse is also true: audiences necessarily experience memory as a more or less conventional modality of time, akin to the blues singer's conventional "woke up this morning." Memory is only the deferred and displaced beginning, a desire for origin.

Exacerbating the difficulty of following this part of the play because of its demands on memory, the language of these sections breaks down, featuring tortured syntax, vaudevillian repetitions and appositions, and references to fractured subjectivity (as in Kin-Seer's "And then my Self came up between us [her "me" and her "uther me"]. Rose up out of thuh water and standin on them waves my self was standin").[74] The dreamed originary site "diduhnt look *like* anywhere *like* [she had] been"; the doubled "like," anticipating a doubled "part" ("The 2nd *part* comes a*part* in 2 *parts*), suggests that the articulated origin is a repetition, that is, nonoriginary: "Half the world had fallen away making 2 worlds and a sea between. Those two worlds *inscribe* the Third Kingdom."[75] This "cleavage," which *creates* the two worlds by an act of inscription, goes a step further to claim that a certain time has ended: "half the world had fallen away." Playing off the inscription here, "Word" replaces "world" on repetition:

> SOUL-SEER: There are 2 cliffs. 2 Cliffs where the Word has cleaved. Half the Word has fallen away making 2 Words and a space between.[76]

This revision, easier read than heard, raises new questions: what is this "space," emerging as it does to mark the distinction of the two Words created after the falling off of "half the Word"? And what of this abyssal Word, out of which comes two spaced Words? What is their relationship to a World? It is in this overlapped cleavage of world and word that the play makes a place for the time of the event, the cracking of the mind to reset it. "Third Kingdom (Reprise)" further revises this scene, from the recitation of names that becomes increasingly referential (e.g., "Sez Kin-Seer sez," "Sezin Shark-seer sez," "Sezin Soul-

Seer sezin sez," and so on), increasingly declined in advance of the recitation of
the dream: "Tonight I *dream* of where I be-camin from."[77] Two figures speak be-
fore the recitation and declension of names and saying:

> OVER-SEER: What are you doing?
> US-SEER: Throw-ing up.[78]

As with the opening section, where Charlene/Chona keeps offering Molly/Mona
food, or "Open House" with its attention to a dental extraction and the smile,
the act of throwing up—vomiting—keeps attention on the mouth. To vomit
may well be a sign of sea sickness, but it also may be a spontaneous, metonymic
sign of disgust. Toward the end of this section, Over-Seer demands such an ac-
count again, with increasing intensity bordering on hysteria:

> OVER-SEER: What are you doing? What'reya doin. What'reya-doeeeeee!
> WHAT ARE YOU DO-EEE-NUH???!
> KIN-SEER: —. —: Throw-ing kisses.[79]

This kiss maintains focus on that which leaves the mouth and does not come
back. One *gives* a kiss to another, but when her lips touch another's, she does
not then *have* that kiss, but the other's kiss. Like the vomit to which it is gram-
matically linked, one cannot immediately and without ambiguity say what the
kiss "means" or "expresses"; neither is immediately recoverable within an econ-
omy of signification. Note, too, the pause, represented by dashes rather than an
ellipsis in the instant Kin-Seer takes before she responds, time enough to throw
a kiss, time enough, perhaps, to think. Figures for this caesura—laughing, vomit-
ing, kissing—cannot immediately or without ambiguity be said to "resist" Over-
Seer's questioning nor to pose a counterquestion of his right to question. Rather,
alongside Rep & Rev and the modalities of blues irony I have been analyzing, these
are moments of excess, mingling the threat of sexual desire with the threat of vio-
lence to make sublime the boundaries of selfhood while also suspending its deter-
mining limits.

BLUES FOR *VENUS*

In arguing that Parks's work constantly opens rather than resolves itself, insist-
ing on its own textuality as part of an overall strategy of affirmative difference
—a bottomless play with the groundlessness of meaning and definition that
unfixes the limitations of black expression to expand the thematic and for-
mal range of black writing—I am using "affirmation" in an unusual way. How-
ever, the term does fold back onto its everyday sense in Mullen's reclamation

of Sapphire as a figure for insurgent poetics and Parks's traffic in the rhythms, tropes, and language of vaudeville and black vernacular culture. What is it to say "yes" to that in the past that seems disabling, disempowering, or abusive? One way to understand such poetics is as positing alternative forms of ancestrality, opening a way of embracing even—especially—that part of history that most hurts, that most wounds, those myths and legends that circulate seemingly without origin, without truth, but are nonetheless solid, real. In American theater understood literally and figuratively, minstrelsy and antiblackness are ineluctable grounds of black representation and performance, a condition of im/possibility of speech and poetics.

As a genre, the blues typically redeems those below the line of respectability, gives public voice to improper desires, and speaks of loving those who for one reason or another may be difficult to love. Parks's controversial 1996 *Venus* conducts such love and redemption as a struggle with and in language and referentiality. The deployment of blues irony in these works, no less than in *Imperceptible Mutabilities*, plays on the gaps in what is only imagined to be total, whole. Both plays are concerned, at some fundamental level, with a history of representation and engage in the deep formal irony related to the "overlap"— that is, the gap—between self-knowledge and self-reference. *Venus*, like Parks's other plays, employs tropes of death and untimely mourning alongside explorations of the norms of representation (and histories of misrepresentation that have resulted in violence) through a language that turns against itself. Its mix of rhetorical registers is discomfiting, presenting allegorical setups that consistently turn into a play of tropes with the cadences of blues irony, mixing the present with the past, the serious with the comedic. Seeming to mock our desire for some clearly articulable transcendental meaning to history, *Venus* confronts us with an estranged present and fails to reassure us that there is anything other than acts of poetics that demand that we rethink what we know, reimagine the terms with which we can relate to history. Its playfulness is finally a means of troubling the affective structures on which a system of rational control, power, and knowledge depend.

Venus also tries to recover the desire of and for "Saartjie Baartman," the so-called Hottentot Venus.[80] This woman's very name is an open question and historical violation: to call her by this name is simultaneously to make her disappear into the colonial system that called her "Little Sarah" (a literal translation of the Afrikaans "Saartjie") in the first place. To represent her, even by calling her name, is to distance her from us, to reinscribe her within a history of violence. To imagine her as a wholly innocent victim and without desire is to produce a stereotype that is as restrictive as Sapphire, but that desire is part of the violence of the episode the play presents to us. Under these circumstances, the act of "recovery" repeats the violence of her misrepresentation, replacing a history of seeing her as a sexual object with what amounts to the same thing: seeing her as a pure victim. *Venus* puts her scandalous desire and her victimization on one level, like a pun that one cannot resolve, showing the ways her incipient victimization shapes her desire and in that process humanizes her. Saying "yes"—embracing the complex, contradictory nature of an identity that always in a sense precedes the speaker—is a step toward unfixing the common-sense truths that take as given the arrangement of peoples and events into hierarchies, leaving selves, and the languages that represent those selves, open to reinvention.

If any historical story required "making up history, and . . . challenging the foundations of that history," this story would, though Parks's approach understandably disappointed and angered many feminist critics, who, for good reason, might have expected a play attuned to the tragedy rather than numbing absurdity of the story.[81] As Sara Warner argues, the play is a "drama of disinterment" rather than commemoration, "subverting the entire Western theatrical tradition in a single play" insofar as it troubles conventional dramaturgical perspective in order to free the Venus "from the burden of representation itself."[82] Fittingly, *Venus* begins and ends with a "death letter": "I regret to inform you that the Venus Hottentot iz dead. . . . There wont b inny show tonite."[83] The pronouncement happens outside the time of the drama, in quasichoral overtures. The "inner" drama is the death, including submission to a plot that audiences familiar with the historical basis of the text know in advance. Throughout the play, staged footnotes, like the serial misnaming of the character the Venus, operate as a continual reminder of the work of dead time, the spacing between inscription and phenomenality that governs any appearance, denying us the usual sense of representation as a genre that makes something absent present. For how can one claim to represent as real one for whom we lack a proper name? What does it mean that claiming her as an ancestor requires calling her by the wrong name? Parks uses the problems of this historical situation to explore questions of posterity (her pun), of "History, Memory, Dis-Memory, Remembering, Dis-membering, Love, Distance, Time," while offering "a Show" that refuses to make the Venus an object of our understanding.[84] Offering a show means disarticulating the woman from the shadow of her name, disarticulating a figure in a show from the woman taken from South Africa to Europe in the early nineteenth century. Then as now she is a powerful emblem of eroticized exoticism the fantasy of a love that demands nothing in return, and the urgent need and difficulty of imagining "another person's pulse." If, as Richard Iton and others have argued, modernity "implies and requires antonymic and problematic others—if it, to put it bluntly, needs 'the nigger,'" then black women have occupied an especially tenuous position, desired and hated for figuring a sexuality and sexual license otherwise disavowed by bourgeois sexual norms.[85] The play draws attention to the Venus's limited agency—marked by her ambiguous, repeated question, "Do I have a choice?"—while also underscoring the interaction of an official record with the representational norms that sustain and animate it, potentially transforming the fact of representation into evidence of the ruling regime's magnanimity: for example, "it is very much to the credit of our great country | that even a female Hottentot can find a court to review her status."[86]

"Do I have a choice?" is not simply rhetorical. *Venus* challenges viewers to remember that power, even colonial domination, is never total. Imagining the Venus's pleasure, shaped by the world in which she lived and died, partially undoes her appearance as a victim wholly separate from us, even as it threatens to make her appear through the lens of another stereotype: the hypersexualized black woman whose desire, rather than her oppression, explains her fate. What Saidiya Hartman has called the "discourse of seduction," the "confusion between consent and coercion, feeling and submission, intimacy and domination, and violence and reciprocity," obscures anything like the "real" desire of this woman who, like Sapphire, does not belong to her name.[87] Without thinking the Venus had a choice, the cornerstone of liberal rationality, she is less than human, even as within the play it is clear that any choice is at best nominal. The play, then, affirms her choice without choice, allowing her an inscrutable desire that is not the audience's, while acknowledging that that desire has been shaped by colonial modernity, especially the nascent science that requires her body after her death. Simultaneously, *Venus* sounds an important caution regarding the limits of the presumption that mere *information* or the presentation of facts—*did* she have a choice?—can serve the function of politico-theoretical work insofar as it underscores the prominent role that scientific knowledge played in determining the fate—in life and in death—of its protagonist and title character.

Venus's scenes proceed in rough chronological order but are numbered in reverse from an unnumbered "Overture" to scene 30, "May I Present to You 'The African Dancing Princess' / She'd Make a Splendid Freak," to scene 1, "Final Chorus." The Negro Resurrectionist introduces most scenes. He most consistently inhabits the choral role, presenting footnotes, drawn from the Baron

Docteur's (the French scientist figure, based on Robert Cuvier, who seduces her and later dissects and displays her body) notebook, Robert Chambers's 1863 *Book of Days*, Daniel Lysons's *Collectanea*, a fictional autobiography called *The Life of One Called the Venus Hottentot as Told by Herself*. The footnotes suspend the progression of the play, placing the Negro Resurrectionist, like Miss Faith in *Imperceptible Mutabilities*, at once inside and outside the play. His footnotes also thematize knowledge production and the weight of factuality, incorporating a margin into the main body of the text. In his very name, the Negro Resurrectionist is a figure of blues irony: "resurrectionist" refers at once to those who illegally exhumed bodies to sell to anatomists, the act of bringing the Venus back to life after announcing her death, and his role in the circulation of knowledge. Given his association with totalizing historical knowledge, he embodies the play's larger concerns with the work of representation obscuring what it would recover. He knows but is powerless to act, unable to do justice to the Venus. Instead, he contributes to the multiplication of real and fabricated texts within *Venus*; dry recitations of measurements and dates that, failing to add up to anything concrete, only point to the insignificance of facts on their own. They amount to little more than babble. The play turns on a question of the means through which resurrecting her—telling her story—will not amount to exploiting and desecrating her all over again by putting her on display.[88] However, by the end of the play the question has become the condition under which we could embrace the Venus—the character and the person on whom she is based—as an ancestor, as pointing to a future we may all share.

The chorus in *Venus* interacts with the principal characters at crucial moments. If the chorus traditionally represents a temporary suspension or interruption of the play's forward momentum, the body that goes by that name suggests openness to such interruption, hospitality toward what may come or what may be brought to the play and its unknown performances or readings of the future. It is the inscribed place of the rabble, the common, the vulgar; it is precisely that which a respectable or well-heeled "political" (that is, concerned with reintroducing the formerly excluded Venus into a common store of now vindicated figures) representation would exclude—either literally not countenance or exclude through staged abjection. Against a backdrop of real and fictional data, readers and spectators confront the discrepancy between the times the Venus might have imagined and the outcomes of those encounters, which we know.

Interweaving disparate times through citation, proleptic pronouncements of events from the future (from the point of view of the play's narrative present), Parks's plays might better be thought of as attempts to articulate two ep-ochs, the time, for example, of the weary blues singer who understands that emancipation has been a farce, that liberty—the right to one's rational choice—is not the same thing as freedom. The struggle of her plays to articulate their staged present with the contemporary present and the unknown past with the known can be considered part of a more general project of considering the place of individual memory and lives in the face of history that runs throughout Parks's work.[89]

Near the end of *Venus*, Wonder #7, a member of the 8 Human Wonders, a chorus that changes identity as the play progresses, sings in his or her song "on behalf of myself and The Hottentot Venus, to the Ladies of New York": "we *appear* comme il faut ["as we must," "as is necessary"]."[90] This conditioned *il faut* is the violence that organizes and ratifies the kinds of "true" statements that we can make about slavery, about sexual violence; it preselects acceptable forms of narration and remediation. It prepares the place for this woman as *our* ancestor. The *il faut* evokes the dense social texture of an ethico-legal system that cannot countenance her repeated question "do I have a choice?" Parks's play maneuvers beyond the dichotomy of appearance/disappearance, speech/silence, presence/absence that govern the *il faut* or law of the Venus's appearance, to the extent that her own desire suggests an obligation for us apart from mourning her or citing her as an example. By suggesting, as the play does, that she could have loved the Baron Docteur—and that he could have loved and then betrayed her—the play asks us to avoid the easy consolation of hating a man like him, while also putting us in a world where her dream fulfilled has proven farcical:

The Venus
I was born near the coast, Watchman.
Journeyed some worked some
ended up here.
I would live here I thought but only for uh minute!
Make a mint.
Had plans to.
He had a beard.
Big bags of money!
Where wuz I?
Fell in love. Hhh.
Tried my hand at French.
Gave me a haircut

and thuh claps.

You get thuh picture, huh?

Dont look at me

dont look . . .

(Rest)

She dies.[91]

Her last speech is a frank, understated narrative whose unsentimental tone would recall the blues but for the apparently earnest turn at the end. Similar to Mona's desire to speak without being heard, the Venus's command "Dont look at me" speaks to its own violation and necessarily seems to command its opposite. The value is in the wish itself, the transformative desire. In the concluding scene, the Venus takes over the Negro Resurrectionist's role from the opening overture, providing the "[t]ail end of the tale for there must be uh end" with the declaration that "[w]hen Death met Love Death deathd Love/ and left Love to rot."[92] She immediately adds two demands: "Miss me Miss me Miss me Miss me" and, the words that conclude the play, "*Kiss* me *Kiss* me *Kiss* me *Kiss* me." Her reiterated death colludes with the other incessantly cited figures and historical data to suggest the marking of time in fundamentally linguistic structures. The announcement of the Venus's death at the beginning and again at the end of the play is affirmative in two senses: in the philosophical sense that there will be a show even though the title character will remain absent and in the related sense that it imagines a call to her in her obscurity, her unlikeness to us.

The ending is sublime: the impossible, unrepresentable union of all the staged times of the Venus and *Venus* into a singularity that cathects so much desire and so much longing via the call and imagined consummation of a kiss and a call not to let the dead stay dead just so we can mourn them. I would add a third sense of affirmation to the prior two: the myth of the Venus, her objectifying use as a trope or allegory for other women, is no longer valid. The death of the myth of the Venus allows for the recovery of the woman to whom that name both does and does not correspond—we can embrace her in new terms, terms through which we can imagine her desire, through which we can imagine loving her.

There are probably as many blues songs about unrequited love as there are about the (frustrated) pleasures of the body. At a thematic level, Mullen's and Parks's respective works ask us to consider both. For to imagine the pleasure implied in both Mullen's and Parks's work is something akin to love, which Richard Iton has called a "subversive gift" that is also "an important public good," because "loving is a significant political act, particularly among those stigmatized and marked as unworthy of love and incapable of deep commitment."[93] To claim the Venus's love—and to claim her as worthy of love for all that she was and was not—is a political act along those lines. The blues has long been a discourse of claiming the right to love in one's own way or the right not to love at all, as well as the right to speak that to others who may or may not have had to same experience. To follow the path of affirmation their texts set out is to be returned to the world without guarantees and to the idea of black culture with a renewed sense of possibility, of productive bewilderment, of pleasure mingled with pain, of new horizons for black writing.

Part of the key to what I have termed a politics of affirmative difference is that it asks us to see the ways the democratic impulse of black vernacular culture is both liberatory and compatible with a history of oppression, exclusion, and antidemocratic practice. To return to some features of the blues and to the figurative sources of the vernacular is to open black experimental writing to a future of black writing not predicated on race in the narrow sense but in a more expansive sense, a mode of belonging for which we as yet have no name.[94] And even if there is no sure basis on which to claim belonging in our atomized, neoliberal present, the politics of affirmative difference reopens our attention to the nonsynchronism of our present, the different paths that our language and culture might still take.

five

Exploding Dimensions of Song

The Utopian Poetics of the Cut

Throughout the piece, one finds the music actively and unremittingly heterospecific. —Bedouin Hornbook

Which exists first, sound, writing, song, or the "we" that hears it? What cures are there, or are desirable, for that insistent sense of previousness, that sense of a missing element that was never a part of any whole? What is the facticity of song if song does not flow from a singular "origin" but marks the fleeting moment of a transit or transfer between poetry and music, music as dwelling in poetry or poetry in music? These are some of the questions that concern Nathaniel Mackey's poetics and theoretical writings, which ask readers to consider "graphicity," a glyphic, "transitional form of writing situated between the visual mimeticism of pictographic script and the more abstract and arbitrary semantics of phonetic writing" that links sound and writing as an ultimately utopian mode of transfiguration.[1] Much of Mackey's writing turns on temporal paradoxes (for example, "each the other's | long lost remnant"); in that spirit, musicality and graphicity are each other's revisionary trace and echo in his serial poetics.[2]

This overlap can make analyzing his textual practices, subject to revision according to the terms of his larger serial project, difficult. The terms shade into and complicate one another. In this chapter, I argue that these components of Mackey's poetics participate in a larger utopian project rooted in "transitional form," that is, his experimental poetics of the cut. "Experiment" here, as throughout *Freedom Time*'s analyses, does not refer to developing the means of solving problems but to expanding the range of the thinkable by calling into question those ideological presuppositions that "everyone knows." Experimentation, rather than naming a method of research, refers here to combinations of elements—musicality and graphicity—that allows the poet to move into areas neither might lead to on its own terms. I have discussed several modalities of graphicity in the preceding pages; musicality—the ensemble of qualities in the broad terrain of sounds we call music that are not exhausted in any listening or analysis—is necessarily excessive: listening again to familiar or treasured recordings often yields new details, reveals the self-differentiation or constitutive incompleteness of a given work. Hence, the centrality of "the cut," referring both to a track on a record and a broader chrono-poetic concept. The cut negotiates conflicts of priority (e.g., does music, writing, or community come first) by refusing to choose an appropriate temporal/axiological order, singular, effectively saying "yes" to all at once. The result is a utopian articulation of elements that continually transfigure each other through a graphic of developmental, serial revision that displaces the logic of progression.

Mackey's poetics of the cut link music to memory, commemoration, the idea that performance of the text changes the text, and an ontological priority of repetition over the "original." His writings, both verse and prose, also invoke an ambivalent orphic capacity for music that connects it to an ecstatic loss of self insofar as music may involuntarily redirect the body's movements. This orphic capacity is not *of* or *in* the music as an indwelling tendency or presence, nor is it the residue or haunting remainder of some history. It refers instead to the not-yet-analyzable part of the performance, song, or lyric: its utopian striving, "the frazzled edge of what remains unsung," unearthed and resituated through a poetics of the cut.[3] That "unsung" or simply missed element addresses itself to a future tense yet unspoken in any language and the aesthetic community that may yet constitute itself in the moment of reception.[4] It is glimpsed in breakdowns, in those gaps between a work as structure or grammar—adhering to conventions—and the work as an iteration through which something unexpected might break through.

Mackey's preference for serial poetics and the repetitions such a writing practice inevitably entails allows for a temporal logic similar to that of the phonograph record or other sound recording. He reiterates, revises, and rearticulates moments so as to highlight discrepancies rather than continuities and thus challenge our assumptions about the literary text, tradition, and, on a direct thematic level, the meaning of repetition. Similar to mechanically reproduced, disseminated sound, Mackey's texts open out unto an unknown audience, one that will have been, as the nature of experience is to be found in the recollection as re-collection, the articulation of one event with another through palimpsestic revision. Abstracted musical techniques—for example, motivic development, serial composition—generate new compositional possibilities. At the same time, Mackey liberally cites recorded musical performances, some real and some fictional, to figure the possibilities of black writing beyond the merely referential and to advance a diasporic sense of black identity as belonging to the "mainstream." As a brief illustrative example, early in *Bedouin Hornbook*, at a press conference that reads as a declaration of poetics for the project, people challenge the musical ensemble to play "more centered somehow," "within the context of the whole culture." Lambert, a member of the band, emphatically declares that their music "churns out of a center other than" the one the challengers have in mind. Another band member, who styles herself Aunt Nancy (a homophone for the trickster Ananse), completes the thought: "[T]he culture you're calling 'whole' has yet to assume itself to be so except at the expense of a whole lot of other folks," even as "Africa, Asia and other parts of the world [are] a part of 'the *whole* culture.'"[5] North and West African, Caribbean, and African American musical traditions, mythologies, and textual practices are important references for Mackey's poetics, related to a larger project of reconfiguring an aesthetic cartography of invention in such a way as to open it to what may otherwise be depicted as alien noise. Subtly ungrounding ethnocentric notions of aesthetic value by undermining judgments rooted in a hegemonic aesthetic community whose power derives from its claims to universality, Mackey offers an unbounded textual wholeness without center produced by a relay between hermeneutic and poetic practices. His work manages to name and participate in global black traditions as an act of elective affinity rather than rooted belonging and in that way conceives of new pathways for black writing.

Thus, Mackey's utopian musicality is an alternative to Larry Neal's famous notion of "the destruction of the text"—the idea that for African American poets "the text could be destroyed and no one would be hurt in the least by it" because the written text was a prompt for future performance within an African American tradition.[6] Indeed, Mackey's musicality is the obverse of destroying the written text: it underscores the ungovernable multiplicity of texts, broadly conceived, revealing that multiplicity to be a constant reopening of horizons. Musicality draws attention to the misfit between score and performance, the many semiautonomous facets of a text activated in repeated listening to a recording or repeated readings. The open-ended textuality of the musical score, which allows for practically infinite "alternate vocalit[ies]," points toward some future revision, moving the emphasis to an underlying conception of a reading or listening in the future anterior.[7] Understood as the textuality of music, musicality figures a "fugitive articulacy," multiplying the contexts or discursive levels of and within the text. The challenge, I argue, is to see the diversity of textual elements as necessary, as harbingers of the genuinely new that does not come as a break with this time but from within this time. Serial work extends the boundaries of the text, making the literary production a kind of running subtheme, an explicit object of thought.

The processual reworking of contexts through repetition understood as a mode of differentiation makes Mackey's work one of encounters, unlikely confluences, mis- and realignments, work committed to a serial poetics that courts repetitions within which new connections become available. Musicality is central to Mackey's serial poetics: in both the prose and verse series, it is a mechanism for the intrusion of one moment on another and allows moments, liberated from a logic of linear progression and development, to rewrite each other. Rather than participating in a logic of time as linearity, musicality produces a graphics of revisable, rearticulable moments that include but do not reduce to individual experience. Any articulated past, such as the personal past or the past of an historical group, is only one possible past cited in the interest of notions of a particular present or desired future. That serialized past is not a passive store of time but remains alive with the fulfilled and unfulfilled dreams of the past and thus serves to keep the past open as a condition of a future imagined on terms other than those of the present. Stated simply, Mackey's serial musicality provides a means to consider time outside dominant narratives of progress and personal development, allowing us to think in positive terms the idea that, as Ian Baucom puts it, "time does not pass, it accumulates."[8] To think that accumulation in positive terms I draw on Gayatri Spivak's distinction between dominant narratives of "Time," which she calls "an implicit Graph only miscaught by those immersed in the process of timing," her term for common ways "of grasping life and ground-level history as events happening to and around many lives," and the practices that give "flesh" to "'time' as a sequential process.'"[9] The accumulation of time marks the pressure and influence of official "Time" on everyday practices of organizing experiences into sequences. Musicality, then, amounts to a performative disruption of the dominant "implicit graph" of progress and the ordinary hierarchies of events to give priority to everyday practices without emplotting them against the official temporal constructs. Uncoupled from official narratives of progress and development, drawing from and rearticulating past sequences and moments, such ambivalent accumulation points to the utopian potential latent within modernity.

More concretely, I locate that a utopian potential in the ways Mackey's work uses musicality to invoke the possibility of another world through reexperiencing and rethinking the past and treating moments as they may be experienced in ordinary practices of timing or making time. My understanding of utopia lies between what Paul Gilroy calls a "politics of fulfillment" (i.e., a model for alternative politics figured by the ensembles of Mackey's related serial works) and the invocations of music throughout Mackey's oeuvre that figure a "politics

of transfiguration" that "[emphasizes] the emergence of qualitatively new de-
sires, social relations, and modes of association . . . by other, more deliberately
opaque means."[10] The politics of transfiguration "points specifically to the for-
mation of a community of needs and solidarity which is magically made audi-
ble in the music itself and palpable in the social relations of its cultural utility
and reproduction," while in my reading music also dissolves existing identities
through its insistent "ecstatic elsewhere." Seeing music as transfigurative re-
quires "a hermeneutic orientation that can assimilate the semiotic, verbal and
textual," which in Mackey's text emphasizes the performative and shared forms
of experience so as to outline utopian praxis.[11] Yet music also satisfies an im-
mediate desire for community, however inchoate. Dialectically, fulfillment—in
whatever form it takes—requires a politics of transfiguration. Any fulfillment
must drastically alter conditions in the present in order to realize its underlying
dream. In different terms, each moment of fulfillment is also a moment of dis-
appointment, revealing a further opportunity for transfiguration, as with James
Baldwin's question "Do I really *want* to be integrated into a burning house?"[12]
The moment of desegregation, like the moment of emancipation, reveals the
narrowness of a freedom compatible with the institutions of oppression. Mu-
sicality, as a graph of fulfillment, is valuable at once for the contradictions it
apparently resolves, for its suggestion of new social relations and modes of as-
sociation, and for the transfigurative possibilities opened up by that apparent
fulfillment.

"Utopian programs" (Fredric Jameson's term for definite schemes of fulfill-
ment)—that is, the ideological positioning of a certain freedom in black music
as proof of the nation's democracy or as insurance against mechanization—
symbolize "a world transformed," while the underlying utopian impulse reveals
"in a variety of unexpected and disguised, concealed, distorted ways" a utopian
desire that will necessarily remain because fulfillment can never be total or per-
manent.[13] To read for the utopian requires, in Jameson's terms, "something like
the structural inverse" of Foucauldian genealogy: "a prodigious effort to change
the valences on phenomena which so far exist only in our own present; and to
experimentally to declare positive things which are clearly negative in our own
world."[14] In this chapter, I trace a utopian impulse in the rearticulation of past
freedom dreams with notions of freedom in the present. As time "accumulates,"
the present continues to be informed by those past dreams and the continuing
state of unfreedom against which the prior dreams defined themselves. I read
"the cut" as utopian insofar as it asks us to look at the temporal trajectories
—the ways things could have been—as imagined in the past alongside the

graphs of fulfillment that fell short but still signal the possibility of different possibilities in the present. The cut, a name for the unresolved contest between Time and timing, is utopian insofar as it resists fatalistic interpretations of time or history.[15]

"Cut" also refers to records, and Jameson's "inverted genealogy" provides one way to view sound recordings, commodities related to the alienation of black cultural producers and their transformation into signs of "successful" incorporation of nonwhite "others," as symbolizing a broader utopian impulse in Nathaniel Mackey's work. Rather than seeing the sound recording as the more or less neutral document of "live" performance, I emphasize the model of circulation sound recording enables as a model of community conceived within and against the urbanization and bourgeois norms associated with modernity. One scandal of recorded sound, from the perspective of those seeking to profit from it, has always been that one does not need to possess one's own copy of it in order to share it freely with one's neighbors. Familiarity with *particular* recordings or nonmainstream genres can be the basis of reimagining community, as can those perverse forms of consumption (connoisseurship or collection) that take recordings out of commodity circulation and render them a nonmonetized form of exchange and value. That form of curatorial collection is a partial demystification: it changes the valences on commodity culture, making the object about relationships between people (albeit not necessarily at the level of its production) rather than between objects. In the verse series, cuts "come on the box": songs play from an unseen jukebox seemingly of their own volition, the music providing oblique commentary or change in mood. But the music also invites readers to remember or discover the songs it cites. In the prose series, Mackey often cites records by catalog number. There, characters communicate with one another through particular recordings or snippets of recorded songs (one character uses John Coltrane's spoken instructions to his band to communicate to band members), and N., the focal character, transmits his band's music via cassette before making a more widely accessible recording.

In the two related series this chapter considers—*The Song of the Andoumboulou* and *From a Broken Perfume Bottle Traces Still Emanate*—curatorial collection and repeated listening to records symbolizes the process of (serial) writing itself, with the cut figuring the movement between fulfillment of one impulse and the transfiguration it intends in the larger world and awaits in revision. The transfigurative and representational dimensions of utopia are not rigorously separable, even as the depicted "world of tomorrow" may prove beside the point for a later utopian practice. The discrepancy between the tomorrow imagined by the past and the present we now inhabit in Mackey's work spurs a utopian impulse, an engagement with what he calls "postexpectant" time, the discrepancy between the dream and its realization, one figure of which is the sound recording, where repetition enables renewed attention and analysis that inspires action.

The utopian moment would be the postexpectant present if one were able to change the valences of the present to revitalize the subjunctive possibilities and unfulfilled collective desires of past moments. Music—especially the music of the African diaspora understood in broad, historical terms—is at once historically and culturally specific, the sign of a broader collective history and collective striving. It serves as the marker of particular moments and the repetition of a singularity that links two moments. Mackey's serial poetics, which advance incrementally through a process that includes revision, are utopian insofar as, analogous to the record, the sequence is at once prospective—each poem leads to another that develops its motifs, themes, and experiments—and retrospective—each new poem subtly rewrites and recontextualizes the poems that have come before it. The poems thereby constantly transfigure their own ground, using every resource of language to produce a text of maximal, multivalent freedom.

"THE ROOT OF WHATEVER SONG"

"Fulfillment" is in some ways an odd word to use in conjunction with Mackey's work, as sensitive as it is to various forms of absence. Each subsequent poem retrospectively makes the poem that precedes it seem to lack, because each subsequent part makes a greater elusive whole more visible. The poetics of the cut is the dialectic of fulfillment and transfiguration in action: each new poem seems to depart from an unfulfilled transfigurative promise, courting the unstable ground such postexpectant "reach" entails, an idea that Mackey speaks to in his discussion of *duende*, an indefinable quality of performance that Lorca and Mackey relate to the dark or "black sounds" at the origin of the Andalusian *cante jondo*, or "deep song":[16]

> It speaks of loss, it speaks of lack, but it also speaks of an insufficiency that's indigenous to the very act of reaching. Reaching wants to go on, in some sense that's troubling to the things it does settle upon and take hold of. It's not that it empties those things. It simply finds that those things are in place in a certain way that the reaching wants to continue to be free of.[17]

Reading Federico García Lorca's reflections on the Moor-influenced gitano music in the context of the African diaspora, Mackey relates *duende* to a phantom limb, "a phantom reach with/after something you have but do not have. It is a kind of re-membering, a mended dismemberment," or articulation.[18] For Lorca, *duende* "presupposes a radical change of all forms based on old structures" and as such interrogates the living on of the past in the "exact present" that defines it.[19] Claiming *duende* as a useful concept for understanding cultures of the African diaspora, Mackey suggests that black culture encodes a response to privation precisely insofar as it revises the structures it might seem to comment on. Insofar as that culture includes the Moors who had conquered the Iberian Peninsula, we get a sense of the ways he stresses the continuing influence of what is largely a suppressed history. Each act of culture, on this view, splits between what is present and what will have been present while seeing something other than exact repetition of old structures as the present's injunction. Like diaspora, *duende* has no proper place: "Through the empty arch comes an air of the mind [*aire mental*] that blows insistently over the heads of the dead, in search of new landscapes and unsuspected accents [*acentos ignorados*] . . . , announcing the constant baptism of newly created things," without the creation of those things becoming the point.[20] Whether a term of musical or poetic analysis, *duende* never makes itself present except as the sign of something absent. It does not belong to the present as constituted. It continues to relate to doorways, that gap between a work as structure and the work as grammar: a "certain arch and | or ache and | or ark of duress."[21]

That play of "arch," "ache," and "ark" in "Song of the Andoumboulou: 7" underscores the many senses of "serial" at work in my analysis of Mackey's poetics, even as it gives a different slant on the privation—refused kinship—Mackey theorizes as central to the birth of song. Music is neither a stable nor an exclusive referent for Mackey.[22] Song, an index of *duende*, functions at least partly as an open-ended textuality that, as Brent Hayes Edwards argues, "foregrounds 'methodologic fissures' not just in terms of broken or doubled voices, however, but also in terms of time," the graphic propulsion of writing.[23] Mackey suggests in an interview that "textual patterns in which staggered patterning and unexpected placement," two hallmarks of his verse, "achieve an unsettled, irregular rhythmicity that you see" producing a "visual syncopation" that I relate to his exploitation of the graphicity of language and sound.[24] This syncopation—an active differing of language against a set spatio-grammatical scheme—relates to the utopian impulse of writing in Mackey's work, which treats language as something other than *logos*, thereby producing a writing directed to an indefinite future in the relay between fulfillment and transfiguration.

Drawing out the initial syllable of music, "mu-" (the name of an earlier series since folded into *The Song of the Andoumboulou*), Mackey's serial poetics speak from and to "any longingly imagined, mourned, or remembered place, time, state, or condition"; crossing "re-utterance and pre-utterance," "pre- and post-occupation," it underscores sound media, including language itself.[25] Musicality, then, indicates a kind of surplus signification—a fugitive articulacy— that tantalizes with the sense of something unfulfilled in this time unearthed through the poetics of the cut. At the level of representation in the ongoing series *The Song of the Andoumboulou*, the poetics of the cut highlights the internal differentiation of the present and interrupts the "now" of enunciation, for example, in the ways "another cut came on the box" in the verse series announces shifts in register while pointing to records as a store of communal memory, from the past, that may be reactivated in the present.[26]

Figures intertwining music and writing recur so frequently in Mackey's writing, not least in the epistolary nature of the prose series, that the conjunction of them is practically a trope. The *Song of the Andoumboulou* series derives its name from a recording, *Les Dogon*, on which an example of the referenced funerary song appears. In lines Mackey cites as the epigraph to the series, François Di Dio writes, "The Song of the Andoumboulou is addressed to the spirits. For this reason the initiates, crouching in a circle, sing it in a whisper in the deserted village, and only the howling of dogs and the wind disturb the silence of the night."[27] As Mackey notes, the Andoumboulou are a "rough draft of human being," a failed advanced form, although, in a reversal common in his poetics, the Andoumboulou are "the work-in-progress we continue to be."[28] Becoming human is a serial procedure but also figures an alternative construction of history as something other than unilinear progress and of the relationships between generations. We are asked to conceive of development as something other than progress, and of time as expanding to encompass more, making our time nearly simultaneous with other times in temporal folds. To whose unrealized ambitions do we still owe an obligation? How many dreams do we share with our kin, unrecognized?

The song is a funeral song directed to them/us that moves from song to eulogy and back, a lone voice "reciting [the deceased's] genealogy, bestowing praise, listing all the places [the deceased] set foot while alive." The directedness of the song, "call[ing] forward and back into question," unites the ancestors to the living.[29] The series to date traces the development and transformation of this collective—"Uninevitable they,|however much it seemed otherwise"—that could be something other than a contingent aggregation of individuals.[30] Mackey relates the song itself to "forms of graphic inscription in Dogon cosmology, the cosmogonic potency and role of sign, figure, drawing, trace, diagram, outline, image, mark, design, and so on" extending this emphasis to the "strikingly tactile, abraded vocality, the grating 'graphic' tone and timbre of the song of the Andoumboulou itself."[31] Writing is "inscribed" in music as much as poetry indexes music; the two together gesture "above where sound leaves off," that is, beyond the constraints of conventional articulacy.

Serial becoming gives the constitutive incompleteness of the Andoumboulou an optimistic character that informs the writing inspired by and written for them, as marked by the centrality given to the act of singing. In the opening lines of "Song of the Andoumboulou: 1," song "speaks" of its own necessity:

> The song says the
> dead will not
> ascend without song.
>
> That because if
> we lure them their names get
> our throats, the
> word sticks.[32]

The varied margin, syncopating the center-justified presentation of the poem, relates obliquely to rhythm, introducing a small visual pause before "our" to match the semantic pause "[T]hat because if" invites. The word sticks in "our throats" without coming forward or revealing itself. The poem performs a definite silence that, in this context, is a syncopation of the "we" that sings to connect itself with its dead. The message issues from the song, but what is the song's "saying"? What speaks in the song or as song? The second stanza suggests a necessity to this song that sidesteps the (tacit) assent often taken to underpin such communal observances. Song thus becomes an apotropaic performance, guarding against some unruly word that "gets our throats"—taking away the breath, enrapturing, suffocating, or disgusting, revealing the contours of community.

The stanza itself is a "breathless" sentence, beginning with a conjunction but refusing direct subordination, eliding a comma between "them" and "their"; its sense may or may not depend on what the song says. The word that sticks and its relation to "their names" is, as in the epigraph to the poem "something secret," something that readers are "not to know."[33] The song of the Andoumboulou, then, is a metonym for communal observance itself, the creation of a "we" connected to a "they" despite and beyond death. It is an observance—"*The dead*, they say, *are dying | of thirst*"— the song being necessary to satisfy them, the part of them that lives on in us, if it is to live on, while threatening always to overflow its bounds: "not even words. | Except it says itself | for days || in your head."[34]

"Something secret" recurs throughout the long poem in such guises as inverted syntax that defers or obscures grammatical subject and propositional meaning (e.g., "Weathered raft I saw myself | adrift on") and accumulates silences generated by the openness of "what" (for example, in lines structured around indeterminacy such as "[n]ot yet asleep I'm no longer | awake, lie awaiting *what* | stalks the unanswered air").[35] Such syntactic dislocations mark the "erosion of the subjective through obliquity" generating what Brent Hayes Edwards, referring specifically to Mackey's "under-the-line" poems, suggestively terms a "poetics of reprise" or a "syntax of love" that marks a postexpectant "closure re-opened to close again."[36] Paul Naylor, in a similar vein, stresses that "love, like song, testifies to the dimensions of reality that exceed articulation, that can only be hinted at in a form of discourse that draws attention to its own limitations."[37] Both of these assessments align love, an unruly gift, with Mackey's celebrated notion of the "cut," which is also a concept of the language's constitutive open-endedness. The cut puts in play a certain "post-," a moment *after* that is also the moment *before* and the moment *of*. The agency of this song, like the agency of the reach, is an absence that inheres "in the texture of things."[38]

His most elaborated sense of "cut" as seriality—a closure that reopens itself—emerges in *Bedouin Hornbook,* the first in the prose series *From a Broken Perfume Bottle Traces Still Emanate,* which, as I have noted, begins in *The Song of the Andoumboulou.* Related to James Snead's discussion of "the cut" as an attempt "to confront accident and rupture not by covering them over, but by making room for them inside the system itself," Mackey's cut refers to the retroactive construction of coherence out of disparate elements.[39] A long dilation of time structures the prose series: published between 1986 and, to date, 2008, only about five years of narrative time has passed. N.'s letters, detailing the daily affairs of an at first five-person and then six-person experimental improvised music ensemble, range between 14 June 1978 and 5 September 1983. This series, related to *Song,* underscores the primacy of the collective over the individual and a suspicion of the givenness of any moment or utterance that marks Mackey's work more generally. Much of the action makes music and sound recordings—those the band listens to and that the band produces—central to quotidian practices of timing, serially staging phonography's temporal rift between source and audience and the kinds of practices that attend such a rift that can emerge with the possibility of repeating an experience of listening.

The prose series, a series of letters between N. and an interlocutor called Angel of Dust that grows out of *Song*, continually invokes nonoccurrence. In "Song of the Andoumboulou: 7," N. refers to "last night's poem (which I've yet to write)," and in the first letter of *Bedouin Hornbook*, dated "14.VI.78," N. declares "I'm not at all sure this won't be the last letter you'll receive from me."[40] The "cut" becomes a specifically temporal concept related to reggae and the epistolary form's connection to "relational coherence." It is a specifically musical term, referring to

> the cricketlike chirp one gets from the guitar in most reggae bands as the echoic spectre of a sexual "cut" (sexed/unsexed, seeded/unsown, etc.)— "ineffable glints or vaguely audible grunts of unavoidable alarm."[41]

In a subsequent letter, N. complains that the Angel of Dust "got [him] all wrong on what [he] meant by "a sexual 'cut,'" clarifying that he does not have in mind "a thinly veiled romance of distantiation":

> I put the word "cut," remember, in quotes. What I was trying to get at was simply the feeling I've gotten from the characteristic, almost clucking beat one hears in reggae, where the syncopation comes down like a blade, a "broken" connection. Here I put the word "broken" in quotes to get across the point that the pathos one can't help hearing in that claim mingles with a retreating sense of peril, as though danger itself were beaten back by the boldness, however "broken," of its call to connection.[42]

Both of N.'s accounts apparently draw on one-drop reggae, a playing style that causes listeners (including the performers) to perceive the same song as having two different tempi or time signatures. Think, for example, of Bob Marley and the Wailers' "Natty Dread"; in this song, the rhythm guitar either accents the second and fourth beat of a four-bar measure or emphasizes the upbeats of a slower tempo, depending on how one hears it. This structural aporia means, for example, that one could justify transcribing the music in two different time signatures or dancing in two different ways, but it also means that such engagement will require imposing a structure on an open form. The cut is an experience of time that does not prioritize one "feel" over another, as N. claims to hear both pathos and peril.

That openness, however, means that the "originating" instance is not singular but iterable, endlessly repeated: there is an insistent "previousness evading each and every natal occasion," an insistent both/and rather than either/or. The cut is "sexual" because *the word* "he" and *the word* "she" rummage about in the crypt each *defines* for the other, reconvening as whispers at the chromosome level as though the crypt had been a crib, a lulling mask, all along. In short, it's the apocalypse I'm talking about, not courtship.[43]

The moment of (conceptual, grammatical, and textual) birth is also death to the extent that the articulation of an origin or singularity of being ("he" or "she") manifests the desire to subvert relational coherence in favor of a singular (given) narrative. This is another example of the "syntax of love": the "broken" or refused connection that precedes connection as end precedes beginning, the empty site of articulation that, the analogy to one-drop reggae suggests, is a matter of perception. That love itself, then, is a name for the originary dispossession and "wounded kinship" that Mackey locates at the "origin" of song in his celebrated essay "Sight and Sentiment, Sound and Symbol": "Song is both a complaint and a consolation dialectically tied to that ordeal [of refused kinship], where in back of 'orphan' one hears echoes of 'orphic.'"[44] It is both a complaint about being abandoned and the voice that calls you back or claims you as kin. As a figure of musicality rooted in broken and reconstituted kinship, the cut is utopian to the degree that it reaches for more complex forms of union and insists on the uncertainly grounded nature of that union. It is also a figure of the temporal and spatial distance between the letter writer and recipient rendered generative: "I see things in your world as *solid* in a way my 'myriad words' can't even hope to be. [. . .] Only an other (possibly Other) sort of solidarity, as if its very underseams—or to be more exact, those of its advent—sprouted hoofs."[45] N. locates himself in another world, identifies as possible Other, and contrasts Angel of Dust's "solid" world with his own, which he insists is not "insubstantial, unreal or whatever else." "The cut" also informs the broader spatial and temporal contours of the serial poem addressing the Andoumboulou—who both never existed and are all that exists of the human—not least through its figures' continued quest: "We knew there was | a world somewhere."[46]

As I have argued, the record is central to the spatiotemporal concerns of Mackey's interrelated serial projects as a figure of the ability to wrest sounds and images from their original contexts and rearticulate them. Though one may have affective investments in particular recordings, the record is a neutral medium; it stores moments and offers a means to reverse or "cut back" to an earlier time without necessarily lending itself to an archaeological "recovery" of origins. The record is not just a means through which a performance is preserved and repeated indefinitely within the limits of the storage medium; owing to the capacities of repetition and the ways repeated listening changes its object, it is also a store of difference. The prose series, with virtuosic analyses of a Joe Henderson miscue that come to seem an integral part of Andrew Hill's "Refuge," dramatizes that process. Mackey refers to such inversions of the relationship between difference and repetition—repeatability making difference prior to self-sameness even, in this case, within static media—as "andoumboulou-ousness," which is also a provisional sense of becoming that prioritizes group identity over individual identity. The repetition that the record invites, and that serial poetics risk, becomes an experience of the impossible: the repetition of a singularity that relates both fulfillment and unfinished transfigurations to a more general promise to iterability, the promise of further writing to come.

"ON THE EDGE OF AN 'IT' OTHERWISE | OUT OF REACH"

I have been stressing musicality as textual and phonography as medium as it interacts with music as culturally specific content in order to stress its position within a broader poetics of the cut. Mackey's serial poetics shares an affinity with the phonograph in another sense, its emphasis on the ability to record, to archive, and preserve more than it may have intended. Commenting on flows of information at the end of the twentieth century, Mackey argues that "the individual consciousness is often being impressed or imprinted upon, impinged upon in some cases, by what's going on in various places at various times and at various levels at various times."[47] His metaphors primarily refer to inscription— the familiar condition of acting (inscribing) as one is acted on in and by other discourses, framed within and by other articulations. The record serves both as a touchstone for the work and as an internal challenge to notions of poetic "expression"—black genius or personal experience, posing as it does a question of the when and where of culture. The play of deixis, especially via prepositional location, suggests a shift from the expression of ipseity—selfhood and self-identity—to one concerned with haecceity—here and now-ness—marking a similar distinction between a cross-cultural *identity* and a cross-cultural *poetics*, between experience *in* the text and experience *of* the text.

Mackey's claims for music as an "alternate vocality" figure an alternate "sounding" attuned to the surplus signification of language that is the terrain of poetry.[48] This "vocality" stretches to the very norms of "voice" as the sign of subjective presence and interiority, highlighting language's graphicity, as in the "mu-" poems and the *Andoumboulou* series, which he claims have become "two and the same," each being, he says, "the other's understudy."[49] They have

in common an interest in a restless musicality that seeks language's self-tran-
scendence while marking that transcendence as internal to language itself:
"Words | don't go there, they said, | no sooner said than they were | there, albeit
there defied location."[50] Even here, however, it's not clear whether the "they"
refers to words or the sojourners the poem follows.

"Knotted Highness" from the now-incorporated "mu-" series, exploits the
slipperiness of pronouns and the graphicity of language through a kind of or-
thographic "declension" centered around pronouns and, through that play, an
engagement with the possibilities of community and narrative:

Carved heart.

Thin bent-over body.

Arced harp cut from

wood

one night brought up

what's under.

Masks

made of trembling.

Paint.

Purgatorial stealth.

Made of

its amends an unappeasable

indulgence.

Makes of them its

then,

of it their

if.[51]

To make sense of these lines requires parsing pronoun antecedents, but one
cannot fully account for their effects by reading them in isolation. These lines
are structured around another "secret" ("*what*'s under"? who is acting?) and
turn on the multiple valences of the phrase "make of/made of" and the struc-
ture of the if/then proposition. If/then relationships are also exemplary tempo-
ral relationships, modeling the grammatical passage of time from one event to
another, contingently. In other words, the last four lines implicate conventions
of writing and spelling and fundamental philosophical or metaphysical pre-
sumptions expressed by the grammar of a language.

If music—the "arced harp"—initiates the action of these lines, their theme
turns on the transformative crossing of grammar and writing that I would

analogize to rhythm, the cut, understood as a more or less regular temporal pattern of discrete events. In music and other forms of timing built around recurring events, rhythm relates events to each other with respect to a given unit of time and necessarily implies a given tempo, a way of experiencing and relating oneself to time. In western genres, musical rhythm typically follows a single pattern of relating events to each other, but the cut implies multiple, simultaneous rhythmic frameworks. Here, rhythm is the relationship between events, between sound and silence. Grammar operates between the paradigmatic axis of language (the semantic relations between words through which sense appears to be immediate) and the syntagmatic axis (the positional or ordinal relationships between words and other signifiers, diacritical marks, punctuation) and is implicated in both. Grammar "is" the relationship between words in ordinary writing and speech. It is to language what rhythm is to sound or events in general—a way of describing regular relationships or occurrences. When more than one rhythmic or temporal meter appears active, the result is a new, more complex rhythm, a polyrhythm. Mackey's play with grammatical elements and recursive, overlapping temporal frames introduces a polygrammar, a kind of double-jointed syntax: the poetics of the cut.

In the passage I have been considering, an unspecified agency ("arced harp" is the grammatical subject) makes of "them" a "then." Some collectivity ("them"—syntactically "[m]asks made of trembling") is temporalized, put into the past, into the narrative of the "it" (still apparently "arced harp").[52] The phrase "made of" changes function as the lines progress. Simultaneously, the poem draws attention to the fundamentally grammatical nature of propositions or declarations of belonging and being, "the thematic after-the-fact constitution of that which never was."[53] At another level, this moment marks a moment of the "birth" of narrative, if not song—constitutively in medias res: the arced harp makes "them" a formative feature of *its* past: its "then." The transition from "it" to "if" reverses the if/then proposition, the grammatical foundation of cause and effect, rendering it a temporally irresolvable "then/if" that interrogates the conditions for the coming of the future or inaugurates a series of contingencies: then, if . . . if . . . . "Then" oscillates between referring to the past and future, and "being" becomes a product—made of—temporality, not vice versa. This inversion, of course, does not abolish causality. On the contrary, it affirms chance. In both instances, the arced harp effects through what it has "brought up"—either unearthed or mentioned—requires only that a single letter be changed to alter the sense of the lines. In both cases, the letter changes to another that is either ordinally or morphologically proximate: *m* to *n*, *t* to *f*.

These two transformations—one word "made of" or into another—illustrate the insubstantial nature of distinctions presumed to be solid. The invocation of music's transformative or generative capacities, its ambivalent position within linguistic semiotic systems and adjacent to those systems, makes temporality of the Andoumboulou at once prior to the humans that "we are" and contemporaneous with "us" to the point of indistinction. The cut here exploits the graphicity of the inscribed work, confronting and thwarting grammar in an attempt to "say" the unsayable.

Repetitions throughout the work make the relationship between the said, sayable, and unsayable into a theme by pushing language further into its own materiality. One example, from "Song of the Andoumboulou: 29," involves the word "loquat," the fruit of the loquat tree but also the third-person present subjunctive of the Latin "loquor," "to speak":

> Loquat exuberance
> got the best of them, loquat
> eloquence, loquat allure.[54]

Repetition underscores and makes meaningful language's sensuousness, its eloquent sensibility beyond the immediate meaning of the words. This sensuousness—the sound and look of the word—anticipates a later moment of fraught etymology:

> Anomalous bed they
> called "loquacious,"   melodious
> word whose root they mistook,
>   took
> to mean loquat-sweet . . .[55]

These lines establish a point of synthesis between the English "loquat," a fruit whose name derives from transliterated Cantonese (*OED*), and the Latin "loquat," which is related to "loquacious." "Root," like the repeated "took," draws attention to the histories of contact and conquest that have shaped English's development. Simultaneously, the connection to the present subjunctive mood returns us to the if/then proposition, insofar as the present subjunctive of "to speak" can be used in the conditional: "if she speak, then . . ." or "whether she speak or not . . ." As "took" is related to "mistook" whether we recognize a commonality or not, so the two senses of "loquat" are bound to one another by a third language that has, so to speak, consumed them both without being able to reduce one to the other. Indeed, as the poem seems to suggest, the confusion of the two, brought out by their common spelling and pronunciation, is a condition of possibility and impossibility for language.

In the collection *Whatsaid Serif*, that surplus takes the form of some of the minimal forms of language: pronouns and the means of their typographic presentation (a serif, rhyming with "seraph," is a term for the "hooks" and cross-strokes at the top and bottom of numbers and letters). "Song of the Andoumboulou: 18," for example, refers to a

> Monophysite
> lament, one we, Ouadada, that
> we would include, not reduce to us ...
> He to him, she to her, they to them,
>   opaque
> pronouns, "persons" whether or not we
> knew who they were ...[56]

Here Mackey invokes the unorthodox doctrine that Christ has only one, divine nature (rather than both a divine and mortal nature) to articulate a desire for a unitary "we" joined by love ("Ouadada"), a "we" of one (*mono*) fundamental nature (*physis*), through a grammatical argument. This would be a collectivity of all subject pronouns where none was made even discursively other, where none was made "him," "her," "them," one that would not speak of an "us." The reference to "opaque pronouns" sounds a larger concern about recognizability, about not only which people can be counted but how they can count. Further, this passage puts the very question of expression in crisis: if the subject pronoun "would include, not reduce to *us*," then this "we" would only ever speak as a subject rather than being the object of its own or another's discourse. In essence, the we that is never an object of its own language has no outside, no others, and perhaps no speech. These lines signify both a utopian desire for a collectivity that would exclude no one and the difficulty of speaking such collectivity.

Direct allusion also raises the question of language as medium:

> [...] "What does 'Language
> is a fruit of which the
>   skin
> is called chatter' mean?"[57]

This chatter, another name for which is speculation, is the necessary attempt to think beyond present conditions through making experimental connections in language and with grammar, putatively nonsignifying elements. That chanced relation poetry risks and enacts is a necessary precondition, here drawing out the surprising correspondence between two unrelated words that poetry relates through homophony and orthography, revealing a "fruitful" arbitrariness in signification and the site-specific bounds of any locution. The interrogation of "root," which also must be read two ways, like the proliferation of anagrams throughout Mackey's work, emphasizes the capacities of language users to more or less arbitrarily redefine or refashion words to suit their needs, to articulate what "conventionally articulate speech" leaves unsayable.[58] Better, such play emphasizes the multiple, simultaneous bases on which language stands, the material bases of the supposed message. The poetics of the cut underscores language's *use* alongside an implicit claim for poetry as a process of tapping language's *potential*, imagining fulfillment as a result of a fundamental transfiguration. This poetry invites us, that is, not to think about what words mean but to look at *how* they mean and how they would mean otherwise.

The Song of the Andoumboulou, chronicling the journey of its eponymous subjects to the surface of the earth, stretches between past and present, engaging a question about the relation of one to the other. Past and present are put in a differential relation to one another through a shifting referential terrain charting movement from and between sites (mythic and otherwise), temporal moments through the "cut" of songs "on the box" of the poem's locations and through pronominal shifts—which I argue for as a play of deixis, the unstable haecceity of the serial poem. The proper names of sites through which the Andoumboulou or sounds travel (e.g., "It was a train | in southern Spain we | were on," "it was a train outside São Paulo on our way to Algeciras we were on," "a | train gotten on in Miami") ultimately serve as simply another form of deixis and deferred identity.[59] The poem's point of view moves between first and third person, singular and plural, often in a self-interrogative tone that locates the "identity" of the poem's speaker(s) outside of the presumptions of language, or speaking, and of identity. As with epic poetry, there is a quest to found a nation—to recover "lost ground"—although, as reference to established territories attests, this founding will necessarily be a refounding or reinscription of space: "each the | other's non-pronominal elsewhere | nominal | out."[60] Unlike epic, these poems do not establish home or nation but instead continue moving toward "some ecstatic elsewhere." The utopian element, then, rests in that trace of the here and now immanent to founded nation as much as lost ground—the not-yet-founded nation that still will not be what it could have been. It marks the trace of irreducible otherness that such myths of origin or emergence suppress. The "outside" sought can only be a "nominal out" that the poetics of the cut asymptotically approaches in its crablike movement toward a potential future embedded in the unfulfilled past.

PHANTOM OBJECTIVITY

The "andoumboulouous" collectivity imagined in *From a Broken Perfume Bottle Traces Still Emanate* is a musical ensemble whose members operate similarly to the subjects of *The Song of the Andoumboulou*, albeit in a world more recognizably "ours." The prose series' interests and methods are more akin to verse than prose fiction—"characters" don't develop, the plot is minimal, and any sense of larger plot is subordinated to the quotidian ways the ensemble creates lived time. *From a Broken Perfume Bottle Traces Still Emanate* advances through a series of meditative letters between N. and the Angel of Dust, detailing the activities of the former's band and his reflections on music. The central conflicts involve inspiration and a concern over the origins of origin, or what N., playing on Wallace Stevens, calls a "Supreme Friction" that invokes a desire to "misconceive or miscarry, to want to be done with any relational coherence, to want to abort."[61] N. is not a fully formed character but a "phantom remainder" from the earlier text who invokes an "originary experience" of earlier texts that retroactively become precursors.[62] He is also the phantom reminder of another, alternative beginning, the invented sense of the past, much as the Andoumboulou are.

The works that comprise *From a Broken Perfume Bottle Traces Still Emanate* are too complex and rich for me to attempt a full account of their textual strategies. Instead I continue my consideration of the poetics of the cut in the prose via the figures of sound recording and the fugue-like states N. refers to as "cowrie shell attacks." These attacks represent the threatening side of inspiration and Mackey's utopian efforts to rework nothing less than the meanings of being human, at once pre- and post-collectivity. N.'s musical ensemble, whose members share dreams and mythologies, posits community as something more than an aggregate of individuals. As such, it describes a utopian imagining of community. Yet the supernatural elements of this ensemble require a more complicated hermeneutic than one that would simply take it as a vanguard or model. At stake is something about the ways culture might be shared, as well as an attempt to deconstruct the collective/individual hierarchy rather than privilege one over the other. In this way, too, the series refuses a simple music-text hierarchy that would have the music somehow be a model for community, using musicality instead as a means by which to imagine other possibilities for writing.

Any possible "expression" must orient itself spatially between two sites and temporally between two moments. Expression, that is, takes place within the limits of deixis, a "there" that always will have "defied location": "No 'it | was' could be made of it, pure | dispatch."⁶³ The epistolary form of this prose work makes both narration's lagging behind the event and the struggle with/against deixis into themes, simultaneously questioning the status of the "correspondence" between the text of the narration and the event itself. This "there," a "'space' we're all immigrants from," is a utopian space available only as a retrospective figuration, "resonance rather than resolution" as N. puts it later. This "space," in other words, is a vertiginous, syncopated "space," *there*, between happening and nonhappening.

The opening 14.VI.1978 letter of *Bedouin Hornbook*, the first volume in the *Perfume* series, thematizes the narrative's uncertain after-the-fact origin, its own fraught and difficult birth. N. writes of a dream he has had in which he comes on an open manhole around which lies an assortment of plumbing fixtures he understands to be a disassembled bass clarinet. Intuiting that the "crowd"—a spectral pressure—wants to hear him play John Coltrane's "Naima," he finds himself playing the version of Coltrane's "Cousin Mary" Archie Shepp recorded on *Four for Trane*. He throws in "a few licks of [his] own" before "coming to the realization that what [he] was playing existed on a record," the vinyl's scratches audible "somewhere in back and to the left."⁶⁴ His own performance, including his own supplemental licks, comes preinscribed on a record, which in the dream serves as a disruption of the performer's identity and emphasizes the performance's iterability.⁶⁵ Though N. throws in "a few licks," the solo's "proper" signatory remains Archie Shepp, meaning those familiar with *Four for Trane* would recognize it, even if initially that recognition takes the form of a teasing familiarity, a "repetition" simultaneously masked and enhanced by being "infinitely more gruffly resonant and varied and warm" than Shepp's swing-inspired timbre.⁶⁶

This beginning, after the initial beginning in an earlier series, promises an end—"please don't expect anything more from me in the way of words"—that has still not arrived, and figures a dream of an original performance that turns out to be unoriginal.⁶⁷ What kind of "origin" is this? What are we to make of this series, from one world and one book to another, which continues after its proffered end, seemingly, like the *Song of the Andoumboulou*, on condition of an end or death that must retrace the steps of the dead? Emphasizing culture *as* repetition and genealogy, the several deferred beginnings and endings of *Perfume Bottle* underscore the negotiations between those marks left behind—for example, tradition or previous occasions—and progression in the present moment, which can never fully dislodge itself from that past that is the condition of possibility for the present. The cut, however, suggests that the past itself is not a simple origin: other possible perspectives that one can imaginatively re-engage or reactivate haunt the articulated past. Such openness to that haunting copresence—at the expense of a secured identity—goes toward explaining the playful allusiveness, which cites both prior texts and albums as "origins." The past emerges as that in and against the flow of time, a rhythmic structure that turns in and against itself "in the way of words."

The text produces a vertiginous effect by its rapid movement through many genres and allusions, not all of which are cited, to philosophers, anthropologists, and musicians, through the recurrent, narrativized descriptions of performance, through N.'s incapacitating visitations from elsewhere (the "scattered cowrie shell attacks"), and his through the "after-the-fact" lectures/libretti. Cumulatively, this multigenre play produces an andoumboulouous sense of locomotive dislocation encapsulated in such phrases as "there's no 'really' when it comes to 'was,'" or "I wasn't really there . . . the 'I' which was was an 'I' which wasn't my own."[68] In a subsequent letter, N. has an encounter with Djamilaa, another member of the ensemble who appears to be under a spell that becomes contagious when N. realizes that it is the "hour of God" and the hour Coltrane died. Upon the spell's subsiding, the phrase "phantom objectivity" haunts N.: "It refers to a situation, if I've got it right, where we find ourselves haunted by what we ourselves initiate."[69]

His discussion of the relationship between (musical) form and conformity to a situation "so pat as to become oppressive" directly invokes Georg Lukács, who understands "phantom objectivity" to refer to the situation in societies in which the commodity is the dominant form, lending it "an autonomy that seems so strictly rational and all-embracing as to conceal every trace of its [the commodity structure's] fundamental nature: the relation between people."[70] In another context, Mackey generalizes phantom objectivity for the neoliberal era, calling it "the veil by which the social order renders its role in the construction of reality invisible."[71] Phantom objectivity, the veil of ideology, effectively erases or suppresses traces of its own mediation of "reality," making the given world seem inevitable, alternatives unthinkable.

Mackey also links the notion of phantom objectivity to the phantom of "phantom limb," and thus back to *duende*; in both cases "phantom" is a "relative, relativizing term that cuts both ways, occasioning a shift in perspective between real and unreal, an exchange of attributes between the two."[72] In other words, what the ruling order tries to suppress necessarily persists in the very appearance of reality itself, providing a postexpectant mechanism with which to undo its own fictions and pretense to totality. Part of that, in this episode and throughout *From a Broken Perfume Bottle*, is attention to additional meanings of time and the present. Observing the hour of John Coltrane's death is one example of opening a moment up to its other, insofar as unofficial but shared commemoration raises questions about the shared synchronicity of an imagined community, locating a revealing discrepancy in the orderly progression of time that might become something articulate.

Thus, encounters such as the scattered cowrie shell attacks, often related to such observances, are not simply revisitations of other times, remembrances of otherwise lost or forgotten moments; they are not events at all but rather the suspension of event, an unwilled suspension of time. Within the prose series, they occur with increasing regularity, serving as a dramatic wedge and an alternate narrative timeline that provides a separate set of characters and possible events. The first such moment, here a "broken-glass" attack rather than a broken cowrie shell attack, occurs in *Bedouin Hornbook* after N. finally manages to orchestrate an encounter with the Crossroads Choir, an "anonymous, axiomatic band whose existence had always been taken for granted," known primarily through rumor, encountered in secrecy.[73] In the presence of an audience "composed of hairless, mannikinlike men and women, each of whose faces wore itself like a tight tautological mask," they play at a scene whose characteristics are not certain: "One moment it seemed like a cathedral, the next a storefront church. The possibilities seemed to go on without end."[74] A flute player solos, during which he has recourse to speech ("'As for me,' he muttered, 'who am neither I nor not-I, I have strayed from myself and I find no remedy but despair'"), leading the audience into bacchant-like frenzy, which "invents" call and response where there had been none. At that moment, "numerous bits of broken glass imbedded themselves in [N.'s] forehead, each of them the seed of a low, breathy growl which seemed to emanate from the stars."[75] Simultaneously "heavensent" and evocative of a past trauma (a car accident), the attack spurs thought of the necessary preconditions to "free the future from every flat, formulaic 'outcome,' from its own investment in the contested shape of an otherness disfigured by its excursion thru the world."[76] The attack spurs his imagining a future on conditions other than those made available as repetitions of the "objective" present. However, this "space" ("the sweet, sour, somewhat acidic hollow in which what was spoken belied the mootness of what might better have been intoned") ultimately proved debilitating, uninhabitable.[77]

A phantom recording announces the onset of each subsequent cowrie shell attack. The letter following his account of his experience with the Crossroads Choir finds N. laid up in bed suffering from what "feel more like shattered cowrie shells . . . tightfisted imprints, fossil imprints" accompanied by a feeling of dizziness and Ornette Coleman's version of George and Ira Gershwin's "Embraceable You" (from *This is Our Music*) "piped into [his] head like *subcoritcal muzak*." He describes them as an "a radical, uprooting vertigo, a rash, an evaporative aspect of [him]self."[78] The spell, whose etiology doctors cannot determine, is broken when members of the band visit N. and, silently, pantomime a performance with their instruments, "playing" at varying tempos (described by analogy to phonographic playback—33, 45, and 78 RPM) that proves to be "an inoculation in the clearest, most radical sense of the term."[79] "Inoculation" may refer to the introduction of the germs (i.e., seeds, as with the initial performance) into the body through a wound, "imbuing a person with feelings, opinions, etc." At once warding off and combining, this inoculation reincorporates N. into the ensemble more primary than himself, formally crystallizing the disparate threads and concerns of the novel, the disparate times of practice as preparation and practice as activity, into a fragile unity.

Almost immediately thereafter, Lambert, a member of the Mystic Horn Society (which later becomes Molimo m'Atet and Djband) expresses his desire to add a new member to their ensemble through the medium of a composition, "Prometheus." His introduction of the composition references an unsigned quotation that gives an added dimension to the cowrie shell attacks: "'To articulate the past historically,' he [Lambert] said, 'means to seize hold of a memory when it flashes up at a moment of danger. This danger affects both the content of a tradition and its receivers: that of becoming a tool of the ruling classes.'"[80] The citation is, of course, the sixth thesis of Walter Benjamin's "On the Concept of History," opposing historical materialism to Leopold von Ranke's view of historiography that would represent the past "as it really was," the condition of making the future thinkable only as the fateful outcome of that articulated past.[81] The juxtaposition of this citation with the reconsiderations of kinship that inform *Perfume Bottle* and with the first cowrie shell attack suggests that the vertigo is a forceful, though involuntary, critical reorientation or reconstellation of memory as a spectral substrate to things "as they are." In this way, they are an answer the problem *Perfume Bottle* (and Mackey's poetics more generally) poses regarding the relationship to loss as originary, the "attempt to raise a metaphysical question of origin, without the pretense that one can ever ask that question from any sure or solid ground," without specific historical or biographical occasion.[82] Uncertainty is an obscured component *within* the prevailing ontological notions, requiring that we imagine an ecstatic 'out,' which may be as involuntary or unwilled, together with that which is excluded in the expression of a "self." Radically, then, the cowrie shell attacks figure the syncopation of the self and the "double-jointed" multiplicity of any moment.[83]

In their most threatening form, the attacks culminate in the introduction of N.'s own avatar, Natty Dredj (a name referencing the Bob Marley composition "Natty Dread," anthropological digging, and a key figure in Rastafarian mythology representing a tear in the self), who writes dateless letters to the Angel of Dust in *Bass Cathedral*, the fourth book in the series. The dateless letters, the first of which evokes the hot Santa Ana winds that occasion Djamilaa's spells, explicitly reference a being "outside of time," that is, not yet or no longer. This datelessness corresponds to a flux in the signatory, "namelessness inversely related to his recent graduation beyond initial constraint."[84] The new signature, making literal the dissolution of self the cowrie shell attacks imply, fundamentally changes N.'s relationship with the Angel of Dust. Within the terms of the prose series, this newest speaking-for (for example, Dredj for N. or the Angel of Dust for their album) literalizes the ongoing concern about speaking with the voice of another, linked with the "voice" from elsewhere, which remains among the novel's central concerns from the opening letter.

While phantom music accompanies the onset of the attacks, the deaths of musicians—Bob Marley and Thelonious Monk, for example—often serve as triggers, linking the prose series and "The Song of the Andoumboulou" in their attention to the need for mourning and the need to claim ancestors who "will not | ascend without song."[85] The aleatory cowrie shell attacks advance a link between poetry, musicality, public mourning, and commemoration. The shattered cowrie shells—suggesting continuity with African traditions but also the mercantile relations at the center of the originary displacement of Africans through the slave trade—also raise the question of "redeeming" the dead or what is otherwise past, a monetary and theological redemption whose status is always fraught. As Saidiya Hartman notes, cowries became currency in West Africa as the Atlantic slave trade was being established, and they were often harvested from the corpses of those murdered or drowned:

> In every place ravaged by the slave trade, stories circulated about the human cost of money: cowrie shells feasted on the bodies of captives. Money multiplied if fed

human blood. Rich men accrued their wealth through the labor of slaves slogging away in cities underneath the Atlantic. Others alleged that cowrie shells washed back into the Atlantic were hoarded by witches or controlled by water spirits like Mami Wata, Mother of the Waters.[86]

Being "shattered," then, has both positive valences, insofar as this breakage allows us to rethink the links between kinship and possession, and negative valences, insofar as breakage makes their edges jagged and more painful, lending wounded kinship, as social relation, a "phantom objectivity" that makes it appear individual. Yet the episodes are ultimately an interruption of the self, an encounter mediated by love as an unheard question in articulation or an unheeded call. The shattered cowrie shells "cut back" to an unavailable origin whose conditions have not yet been realized. Underscoring something absent from the phantom objectivity of lived experience, they bring "up what was under," what persists unacknowledged in historical narrative and subjective plots, suspending the prose series between the fulfillment of an imagined realignment with Africa and a transfiguration of that relationship that accepts the nonheroic alongside the heroic. The shattered cowrie shell episodes' temporal caesura is, from the point of view of the narrative, a figure for the communicability of another time that coexists, unredeemed, with this articulated now, the irruption of a past and form of pastness awaiting its moment of recognizability. These episodes of temporal arrest or stilling, often triggered by death, differ from individual melancholia and public mourning; they are untamed by a "common denominator" or singular signifier (i.e., "culture," "diaspora," "revolution"), not curable by a substitute object. To redeem is to re-deem, to change or name again.

"TIME NOW HAD A HOLE IN IT": POSTEXPECTANT TIME

The cowrie shell attacks introduce another, extra-narrative time, suspending the coherence of the speaking/writing subject and time's already slow pace through these prose works (although the reader does not sense the gaps in time that N. habitually mentions between his letters to the Angel of Dust). I want to return to the record, to which the attacks are linked, as a representation that plays on the vacillation between noun and verb, between sound writing and figure writing. Records, like the music they convey, serve as a kind of "technical-ecstatic" foundation for thinking and thinking otherwise, privileging a density of subjective and intersubjective experiences, while troubling the line between the two. At issue seems to be the communicability of sound. Somewhat schematically, this communicability relates both sound's *extensive* aspect—its distribution across defined space and especially across differing "uses" or interpretations—and its *intensive* aspect—its "own" temporality, materiality, and "inoculative" capacity. Though a record may help one imagine oneself in a community with others listening to the same sounds, the alternation of intensive and extensive listening —the former catching what is most peculiar or personally striking, the latter what is most familiar and locatable within traditions or histories—means that the two modalities of listening to the same record produce at least two different objects, multiplied across an unknowable number of anonymous listeners.

The metaphors regarding music's tactile caress or "gruff embrace"—the "song so black it | burnt | my lip"—are one means through which Mackey's writings problematize any simple privileging of the aural or the phonic, reminding us that listening is not a passive activity but an active one. Recorded sound indexes a performance and the framing of that performance for an audience that has conditioned its hearing. The prose series, like the *Song of the Andoumboulou*, figures recorded music as a dense labyrinth of connections and reconnections, linked through a reciprocal anticipation: the audience anticipates the next sound, and the record anticipates an audience. This structure is thematized and complicated by the appearance, both during live performance and on records of the band, of comic strip balloons—later given the name B'Loon and a corresponding mythology—that come to accompany the performances, seemingly according to their own will. N. connects the balloons to the cowrie shell attacks (which briefly become bottle caps before returning to being shells) through the curative lip of a conch shell: "Every cowrie, the conch's lip insisted, had to be removed, all pretense to unwoundedness let go," each "exiting Dredj's brow and, balloonlike, rising skyward, joining the night's garment of stars."[87] On the one hand, the balloons parody N.'s own tendency to describe improvisation as conversation, lecture, or story. On the other hand, in line with the interrogations of speaking and identity traced throughout this chapter, the balloons also figure the inverse of the anxiety of merely repeating another's voice by being the voice that speaks otherwise than the speaker's, the voice whose words say otherwise than what the speaker's words "want to say."

The balloons, which are central to the thematic conflicts of *Atet A.D.* (where they appear during live performance and elude photographic documentation) and *Bass Cathedral* (where they accompany the band's record), first appear in Mackey's "Song of the Andoumboulou: 25," subtitled "'zar' nth part," in refer-

ence to one of several of that poem's mythic locations. There, the balloon func-
tions as an extension of a theme of volitionlessness:

> Heard
> my head say cradle me, myself cradle
> my head. Wondered whose head I meant,
> what voice I spoke with, *volitionless*,
> feet
> stuck to the floor . . .
>
> A balloon tore
> loose, floated off, I called it
> back . . . B'Head looked in from
> on high . . .

In these lines, the irregular margins situate "heard" rather than "head" above
"feet," implying sensation—that is, having one's ears impressed with sounds
from elsewhere—as a condition to an *ecstatic* experience separate from an "I."
The theme of speaking with the voice of another returns, whereupon a "balloon
tore | loose," a pun on inspiration, the fraught or illusory nature of the artist's
freedom and privileged perspective, and a literalization of the theme of "lost
ground," the groundlessness of a thought from the impossible perspective of
redemption.

During N.'s performance with the Crossroads Choir, the audience chant-
sings select lyrics—"my house of cards has no foundation" and "my life revolves
around her/ What earthly good am I without her? | My castle has crumbled, | I'm
hers, body and soul"—while N. tries "to sound as much like [Eric] Dolphy
as [he] could," using a "borrowed voice," feeling himself to be in the endless
eighth day, after the end of a love affair he remembers and after the creation
of a world, a day that "prolonged itself into eternity."[88] As N. plays his bass clari-
net and meditates on this eddy of time, the audience bursts into spontaneous
song, accompanied by "a ball of light [that] bounced from syllable to syllable as
in the sing-along cartoons we saw at the movies when I was a kid."[89] This sing-
along refers to his utopian everywhere-and-nowhere sense of having a "blank
check drawn on a closed account," the forms of community that separate but
shared experience make possible, with implied, idiomatic "bounce" mixing the
religious or ecstatic ascent with the mundane here and now. The "cabalistic ball
of light" becomes a white balloon bearing the words "Only One." This balloon
—which, like the beads of glass N. feels have "imbedded themselves in [his]

forehead," comes apparently of its own accord from elsewhere—materializes metaphor. The response invents the call, both the song and the obligation to repeat, which does not burnish N.'s spirit but "takes [his] breath away" as it rises.

A later balloon visitation, narrated in a letter dated 28.IV.81, reaffirms the dual nature of the balloons as threat and promise. Complaining that the Angel of Dust has lapsed in their correspondence, N. describes the ways that "inarticulacy *spoke*" in a street guitar performance as a "loud critique of available options," but a sense of "being ushered . . . beyond oneself," for which he offers the borrowed blues-inflected term "jellyroll," accompanies that critique.[90] Throughout his account of this performance, N. refers to his desire to escape the strictures of bourgeois ideology, to his understanding (and the band's imputed understanding) of "the resident hollow one's apparent solidity concealed," expressed first through Penguin's face as he performs, its left side "tend[ing] to bulge with a wad of breath at the outset of each run."[91] N. considers this "wad of breath" a "cud" on its way to being a homophonic "could" that in turn will move from "conditional 'could' to unconditional 'will.'"[92] Lambert devises the solution of adding a "new proportion," taking the baritone sax from the performatively supine Penguin and replacing it with a sopranino saxophone, out of whose bell issues "bubble after bubble of the sort children make with soapy water." This figure links child's play, amniotic fluid (N. refers to it as an "embryonic proportion"), tactility, and fragility, which in turn figures a connection between audience and band members: a "transitory, nameless oneness" initially attempted by guile, retroactively felt.[93] The balloon visitations "initiate" a synaesthetic encounter with music as a kind of thinking in its own right, that must be attended to on its own "terms" and that must continually reinvent terms so as to avoid the temptations of imagining any word to be final.

By 4.VI.82, the balloons, as emblematic of all such revenant visitations (reminders of the openness from within of any ensemblic designation), take the form of gender-specific shared dreams and hauntings related to the search for and ultimate addition of a new band member, the drummer Drennette, that comprises much of *Djbot Baghostus's Run*. The band is in Seattle; a "comic strip balloon" literalizes Penguin having "something to say" on his oboe. The text of that balloon adds an erotic element to the band's internal mythology of Drennette, who had been imagined/envisioned in shared dreams before the fact to be a demiurgic figure alternately named Djeannine (for the males of the band) or Penny (for the females). This scene suggests a relation between the balloons and the "speaking" of articulacy. That which speaks in articulate speech, a concern that includes N.'s retrospective narrative accounts of his music or of records, is linked to the notion of postexpectancy, the in-turning of one moment to recuperate possibilities not pursued, "like walking up a stairway and reaching for a step that isn't there."[94] This is a narrative description of the poetics of the cut: it is not concerned with the moment of the fall but with the reinterpretive, recuperative moment after that changes the sense of time.

The balloons, like the cowrie shell attacks, "cut" the narrative. They are "playful" mechanisms that counter limiting binaries, commingling fulfillment and transfiguration by retroactively understanding transfiguration as authentic fulfillment. The balloons are a *demand*, concerned with the communicability of the message, with the possibility of communication more than the message itself. Rather than raising a material question about access or technical limitations in the recording or broadcast of sound (the question, indeed the thought, of playing the band's record on the radio has not been brought up), the balloons in particular raise a philosophical question about the *stance* and *substance* of listening. The two-dimensional balloons' "volitionless" appearance and the relation of that appearance to respiration (or to the length of musical phrase) becomes evidence. Rather than asking what the balloons say, or what the text means in relation to the music, people question *whether* the balloons, which refuse to be photographed (leading some to enlist the aid of police sketch artists) exist, what their mode of being is. They ask each other, "What was that?"

N. invents a syncretic mythography for the balloons, invoking a sense of prehistorical, future-oriented origin. The balloons become the material aspect of B'Loon, a Gnostic figure combining earth-diver myths of the loon who "plunges into primeval waters and brings up a mouthful or beakful of mud . . . from which the earth is then made" and the pseudo-Bahamian "play with B' [for "Brer"]-*Ba* [the Egyptian term for "soul"], . . . the spirit or embodied soul of namesake play."[95] The loon who founds and refounds a world is also soul kin (a literalized "soul brother") to the inhabitants of worlds coming into and going out of being. B'Loon belongs to a postexpectant time, another timeline immanent to this one that has access to a futurity and to a past that has not passed, a revenant past that he does not so much figure as point to. He is emblematic of a counterenchantment that "muddies our mouths with the way the world is."[96] Accompanied by words or not, the balloons call into question the conditions of articulacy and communicability. The appearance of the balloons during performances suggests an ongoing demand to reconstellate concepts, an ongoing deconstruction that puts origin "outside" any law of general equivalence, making it a nonsubstitutable (but not irreducible) central category that must be problematized (and, as B'loon's hybrid name and origin story suggest, points to a plural rather than singular origin).

Postexpectancy crosses the personally monumental—that which matters in the individual life—with the publicly monumental, the intensive and the extensive, without reducing one to an "expression" of the other and thus without trivializing one at the expense of the other. Thus Seattle's Space Needle, a symbol of "the datedness of what was once thought of as 'things to come,'" becomes its own "ecstatic elsewhere" a "tomb to the elapsed expectancy it turns out to have been."[97] It is, in the moment of the encounter, its own double or repetition. Postexpectancy, then, names that feeling of time "falling behind itself" but also getting ahead of itself, a figure of *tempo rubato*, literally, "stolen time," that keeps time with itself if not with other rhythms to which it might be attached. Less a quality of things "in themselves," it is a utopian method of "seizing" an image or memory that is not merely additive or synthetic on the model of "recovery" but syncopated, antithetic: it demands but largely eschews proffering solutions. Temporality is internally haunted by its pretenses to fullness, to self-adequacy, by all that could have happened but has not yet—and thus opens onto the utopian thought that the present is neither inevitable nor immutable.

ORPHEUS CALLING

The cowrie shell attacks and balloon visitations figure a postexpectant time always on the verge of switching places with our notion of everyday reality, transfiguring the present as a betrayal rather than fulfillment of the past. They mark the word that can inspire the self as well as suffocate it, make it literally "both I and not-I"— just a name or pronoun. I have alluded to the relationship between music's orphic capacities in Mackey's work, which the cowrie shell attacks and related balloon appearances make at once a thematic and formal component that partially undoes the "phantom objectivity" of the book as solid object. Throughout the prose series, music and musical performance relate to the boundaries separating disclosure and enclosure, the enclosure of public space for private enterprise, the spectral "invisible hands," and the force of law. In a semipublic Santa Cruz space called Pacific Garden Mall, the band performs, circling "counterclockwise . . . an uroboric strut, marking every eight beat with an ever so slight stutter-step" for a small, transient audience.[98] Considering a spectator's complaint that the band's music is too esoteric or "overly elitist" for public performance, N. concludes that revolution, in all senses, must make "for a lateral displacement (a stepping aside from whatever one thought 'upward' and 'downward' meant)," lest one find oneself merely spinning in a rut or groove.[99] The ecstatic possibilities of the postexpectant, animated by a poetics of the cut, call for such a displacement of our accustomed understandings and point toward such a revolution.

As with much of Mackey's work, "revolution" retains another meaning: spinning and circling recur both as literal ambulatory circling and as figural recumbent appeal. At an early audition for a new member of the group, the two females of the group stage a musical protest, Djamilaa singing what N., recalling that she is an orphan, describes as "a wordless wrestling with sound as in flamenco singing . . . part wail, part suspended sentence" that eventually takes an "orphic turn."[100] She lowers her volume at one point to allow "the rest of us [Lambert, Penguin, N., and the would-be new drummer Sun Stick] to catch up with the 'not-of-our-time intensity' of her singing.[101] The play seems to involve a temporized excess of embodiment, ahead-of-its-time embodiment that participates in the logic, meaning the structuring effects, of the secret. The men sit transfixed at her voice's "textureless appeal," its text without text. When she takes up a song recorded by Nancy Wilson, "China," her interaction with the tricksterish Aunt Nancy (nicknamed "Ain't Nancy" for the occasion) invites the intervention of a "curious compound play of identity and difference."[102] There are many levels of play here between naming and negation, between what is contingent to meaning (the phonological) and necessary, which are underpinned by the assumption that the music, as well as musical performance, is intelligible, that meaning is a matter of the unconcealment of truth. What power the name has lies jointly in its being concealed as secret and subsequently revealed: neither I nor not-I but in a vital sense both.

The "orphic turn" is a pivot between material and immaterial, sensuous and nonsensuous, or known and unknown, an ahead-of-its-time "knowledge" for which "intuition" is too fraught a term. An orphic turn, "turn" being both a noun and a verb, finally, is the trope of musicality, related to the repeatability of performance, the modifiability of traditions even unto their transformation. It is that which in Mackey's utopian poetics of the cut mediates fulfillment and transfiguration to escape the "centrist ordeal" N. frets about. Figured by inscription at multiple levels, the orphic turn also mediates the contradiction between tradition as the precondition of legibility and that intensive component of the recorded performance that retains its ability to surprise.

With that in mind, I now turn to two scenes of performance from *Bass Cathedral* that combine spectacle and orphic enchantment. In the first, recounted in a letter dated 18.IX.83, the band has listened to the test pressing of their album and are somewhat alarmed at B'Loon's appearance during Aunt Nancy's solo on a composition called "Dream Thief." She considers the text a "time-lapse translation" of her "thoughts and feelings extending much further back than the moment of her 'Dream Thief' solo."[103] During a live performance of the same song, she plays a cigar-box guitar, which figures in the story for which B'Loon is supposed to be amanuensis. Penguin joins in strumming a broom as if it were a guitar, "seeking leverage on Drennette and Aunt Nancy's churchical exchange," then Djamilaa joins in, delaying time with her percussive foot taps, seeking "leverage, an oblique, dislocating fulcrum furthering her own blue-ictic stroll, pianistic strut," followed by what N. refers to as Lambert's "dance":

> he extended his arms in front of his body, hands hanging limp, the classic or ste-reotypic sleepwalker's pose though his eyes remained open. His arms were ex-tended for balance one soon saw, as he now leaned back on his heels, letting the front of each foot come up off the floor. His heels alone touching the floor, his legs locked at the knee and at a 75° angle with the floor, he proceeded to step in time with the music, walking backwards in a counterclockwise circle.[104]

N. subsequently emulates Lambert's improbable limbo "in time," feeling him-self "possessed of a non-predicative truth" related to Mackey's deferral of propositional content; he puts his horn to his lip to play, only to surprise him-self by joining Lambert's "backwardswalking circle," becoming a follower and, because he's behind Lambert and thus in front from the perspective of their movement, a leader as well. The phrase "in time" is likewise ambiguous, re-ferring equally to the rhythm of his dance and to the layers of temporality the performance avails itself of. There is at once the time of Aunt Nancy's haunted childhood (her father dies shortly after giving her the initial cigar-box guitar), the time of the balloons that "see deep into the past and present," the recur-sive time of the ensemble's shared dreams, and the "seemingly endless instant" of the performance, among others.[105]

The dilation of time, both on the level of this scene and on the "macro" level of the prose series' four parts to date, which largely thwarts conventional char-acter and plot development, suggests a change of scale. It is not that "personal" or "private" time trumps or overshadows "public" or "political" time but that the lingering development of the former interrogates the latter, implicitly ques-tioning those hierarchies that privilege the latter without carefully consider-ing those whose names and actions will not be considered when "historical" accounts are given. The prose series' dilation of the everyday magnifies the de-tails of timing to such a degree that it challenges ideas of incremental "progress" and "development," focusing instead on the ways the present shapes possibilities for living and making art. Lambert and N.'s limbo without bar suggest tactics for getting around an ongoing ordeal—called variously marginality, centrism, patness, or banality—a concern Mackey's poetics, especially its commitment to surprise, share.

A later scene more directly thematizes such audience interaction, the confusion of leader and follower, of cause and effect, that runs throughout all the work considered here, returning us more directly to questions of the body and so-called lived experience. In a letter dated 13.II.83, N. recounts the band's record-release gig at a club called the Studio. For the encore, they play a tune "off the record" called *Djam Suasion*, a modified jam session "that avails itself of the impromptu impulse and proceeds on a very bare outline of structure and motif" Djamilaa calls "drift conduits," set performance concepts whose order she arranges in the moment to allow opportune mistakes to dictate the shape of the piece.[106] Extending one of the "drift conduits" that is used to signal soloists and using it to end a solo of her own, an "anacrotic run [, . . .] reminiscent idea's utopic wish, would-be return to reminiscent flesh's first awakening."[107] The passage concludes by crossing James Brown's "Sex Machine" ("the way I like it is the way it is") with Walter Benjamin's "On the Concept of History": "'the way it was' the way one wanted it to be."[108] Further alluding to James Brown, the rhythm shifts to a "4/4 shuffle meter" (akin, I take it, to James Brown's "Doin' it to Death"), which provokes the audience to "dance": "knees bent, asses lowered to the floor but short of outright squat, they assumed something of a jockey's position," seeming to celebrate embodiment as such, "the wonder of arms and legs having a torso to attach to and extend from."[109]

The members of the audience have no formal or "historical" connection to one another save a common besiegement of abstraction that they attempt to escape in the retroactive moment of awareness, the dance itself. In the following passage, B'Loon visits, corresponding with the movement of the audience rather than the band:

> Each dancer raised and lowered his or her right arm, pounding his or her right thigh as with a hammer, an ever so restrained hammer whose handle was the dancer's forearm, its head the dancer's fist. It was a methodical, all but robotic pounding, deliberate and insistent yet of a soft, slow-motion cast, as though the air were a viscous liquid the arm strained against, fought to rise and fall, move at all within.
>
> As fist hit thigh, at the exact moment fist hit thigh, a balloon emerged.[110]

The rhythmic and aural patterning emerges in part due to the insistent "his or her" used to maintain gender neutrality. The short a ("hammer," "handle"), o ("robotic," "methodical"), and i sounds ("liquid," "viscous"), along with the repeating p and b draw attention to themselves; they constitute a phonetic supplement to the methodical movements described, insisting on language's specific modes of embodiment, writing's labor. The gender-specific balloons, which recur with each strike of fist to thigh, narrate a man and woman engaging in oral sex, each beginning with the phrase "I lie on my back," each insisting on the nose pressed to the "crack of [the other's] ass," insistently referring in explicit detail to the genitals with frank vulgarity (e.g., "balls," "cunt"). This, coupled with the formal repetitions of words and vowel patterns, leads one to the sense that these members of the audience have become literal "sex machines." The "enjoyment" of the body becomes explicitly sexual, recalling the word "jazz"'s carnal roots, explicitness becoming the austerity of the martinet, a form of the *cante jondo*, informed by the hammer-and-anvil suggestion of the dance's fist strike.

After the band shifts from 4/4 to a slower "duple time," Djamilaa reinscribes the hammer-and-anvil implication of the dance through the martinet, abetted by Drennette, who accents the dancers' movements with well-timed cymbal accents. Invoking cultural crossings—"an Andalusian Ogoun and a Gypsy John Henry"—Djamilaa's voice "erase[s] the balloon's X-rated script." The balloons become blank, and the focus shifts more decisively to work, "sacred labor," which must include the possibilities for reinscription as an erotic, if not loving, act. These crossings, that is, are a "transitive equation," a way of thinking that even questions labor's sacredness precisely by keeping labor open as a question, a question extended by the invocation of "Work Song."[111] Oscar Brown Jr.'s lyrics to "Work Song" locate this labor on a chain gang, tacitly invoking conviction without due process, conviction for a crime of necessity, the criminalized act of stealing for sustenance once living off the land has become impossible.[112] Labor is a modality of "serving time," a modality referenced by Drennette's "monotonous marking of time—a corroborating but . . . complicating witness" that bespeaks "abject, alienating duration while the very manner of its production seemed intent on underscoring *strike*."[113] "Strike" is another turned word, referring to "would-be liberatory" labor action as much as discipline or labor itself, implicating the body's actions or withheld labor within juridical and social forms of discipline. It is a reminder that that the body's pleasure can be recuperated by a repressive state apparatus. The band, "*possessed* agents of iterativity," also mark time, repeating the head of "Work Song," at once extending the moment and refusing to let time pass, labor here also being a punning reference to postexpectancy.[114]

The balloons' blankness anticipates the "supple oneness" between band and audience, a graph of fulfillment "that no named aggregate enclosed or could caption."[115] "One" is an apparently singular pronoun that inscribes a collectivity, keeping open that strand of Mackey's poetics: every social unity passes through figuration, communicates itself *in*, rather than *through* language. Insofar as this oneness is available retroactively through narrative, it *is* a named aggregate, an effort to supply captions to the blank balloons, which themselves figure the blankness or contingency of an encounter. This oneness, as a tactical naming of the unnamable, is a revolutionary, orphic turn, participating in multiple, irreducible times without itself being timeless or necessary. That this oneness, and the feeling it describes, would be the impossible resolution of the planned and the accidental, the intentional and the aleatory, available only through the mediation of the record or narrative more generally, returns throughout the series. Joe Henderson's flubbed, premature two-note would-be unison riff on Andrew Hill's *Point of Departure*, a flub that becomes obvious as a flub only on replay, becomes the occasion for N.'s reflections on the links between repetition and necessity, repetition and experience, and the recording's vitality. By the end of the scene one is left with N.'s inverted Orpheus, uncertain whether one leads or one follows, the fragile, aleatory "community" formed through a repetitive, iterable experience, namely, the retroactive imputation to music and poetry of the orphic capacity to create and sustain erotic conjunctions, an imputation that temporarily lends them that power.

The audience's dance and N.'s posited "supple oneness" amounts to an encounter with the impossible: figuratively, the audience has an encounter with itself as something other than an aggregate of atomized individuals and achieves a synchronicity that excludes no one. Though the mechanical dance recapitulates the struggle with and for freedom following the end of slavery, highlighting the disciplining of the body that underscores the dance's being understood as freedom, tactical oneness suggests a reinscription of that discipline into another scene. The dance and the relay that moves the performance from "Sex Machine" to *cante jondo* to "Work Song" to *bulería*, from certain meaning to an invitation to articulate new meanings, suggest a turn away from the body's apocalyptic freight. The undecidable moment of song's origin remains always before us, not as a fulfillment of the past but as a cut back to that freedom time yet unfulfilled.

postscript

Destination . . . Out!
Experimentation, Aesthetics, and Racial Time

Sleet sheet of outfulness,
awayfulness,   numb,
                    long-
        fisted stir . . .   —Nathaniel Mackey

Bang/Bang Outishly. . .   —Amiri Baraka

Throughout *Freedom Time*, I have emphasized the resonances of black experimental writing, its opening new horizons of thinking by calling into question the grounds of knowledge. In this postscript, an afterword to argue for the continuing resonances of experimental texts, I extend my arguments about "the cut" in Nathaniel Mackey's work to more general claims about the poetics and politics of black experimental writing, its methodological chances and demands. Borrowing another of Mackey's terms, I want to consider the practice of "outfulness," as it helps to constitute and advance a larger contest over racial time, reimagining the connections between race and history and stressing forms of nonsynchronism in the present, both of which have been abiding issues in this book. To use a jazz idiom, black experimental writing represents an instance of "taking it out," a practice of "outfulness" cast as freedom. The phrase "taking it out," like so many idiomatic expressions, is polyvocal. On the one hand, it is an imperative to play the final chorus, including any special tag endings or cadenzas, and end the song. On the other, it refers to following a melodic, rhythmic, and harmonic logic that conflicts with prevailing aesthetic norms, to violating the notion of a single tonic or harmonic "home" so as to expand the basic structures of the tradition and allow for novel forms of musical expression, novel forms (and standards) of aesthetic competence. Commonly associated with players of "free" or "avant-garde" jazz, playing "out" has been an important tendency of African American musical traditions, serving as a means of challenging what W. E. B. Du Bois termed "the limitations of allowable thought," the ideological limits of thinking and imagining I have invoked throughout this book. Rather than casting intensity as rage or difficulty as resistance, I have instead stressed the production of "outfulness" as self-liberation from constraining norms and ideologies. But it is also self-liberating to combine aesthetic techniques, genres, and cultural materials in new ways. Experimental violations of established norms evince both dissatisfaction and the contingent extension of techniques into new areas of thought, feeling, and desire whose effects are not known in advance. The "blue" notes, smears, slurs, glissandi, and so on all mark instances of playing "outside" the Western tradition, as do the polyrhythms: each mark moments of transformation through importing "foreign" elements.

Just as those musical traditions rarely register in accounts of American avant-garde music, black experimental writing rarely receives attention in more general accounts of American experimentalism save as a footnote. It is important to acknowledge the ongoing production of a black experimental tradition even though scholars and critics of an unmarked experimental tradition have tacitly understood that tradition to be white, for doing so changes our sense of broader literary history. Part of the newness of black experimental writing comes from its novel combination of techniques, which I have argued rearticulate race and writing, pointing each toward new ways of imagining and thinking. If forms and genres encode social and historical meaning, then attention to repurposed techniques as part of a larger poetics is a necessary step to analyzing the politics of literature. To start to see the full radical potential of black experimental writing, to some degree analogous with "out" playing (and emerging at roughly the same time), requires starting from recognizable structures—genres and techniques—and interrogating precisely how a work "takes it out": how it violates readers' expectations and literary conventions to make qualitatively new statements. But it also requires registering the particularity of black demands for alternative modes of attention without assuming one knows in advance how to answer that demand. Understood in historical terms, we might think the black demand for restitution in terms of the unimaginable itself, which Paul Gilroy calls the "slave sublime." Read in slightly different terms, the demand is for a share of the future, and for a future conceived on different terms. In either case, I have tried to link the concept of a black demand to another way of thinking and imagining the terms and conditions of our being together.

One of the most important voices for seeing and hearing the kind of broad revision I have in mind is the recently departed Amiri Baraka, who heard in Albert Ayler's playing, for example, the sounds of the black church and heard in the black church not only refuge and spiritual re-creation but sounds yet more out. More than that, he consistently figured black writing as doing something more than "resisting" or "subverting" nonblack traditions. In his famous poem "Black Art" he intones, "Clean out the world for virtue and love, | Let there be no love poems written | until love can exist freely and | cleanly."[1] The poem clears a space for the love it participates in. It clears a space for black love and unencumbered being. Baraka calls for a poetry of getting and being free, a poetry that risks defining and redefining freedom. This is the tradition of black experimental writing I have analyzed throughout this book, stressing its radical, world-making inventiveness—and radical, transformative new modes of politics that help us reclaim past techniques and the dreams they carry as a future. If Amiri Baraka seems a conspicuous absence from this book, his challenging writing—poems and criticism—inform my approach throughout.

I have advanced a critical methodology attuned to the intergeneric borrowing, mixing, and transformation of techniques at the same time that I have considered the positive articulations of freedom and alternative forms of community figured by the work, asking what new thinking might literature make available, what new worlds it might make seem inhabitable. My question has been and continues to be what literature does *as* literature and what it does within the domain of the literary to affect the world if it is not as directly political as, say, the slave narratives were or if it is not imputed to be political, as, fore example, Kenneth Warren argues black writing was through the period of Jim Crow. My basic answer throughout this book is that its political value is in the questions it raises, in its call for thinking beyond the prevailing assumptions of the institutions that shape and limit thought in a given moment, in its "outfulness." We do not study the slave narratives just to learn about slavery or earlier moments of capitalism but also to glean the unrealized visions of freedom they encode and unearth something of the broader culture within which they emerged. We do not continue to study something under the name "African American" or "African diaspora" literature to understand an earlier period's politics of racialized authorship but because there is something more, a politics that exceeds the ideological confines of its moment, as I have tried to demonstrate with my reading of W. E. B. Du Bois in the introduction. A historical approach to poetics can tell us what a particular set of techniques might have meant in its moment, and a more general historicist approach will tell us a good deal about the larger placement of a text within its moment. I have learned from and used both approaches throughout this book. But I have also stressed that a text is not just its ideology or a token of its social order and is valuable for more than the forms of life it may model. The uses of a text does not tell us all that we want to know about the politics of literature and black imagination.

Simultaneously, a formalism that does not understand literary techniques and genres as historical takes too much for granted and may reproduce consensus rooted in erroneous assumptions. More than themes and topical references, form—or, to use a more old-fashioned term, "style"—is where the literary text is most historical, making poetics a valuable critical method with which to raise questions of literary politics as I define them: the thinking literature promotes, the new aesthetic communities it seeks to bring into being, the questions it raises. At once idiosyncratic and historical, style— those sensual qualities of language and novel usages through which literature evolves—seems to me primarily a matter of organizing and combining techniques, which are rooted in common forms of life and norms of expression. Considering the historical situation of both race and techniques, I have stressed literary politics as a means of negotiating larger political situations including the social meanings of black authorship. Most of my analyses in the preceding pages start from the assumption that this innovative work draws on and transforms past techniques and use the difference from an older technique—concrete poetry, the lyric mode, African American music—to conceptualize the nature of experimentation. Each of those older techniques, insofar as it names a shared *poiesis* or way of reading (or both), refers to shared ways of inhabiting the world and mutual intelligibility. The work rides that division between speech and noise. To "take it out" risks being mistaken for producing mere noise, for being undisciplined, unserious, or in short not "one of us." I propose instead that we see these novel ways of resolving technical problems—representation, expression, the range of acceptable metaphors or limitations of allowable complexity—as indicative of writing that *thinks* differently.

By "thinking," I refer to the ways literature works the given—prevailing ideologies, a history of techniques and genres—to approach what remains unthought and unthinkable within the regimes of common sense I have referred to throughout *Freedom Time*. *Poiesis*, as "altering force," is the medium of literature's thinking, whatever other meanings form may have.[2] This, for me, is the political meaning of poetics, which simply refers to the processes of making the text and those that surround that making: insofar as it produces literary effects and extends the range of effects that count as literary, *poiesis* is where literature may change the "sensory fabric" that defines a particular way of being together. *Poiesis* is where the conflicting punctualities of a text—those to whom it addresses itself now, those to whom it will have addressed itself, ways of understanding the "now"—are put into motion. Tracing the interaction of techniques and theme can change the terms of hermeneutic analysis, revealing new challenges and questions than those we may have brought to the text. As I have stressed throughout my analyses, each era dreams its different "worlds of tomorrow" in the shadow of the unrealized dreams of tomorrow from the past. They resonate in our own present, alongside our own configurations of inhabitable futures.

Du Bois seeks such freedom in *The Souls of Black Folk* in the rhetorical strategies I briefly discussed in the introduction and in his musical epigraphs. Recalling an earlier era when one might entertain oneself and one's company by playing the piano in one's parlor, those epigraphs signal the repetition, temporal displacement, and especially the differentiation citation suggests. In this sense, they are a textual analogue for "playing out": citing and reconfiguring another era's texts to create new, intergeneric texts, while reminding us of the still unrealized freedom toward which the spirituals sang.[3] Here, we can see a similarity between Baraka's project and certain way of reading Du Bois as concerned with transformations more fundamental than a narrowly conceived "propaganda" would suggest, especially if we recall that the sound implied is not simultaneous with the inscription of the musical bars. That disjuncture, like Du Bois's reclaiming these songs from minstrel imitation, re-marks the promise of being both "a Negro" and "an American," the former term being wholly contingent upon the latter and that the latter having no meaning apart from the former. Yet, inescapably, minstrel imitation and plantation nostalgia conditioned Du Bois's readers' to mishear these songs and their unfulfilled desire for freedom. The challenge is to think the ancestral as a demand, without the reassurance that we are the ones the ancestors might have intended, and to see in past cultural forms the call to a future anterior that may still be yet to come.

Throughout *Freedom Time*, I have stressed the ways the poetics of black experimental writing engages the norms and conventions of writing in order to configure new ways of thinking, including new ways of conceptualizing the present, and futures imagined on other terms. In these final pages, I want to stress this way of reworking past techniques within a broader reworking of temporal concepts and givens to articulate a different understanding of what Michael Hanchard calls "racial time." Hanchard argues that history, imposed modes of time, and the "temporal understanding of racial and colonial orders" transect the space-time of the African diaspora, down to the temporally understood regimes that divide history into "epochs of slavery, freedom, and emancipation, and in the post–World War II period of civil rights, black nationalist and anticolonial movements."[4] "Racial time" as political practice involves an "appropriation of time," a collective action wherein blacks "seiz[e] another's time and mak[e] it [their] own."[5] For my purposes, this can happen at different scales from designating "outfulness," the New Negro, the New Thing, the New Black Poetry, or more recently the New Black Aesthetic and the subsequent "post-"s, all of which make a case for the political urgency of the present, as they highlight something in the past that has grown outmoded or oppressive. While I have used the term "appropriation" throughout this book to refer to making cultural practices into objects of knowledge, Hanchard uses the term to name the act of seizing and repurposing the "means of culturo-temporal production." Hanchard's account helpfully reminds us of the copresence of races in constructions (if not conceptions) of modernity and that race is a temporal concept that attempts to order contingent differences into racialized destinies. I argue that this literature asks us to think beyond the limits of the age insofar as it seizes a role in defining this age, revealing simply that another order remains possible.

I have linked the emergence of these particular modes of experimentation in the postsegregation, postcolonial era to a larger demand for freedom, to a demand for more broadly defined forms of freedom, suggesting some of the ways these authors' work responds to the need not just for new forms of politics but also new temporal regimes, insofar as regimes of governmentality are also temporal orders, referring to a shared set of myths of the past that set the terms of imagining the future. To my invocation of the demand for a share of the future and for a future conceived on different terms indexed in the repurposing of existing techniques, I would add a rearticulation of racial time. It does not seem coincidental how many albums of "the New Thing" refer to changes in temporal order, from Eric Dolphy's *Out to Lunch* to Jackie McLean's *Destination . . . Out!* The jazz player's "taking it out"—not strictly a refusal of traditional aesthetics insofar as it relies on (and displays a deep knowledge) of the structures of such aesthetics—refers to a set of techniques reworked with experimental approaches to history and to time in mind that begin to fulfill W. E. B. Du Bois's injunction that black art "let this world be beautiful," implying new ways of understanding and experiencing beauty.

By way of a closing gesture, I want to propose a history of the period rooted in a radical idea of beauty related to changing the very grounds of experience. Famously, in his 1926 lecture "The Criteria of Negro Art," Du Bois linked beauty with propaganda, a term he did not define and which critics have typically taken to refer to positive representation. Propaganda, etymologically related to "seeds" and "propagation," is the tactical means through which Du Bois links aesthetics and politics, rewriting the conditions of the sensible while making beauty itself, in Russ Castronovo's terms, "an area for crafting hegemony."[6] One could chart the politics of contemporary African American poetry through the term "beauty." In 1966, Robert Hayden, as we have seen, defined poetry as "the *beauty* of perception given form" before calling it the "art of saying the impossible." Almost contemporaneously, in 1969, Clarence Major, in his introductory essay to *The New Black Poetry* argued that a vision of the world rooted in an emergent, radical black aesthetic and "black vision" "broadens and deepens the beauty of this nation, of the world," which, like Anselm Hollo's praise for LeRoi Jones, would advance a " 'new beauty' in his native America."[7] A few years later, in 1972, Stephen E. Henderson argued that "literature . . . is the verbal organization of experience into beautiful forms," though both "beauty" and "form" are "bound up with the truth of a people's history, as they see it themselves."[8] It is unlikely that these authors intend exactly the same concept with the term "beauty." However, although Larry Neal criticizes Du Bois for being insufficiently radical, his idea that literature could be integral to aligning a community's life and history, that is must be aimed at the "destruction of the double-consciousness," owes a debt to Du Bois's claim that black art must "let this world be beautiful" and to Baraka's "cleaned out" world.[9]

In the command to "let this world be beautiful," I want to emphasize the capacity (and obligation) to make and to change the grounds of evaluation and experience. The designation "this world," for instance, points to the historicity of our aesthetic categories. Though Du Bois refers to the NAACP as "group of radicals trying to bring new things into the world," his insistence on "this world" in my reading indicates that if the world will remain constant, beauty will come through human actions to change the sensorium. Marx's oft-cited claim that the "*forming* of the five senses is a labour of the entire history of the world down to the present" names a reciprocal, historical interaction between the world and the senses.[10] As Susan Stewart has argued, Marx "considered the senses to be both shaped and shaping forces, productive of forms, influenced by and influencing historical developments in the species beyond the agency of individual subjects."[11] That dialectical sense of the relationship between the senses and history, interpreted through the understanding that the meaning of the senses—aesthetics—is similarly historical, is behind my own understanding of beauty.

Within Du Bois's argument, then, beauty is both product and spur to ethical and political action, redemptive—bringing forward what would otherwise be lost to history—as well as creative, initiating a demand that cannot be fulfilled as such. "I am one," he asserts, "who tells the truth and exposes evil and seeks with Beauty and for Beauty to set the world right." The artwork, which Du Bois's lecture primarily identifies with literature, intends an audience that will have encountered it "beyond the narrow now."[12] Propaganda in the narrow sense might be exposing evil and telling the truth, but linked with beauty, it sews seeds to a future, addressing a speculative, unimaginable audience. More figuratively, propaganda orients us to a possible future, establishing "roots" in this present, attempting to subvert or elude the calculable possibilities of the present. Linked with beauty, propaganda makes possible a thinking of the future (and a redemptive, undisciplined rethinking of the past and present) by departing from the boundaries of the sayable and thinkable. Propaganda is seeking emancipation, but has not yet escaped.[13] It orients itself toward freedom, addresses an audience that will have been.

Producing a sense of "fugitive," unfulfilled time, changing the conditions of the beautiful, black experimental writing presents a challenge to that conception of time as a succession of static presents and appropriable moments. Mixing and combining these epistemological modes and aesthetic techniques, it creates and multiplies temporal registers. In so doing, the world may appear to us again not just as a historical outcome but also an unfinished project, like freedom itself. This work, led by beauty and seeking with beauty "to set the world right," is compatible with "tell[ing] the truth and expos[ing] evil."[14] Telling the truth and exposing evil are only part of the story and are ineffective without some positive sense of beauty, the beauty of this world and that to come. This point bears repeating: politics worthy of the name requires not just dismantling what we oppose but engaging in the complicated processes of making a new world together. The concept of racial time understood as political practice requires an aesthetic component related to the terms of our living together, to our partitions of intelligibility from noise, to our discontent with the present, and to our demand for some future moment when we may yet be freer.

Notes

INTRODUCTION. Visions of a Liberated Future

1. In these opening sentences, I am drawing on Elizabeth Grosz's "The Time of Thought" and Erica Hunt's bracing "Notes for an Oppositional Poetics." Hunt's discussion of co-optation is especially helpful: "Opposition is alternately demonized or accommodated through partial concessions without a meaningful alteration of dominant culture's own terms," she writes, while "opposition is characterized as destructive to the social body and to itself," which has the effect of reducing conflicts to matters requiring policing rather than politics (202). Hunt's dialectical sense of opposition informs my own sense that resistance alone is an inadequate slogan for considering literary politics, and it informs my methodological privileging of poetics as historical and future oriented. Merely referring to "resistance" without defining a positive aim can make the resistance itself a difference that makes no difference.

2. In addition to Kelley's text, I have in mind Richard Iton's *In Search of the Black Fantastic* and, from a different perspective, Hortense Spillers's essay "The Idea of Black Culture," which sees that formation itself as one all the more necessary in our postsegregation moment. None of these works is nostalgic for segregation; rather, I draw from them the importance of beginning one's analysis of culture and race from their particular moment and articulation and of including the shaping "ideas" that inform their articulation and circulation.

3. Timothy Yu persuasively argues that "the aesthetic and the social are inseparable" the "question of race" assuming a central place in "the constitution of *any* American avant-garde" especially after 1970, and that an "avant-garde is an aesthetic *and* a social grouping, defined as much by its formation of a distinctive kind of community as by its revolutionary aesthetics" (*Race and the Avant-Garde*, 1–2). Michael North situates an awareness of race within avant-garde practice earlier in *The Dialect of Modernism*, demonstrating the ways racially marked vernaculars spurred avant-garde practice. In a different register, although Fred Moten and George Lewis have pushed back against the notion that blackness and the avant-garde are mutually exclusive, there has still been relatively little scholarly attention to the practices of black experimentalism, with the exception of Aldon Nielsen's scholarship and Evie Shockley's *Renegade Poetics*. New scholarship of the Black Arts movement, including James Smethurst's *The Black Arts Movement*, Margo Crawford and Gail Collins's *New Thoughts on the Black Arts Movement*, Cheryl Clarke's *After Mecca*, and Howard Rambsy's *The Black Arts Enterprise and the Production of African American Poetry*, augurs renewed interest in the experimental writing of the Black Arts era and the communities that have supported it.

4. Foucault, *The Birth of Biopolitics*, 77.

5. Richard Wright's 1939 "A Blueprint for Negro Writing" is an early, influential instance of this argument, later taken up by members of the Black Arts movement.

6. Melas, *All the Difference in the World*, 43.

7. Ibid.

8. Edwards, "The Uses of Diaspora," 55. I am also drawing on his expanded arguments in *The Practice of Diaspora*.

9. Ibid., 64.

10. Hall, "Race, Articulation and Societies Structured in Dominance," 38.

11. Macherey, *A Theory of Literary Production*, 46.

12. Fred Moten's *In the Break* troubles the presumptive whiteness of the avant-garde, and George E. Lewis's *A Power Greater Than Itself* provides a very compelling genealogy of the historical processes that led to black and white experimental movements developing separately in places like New York and Chicago. Likewise, I would highlight several recent studies of cross-cultural modernist and contemporary "transnational" poetics important to my own articulation of black experimental writing, especially the notion that literature offers resources for reshaping rather than expressing identities. Charles W. Pollard's *New World Modernisms* traces the relationship between modernism (figured by T. S. Eliot) and Caribbean poetry, arguing that Caribbean writers engage with and transform Eliot's terms rather than simply adapt a reified or oppressive modernist form. In a similar, broader study, Anita Patterson traces lines of influence between Eliot, Saint-John Perse, Derek Walcott, Langston Hughes, Wilson Harris, and others in *Race, American Literature, and Transnational Modernism*. Considering the later twentieth century, Paul Naylor's important study *Poetic Investigations: Singing the Holes of History* takes up the relationship between experimental poetics and history, comparing Nathaniel Mackey, M. NourbeSe Philip, Lyn Hejinian, Susan Howe, and Kamau Brathwaite. In *Writing Plural Worlds in Contemporary U.S. Poetry: Innovative Identities*, Jim Keller takes contemporary U.S. poetry as an occasion to consider the relations between "the avant-garde of marginalized social groups" and a "plural-world" philosophy (13) as a counterdiscourse to Western universalism. Jahan Ramazani considers the interrelation of English as medium and institution and traces connections between Anglophone poets in *A Transnational Poetics*. Finally, in *Nations of Nothing but Poetry*, Matthew Hart argues for a "synthetic vernacular" through which socially marginalized authors can negotiate what I am here calling a politics of expression.

13. Here I am drawing on Virginia Jackson's notion of lyricization, whereby the expressive romantic lyric becomes model for all adjacent poetic genres, affecting which poems come to be canonized and which poets and forms come to be neglected. See *Dickinson's Misery*.

14. Using the fraught term "appropriation," I follow such thinkers as Roger Chartier and Jon Cruz. In *Culture on the Margins*, Cruz's study of the role of the African American spiritual in the larger "cultural turn" that created culture as a semiautonomous sphere separate from the political sphere, Cruz argues that the process of understanding social practices makes those into objects of knowledge, which then "become part of the constitution of cultural realities, and thus worthy of appropriation. A culture's appropriation of objects thus refracts culture as practice rather than culture as already embodied in material things" (214n36). I would distinguish appropriation, then, from co-optation, which Erica Hunt succinctly defines as the attempts of the dominant culture to "transfer its own partiality onto the opposition it tries to suppress" (202).

15. Marjorie Perloff, for instance, recently claimed that in the 1990s "Language poetry felt compelled to be more inclusive with respect to gender, race, and ethnic diversity" and so

made room for female and nonwhite writers without questioning why nonwhite, nonmale writers had not been more involved in the first place. Nor is it clear what would account for the strangely personified Language poetry's moment of largesse (or what those writers had been doing before), but in Barrett Watten's account, they were engaged in a naïve "expressivist" poetics located in "the self-presence of the expressive subject." See Perloff, "Poetry on the Brink," and Watten, "The Turn to Language and the 1960s."

16. Moten, *In the Break*, 33. I am here indebted to Michael North's arguments in *The Dialect of Modernism*.

17. Quoted in Hayes and Shockley, "African American Experimental Poetry Forum," 130.

18. I am again drawing on Stuart Hall's concept of articulation, which he develops from Althusser and Marx. Hall critiques theories that assume race to be simply part of the "superstructure" that will be overcome dialectically with the overcoming of class antagonism and that thus treat it as secondary or external to economic or class concerns: "Dominated subjects—those subordinated ethnic groups or 'races' . . . live their relation to their real conditions of existence . . . in and through the imaginary representations of a racist interpellation and . . . come to experience themselves as 'the inferiors,' *les autres*," as a consequence of those structures ("Race, Articulation and Societies Structured in Dominance," 57).

19. Rancière, *The Politics of Literature*, 4.

20. Paul Gilroy, "'After the Love has Gone,'" 55, my emphasis.

21. Neal, "Black Art and Black Liberation," 54–56.

22. Du Bois, *Writings*, 536–37.

23. Baraka, *Black Music*, 207. Somewhat surprisingly, Baraka does not note that "Blowing in the Wind" derives from the spiritual "No More Auction Block."

24. See especially Shamoon Zamir's *Dark Voices* (113–68) for an account of the prevalent, contradictory American Hegelianisms and an argument linking W. E. B. Du Bois to them.

25. Gooding-Williams, *In the Shadow of Du Bois*, 97. Despite Du Bois's avowed political commitment, his position looks different apprehended from the point of view of his writing.

26. Kelley, "Notes on Deconstructing 'The Folk,'" 1402.

27. I have in mind the essay "Scattered Speculations on the Question of Value," in which, beginning with the necessity of theoretical subject predication (i.e., understanding the subject in either "idealist" terms as the subject of consciousness and intendedness toward the world or in "materialist" terms, as Marx does), Spivak critiques structuralist accounts of Marx. She singles out Jean-Joseph Goux's posited isomorphism between the money form and Lacan's account of genital sexual organization: as money is the universal equivalent (but not part of the commodity function), so the phallus is a kind of universal equivalent—a principle of exchange—in the libidinal economy. Amy Villarejo's reading of Spivak's argument has influenced mine, and her arguments, especially regarding the ways attempting to bring "the" lesbian into view as a nominal person (or thing) conceals—or veils—the subject at the moment of revealing her, greatly inform my arguments throughout this book, especially my conception of the adjectival "black" in "black experimental writing" (*Lesbian Rule*, 27–36).

28. Benston, *Performing Blackness*, 5.

29. In different terms, double consciousness is a conflict between the metaphysical and the exegetical, turning on the aporia where the fixed location and function of race might be imagined. I draw the terms "metaphysical" and "exegetical" from a poetic "debate" between Robert Penn Warren and Sterling A. Brown that Houston A. Baker Jr. restages in his *Mod-*

ernism and the Harlem Renaissance. In the poem "Pondy Woods," Robert Penn Warren wrote "'Nigger, your breed ain't metaphysical.' Brown's response: 'Cracker, your breed ain't exegetical'" (72).

30. Coleridge, "Shakespeare, a Poet Generally," 55. Coleridge contrasts "mechanic form" and "organic form," the latter of which "shapes as it develops." His argument is specifically about organic poetics, and thus my citation in this context is slightly misleading. However, in the sentences that follow he praises organic form for its proximity to nature. It would seem to follow that the perfection of organic form inheres in its organic connection to nature and thus that the work is fundamentally expressive or representative of nature.

31. Izenberg, *Being Numerous* 54. Izenberg's call to consider the "role that poetry can play in social thought" is salutary. Explicitly, Izenberg sees poetry as "an ontological project: a civilizational wish to reground the concept and value of *the person*" (1, his emphasis). This commits him to an ahistorical view of poetry and makes embarrassing anything that doesn't rise to the level of abstraction implied by "personhood," which he seeks to recover from a recent history of denying personhood in the Holocaust. Of course, the problem with personhood is that, given its place within legal discourses, it is always subject to sudden revision and exclusion. Left to fall back on a notion of personhood that is "minimal" and "universal," the "new humanism" resembles the old, for while the notion of humanism "tolerat[es] no exemptions or exclusions" (4), only a few may speak in its name.

32. I am indebted to Lytle Shaw for the phrase "social languages" as shorthand for the myriad ways identity enters literature without subsuming everything else under it and as a subtle reminder that language is always social whatever other claims we would make for it.

33. Izenberg, *Being Numerous*, 4.

34. Warren, *What Was African American Literature?*, 10.

35. Larry Neal indicts the concept of double consciousness for its "general lack of clarity about how to proceed" in his concluding essay to *Black Fire*, "And Shine Swam On." Neal finds that needed clarity in black nationalism, which acknowledges the "political status of over ten million people of African descent who, against their wills, were being forced to eke out an existence in the United States" and resolves matters of representation through expressive politics (641). Du Bois, as Neal acknowledges, worried about the same thing throughout his life, asking at one point, "But how far did we really represent and voice them [i.e., black men] and how far are we were we merely floating in the air of our dreams and ambitions? . . . Who shall say until Time itself tells?" (Du Bois, *Reader*, 667).

36. Du Bois, *Writings*, 365.

37. Derrida, *Margins*, 55, his emphasis.

38. Du Bois, *Writings*, 363, my emphasis.

39. In both *Dusk of Dawn* and *Autobiography* he writes only that he has written of this incident previously, reproducing its performative silence.

40. Du Bois, *Writings*, 363–64.

41. I thank Gerald Jaynes for pointing out that Du Bois's sequence of races duplicates Hegel's sequence in *Lectures on the Philosophy of History.*

42. James C. Hall offers an invaluable account of this conference in *Mercy, Mercy Me.* Among other things, he points out the ways David Llorens's account silences Margaret Walker's (and Arna Bontemps's) contributions to the panel and underscores the masculinist terms of the reception (52).

43. Killens, quoted in Llorens, "Seeking a New Image," 54–68; Du Bois, *Writings*, 364.

44. One famous instance of this is the black aesthetic of the mid-1960s, which was in part a return to black folk forms on the grounds that this would result in better black art because it would be further from the corrupting influence of white culture. In the wake of that moment, Evie Shockley proposes attention instead to the current era's "'black aesthetics,' plural: a multifarious, contingent, non-delimited complex of strategies that African American writers may use to negotiate gaps between their artistic goals and the operation of race in the production, dissemination, and reception of their writing" (*Renegade Poetics*, 9). A plural "black aesthetics"—an alternative to the expressivist black aesthetic, which was a hermeneutic as much as an aesthetic program—provides a very useful lens through which to think the different ways black authors have called different aesthetic communities into being, without reducing the texts to artifacts.

45. Llorens, "Seeking a New Image," 62, my emphasis.

46. Brooks, foreword, 13.

47. Ibid.

48. Llorens, "Seeking a New Image," 62.

49. Ibid., 63.

50. "We who are dark can see America in a way that white Americans cannot," Du Bois argued. "And seeing our country thus, are we satisfied with its present goals and ideals?" (*Writings*, 993). Though "The Criteria of Negro Art" is famous for Du Bois's claim that "all art is propaganda and ever must be," Du Bois also gives art the more ambiguous task to "let this world be beautiful" (*Writings*, 993, 995).

51. Hall, "Race, Articulation and Societies Structured in Dominance," 55.

52. Nielsen, *Black Chant*, 7–8.

53. These phrases are from Stephen E. Henderson's introduction to *Understanding the New Black Poetry* and Clarence Major's introduction to *The New Black Poetry*. The question of knowledge is not insignificant: Major writes that early in his publishing career "several journals, some located in the South, printed my work without realizing I am black and their editors later experienced deep frustration when this incidental information came their way" (18).

54. To some extent, my methodology is compatible with Stephen Best and Sharon Marcus's notion of "surface": "what is evident, perceptible, apprehensible in texts; what is neither hidden nor hiding; what, in the geometrical sense, has length and breadth but no thickness, and therefore covers no depth. A surface is what insists on being looked *at* rather than what we must train ourselves to see *through*" ("Surface Reading," 9). Unlike Best and Marcus, I have no interest in advancing a "new formalism," and I am not wary of symptomatic reading or totalizing discourses. Attention to the surface of black experimental writing encourages interrogation of the specific ways and meanings of its avoidance of conceptual or aesthetic closure.

55. Rancière, *The Emancipated Spectator*, 56.

56. Fred Moten makes a similar argument in *In the Break*, seeing blackness itself as a disruptive force that prevents the self-enclosure and self-identity of the concepts of Western philosophy and modernity, submitting an ever-unanswered demand or "objection." His conception of a black radical tradition, meaningfully informed by Cedric Robinson's *Black Marxism*, enables my own study of black experimental writing to the degree that it makes such a tradition visible.

57. Rancière's term is "dis-identification": "a multiplication of connections and disconnections that reframe the relation between bodies, the world they live in and the way in which

they are 'equipped' to adapt to it" (*The Emancipated Spectator*, 72). I prefer "desubjection" because one of the effects of this literary "call" is the sense that what is being addressed is a community that does not yet exist. I draw the notion of undisciplined thought as a radical unlearning of categories from Grant Farred's engagement with Heidegger in his essay " 'Science Does Not Think': The No-Thought of the Discipline."

58. I thank the anonymous reader for inspiring this sentence.

CHAPTER 1. Broken Witness

1. I am drawing on Rancière, *The Emancipated Spectator*, 60.

2. Mitchell, *The Language of Images*, 9, 274.

3. Mitchell's more radical formulation is relevant here: "In literature, our sense of continuity, sequence, and linear progression is not nonspatial because it is temporal. Continuity and sequentiality are spatial images based in the schema of the unbroken line or surface; the experience of simultaneity or discontinuity is simply based in different kinds of spatial images from those involved in continuous, sequential experiences of time" (*The Language of Images*, 274).

4. I draw the term "ancestrality" from "Ghostwriting," Gayatri Chakravorty Spivak's reading of Derrida's *Specters of Marx*. Relating hauntology to the Sioux ghost dance, Spivak suggests that "the 'end' of the ghost dance—if one can speak of such a thing—is to make the past a future, as it were—the future anterior, not a future present. . . . Now we can see that this is an alternative way of reading Marx—relating him to an ancestrality that can appear as a future" (70). Throughout my analyses, I use the term also to mark ways of considering the past that do not have it lead to us but that ask us to rethink our understandings of who we are in the present as a line through which to consider alternate forms of futurity against the "end of history."

5. De Campos, "Concrete Poetry," 213.

6. Marcuse, *An Essay on Liberation*, 38, cited in Perloff, *Unoriginal Genius*, 52, who in turn is cited by Bayard, *The New Poetics in Canada and Quebec*, 171. The perennial citation of Marcuse in concrete poetry scholarship indicates a long history of ascribing utopian aspirations to disparate concrete poetics and of voicing a suspicion of those aspirations. Perloff emphasizes Marcuse's skepticism toward these programs of mental liberation and suggests that concrete poetry anticipates Language poetry's "attention to the anagrammatic and paragrammatic play *inherent in language*" rather than to "such concretist elements as font, color, and spacing" (this attention being one of the hallmarks of what she terms a "more adequate poetics") that, history has shown, are themselves vulnerable to being subsumed by capitalist regimes of experience (52). With respect to presence, Johanna Drucker, for instance, has argued in the context of an analysis of what she calls the "visual performance" of poetic work that "*the visual performance of a work, rather than being about the presence of the author/reader, is about the presence of a poem*" ("Visual Performance of the Poetic Text," 131), a claim I take up in the context of my discussion of Philip's poem sequence *Zong!*

7. Madhubuti, *Directionscore*, 85.

8. Baraka, *Black Music*, 184. Baraka is discussing Muhammad Ali's style, but the broader context is his identifying rhythm and blues as participating in a "changing same" impulse that informs the culture as "the exact replication of The Black Man In The West" (180). This is not exclusively a U.S. conception: in a later reformulation of his notion of "nation-language," which I discuss in chapter 2, Kamau Brathwaite claims it as part of a cultural line extending from Baraka back through Sterling Brown, Aimé Césaire, and "the Black Church generally" (*Ark*, xv).

9. Henderson, *Understanding*, 68.

10. Fred Moten teases out a potential link between Black Arts theorists, especially Amiri Baraka, and Martin Heidegger, at length in *In the Break*, 87–149. It is no accident that a group of black experimental writers at Howard University in the 1970s called itself the "Dasein group." My own linkage of them has to do with their sense of spirit as discussed in the introduction and with the importance of the concept of authenticity to both.

11. Heidegger, *Being and Time*, 56.

12. Draper, "Concrete Poetry," 334. Draper goes on to cite Dom Sylvester Houédard's claim that the origins of concrete poetry are in treating words "as friends, not slaves—as holy not débris," a distinction that resonates with Philip's turn to concrete poetics in *Zong!*

13. Waldrop, "A Basis of Concrete Poetry," 57.

14. I am condensing and mobilizing part of Jacques Derrida's reading of Husserl (and Heidegger) in *Edmund Husserl's "The Origin of Geometry,"* 34–51.

15. Hayes, *Hip Logic*, 13.

16. Vendler, *The Art of Shakespeare's Sonnets*, 19.

17. Omi and Winant, *Racial Formation in the United States*, 55.

18. Eugen Gomringer's famous (and frequently cited) "Silencio," for example, prints the word "silencio" in three five-word columns, omitting the third "silencio" in the middle column, thereby creating a blank space in the center that connotes the silence the words designate. The effect of the poem depends on our reading the blank space as a signifying gap, but once we do so, space and text effectively cancel each other out because they mean the same thing. It seems superfluous to ask what or who is being silenced, whether this is the spiritual silence of meditation or the imposed silence of murder. The poem is not, however, "about" silence—one could achieve comparable effects with the word "blanco" or "espacio."

19. Jerome McGann argues in *Black Riders* that Dante Gabriel Rossetti is among the first Anglophone poets to imagine a function for the spatial arrangement of elements in a poem other than emphasizing its oral/aural features.

20. I take this definition from Draper, "Concrete Poetry," 330.

21. I am drawing on Marjorie Perloff's arguments in *Unoriginal Genius*, 50–75.

22. Fredric Jameson defines an "ideologeme" as "the smallest intelligible unit of the essentially antagonistic collective discourse of social classes" (*The Political Unconscious*, 76).

23. Bayard, *The New Poetics in Canada and Quebec*, 178.

24. Young, "Signs of Repression," 37.

25. Pritchard, *EECCHHOOEESS*, 28.

26. Clüver, "Reflections on Verbivocovisual Ideograms," 138.

27. Pritchard has more paradigmatically concrete poems, such as "VIA" in *EECCH OOEESS*, which, for example, prints the word "spilling" upside down on one page, then backward on the opposite page. He also wrote (or designed) enigmatic shape poems like "#," which composes a capital *A* from multiple lowercase *z*s, and ":" and ".-.-.-.," which create abstract graphic structures using only punctuation marks. Those poems are collected in Adam David Miller's *DICES; or, Black Bones*.

28. Nielsen, *Black Chant*, 140.

29. Thomas, "The Shadow World," 54–55.

30. Pritchard, *The Matrix*, 30.

31. Because many of the poets I quote in this book use slashes in their poems, I use a vertical line (|) to indicate line breaks.

32. Cited in Nielsen, *Black Chant*, 13. Nielsen makes much of that latter claim as proto-poststructuralist and as evidence of a moment prior to "the all too common assumption that experimental approaches to expression and theorized reading are somehow white things."

33. Jameson, *Postmodernism*, 146, his emphasis.

34. Claudia Rankine, whose work I discuss in chapter 3, has a wry moment that touches on this phenomenon in *Don't Let Me Be Lonely*, when a speaker watches a commercial for the mood-altering Paxil: "Parataxis, I think first, but then I wonder, for what, for what does it wait? For life, I guess" (29).

35. I draw the notion of an aesthetic break from Rancière, *The Emancipated Spectator*, 51–82.

36. Pritchard, *The Matrix*, 48.

37. Ibid.

38. Ibid., 87–95.

39. Philip, *A Genealogy of Resistance*, 120. Philip's proposed solution to this dilemma is fashioning "a tongue | split—two times two times two | into | poly & | multi & | semi | vocali-ties" (121).

40. Philip, *She Tries Her Tongue*, 15.

41. Ibid., 15–16.

42. Ibid., 12.

43. Philip, *A Genealogy of Resistance*, 120.

44. Kinnahan, *Lyric Interventions*, 110.

45. Davies, *Black Women, Writing and Identity*, 163.

46. Philip, *She Tries Her Tongue*, 17.

47. Ibid., 12.

48. The number of Africans drowned aboard the *Zong* is far from a settled matter, with the number being put between 123 and 150. I draw 133 from Ian Baucom's account: sixty of the Africans (and seven of the crew) died at sea. On subsequent days, the ship's crew handcuffed and threw fifty-four slaves into the ocean, then handcuffed and threw overboard forty-three more (one managed to climb back aboard), then twenty six were brought on deck; sixteen were thrown overboard, ten jumped. "One hundred thirty-three beings thrown or driven overboard over a period of three days. One survivor" (*Specters of the Atlantic*, 129).

49. Hartman, "Venus in Two Acts," 9.

50. Philip, *She Tries Her Tongue*, 90.

51. Ibid., 98. Philip cites these lines in *Zong!*, 207.

52. Philip, "Fugues, Fragments and Fissures," 1.

53. Philip, *Zong!*, 207.

54. Walvin, *Black Ivory*, 16.

55. Ibid.

56. "Ontopology" is Jacques Derrida's term for "an axiomatics linking indissociably the ontological value of present-being [*on*] to its *situation*, to the stable and presentable determi-nation of a locality, the *topos* of territory, native soil, city, body in general" (*Specters of Marx*, 103).

57. Philip, *Zong!*, 211. This language is from the court record of *Gregson v. Gilbert*.

58. Philip, *A Genealogy of Resistance*, 124–25.

59. Philip, *Zong!*, 199.

60. Philip, "*Zong #1*."

61. Baucom offers a tangentially relevant and compelling interpretation of insurance

value as a notion that "annuls the object, abolishes it as a bearer of value, and so frees it from the degradation of thingly existence" by making the vicissitudes of that existence themselves objects in which one can invest. Insurance value itself becomes the abstract, surrogate object: a "pure" instantiation of value as ideal, achieving an almost autonomy complete autonomy from use value understood as bound up in the bodies of the workers (or slaves) or the objects exchanged but rather located in the abstract ideals of exchange in general. See *Specters of the Atlantic*, 95–107.

62. Philip, *Zong!*, 23.

63. Philip, *Zong!*, 5.

64. Martin, "The Language of Trauma," 303.

65. In a terrific analysis of *Zong!* (and Douglas Kearney's "Swimchant for Nigger Merfolk (An Aquaboogie Set in Lapis)"), Evie Shockley suggests that we read these names as the "underwriters" of the poem, an intriguing reading in the context of a poem concerned with lives treated as either abstract labor power or "insurance value" ("Going Overboard"). Philip herself likens them to footprints, "acknowledgement [that] someone else was here before," but given the names' derivation from Modupe Oduyoye's *Yoruba Names* (*Zong!*, xx) and the conspicuousness of familiar names like the Akan "Nkrumah" and the Kikuyu "Kamau," they signal the continued presence of the ancestors.

66. Hartman, "Venus in Two Acts," 10.

67. Philip, *Zong!*, 172.

68. Ibid., 107–8.

69. Baucom, *Specters of the Atlantic*, 324.

70. Wright, *The Guide Signs*, 69. A few lines later, Wright pertinently repeats "[a] grammar of distraction. | The pun raises the dead."

71. Philip, *Zong!*, 201.

72. Derrida, *Specters of Marx*, 202.

73. Philip, *A Genealogy of Resistance*, 11.

74. Philip, *Zong!*, 199.

75. Ibid., 7.

76. Baucom, *Specters of the Atlantic*, 305.

CHAPTER 2. Establishing Synchronisms

1. I draw the concept of mediality from Walter Benjamin's early writings on language, which stress that the concept of medium is inseparable from the concept of language "as such." See "On Language as Such and on the Language of Man," *Selected Writings*, vol. 1, 62–74.

2. As Marcy J. Dinius has shown, texts as early as David Walker's *Appeal to the Coloured Citizens of the World* (1829) exploited typographical technology of their day to create a performative, hybrid text. Aldon L. Nielsen discusses Harrison and Atkins's work in *Black Chant*. For Black Arts visual poetry, I am thinking in particular of Sonia Sanchez's "a/coltrane/poem," Haki Madhubuti's "Don't Cry, Scream," and Amiri Baraka's "AM/TRAK," as well as other poems from the era whose typography exceeds the supposed transfer of orality. The phrase "trope of orality" is Harryette Mullen's, from her essay "African Signs and Spirit Writing."

3. My own analysis highlights his notions of ac/culturation—the attempt of a dominant group to impose its culture on another—and inter/culturation—the unpredictable syntheses of cultures due to historical mixing. His key texts are *Development of Creole Society in Jamaica, 1770–1820*, and *Contradictory Omens*.

4. Brathwaite, *History of the Voice*, 10, 8–9.

5. I am drawing on Jon Cruz's argument that African American slave songs went from being valued for their truth value as testimony to slavery to their being valued according to an autonomous truth regime that saw them as artifacts of "authentic" African American "folk spirit."

6. Brathwaite, *History of the Voice*, 13.

7. Brathwaite, *Golokwati 2000*, 238.

8. Savory, "Returning to Sycorax / Prospero's Response," 209.

9. Cited in Brathwaite, *DreamStories*, iii. In a later account of his attack in Jamaica, Brathwaite claims his assailants shot him with a "ghost bullet," going so far as to narrate his own death in "I Cristobel Colon."

10. Brathwaite, *The Arrivants*, 263.

11. Dash, *The Other America*, 71.

12. Brathwaite, *MR/1*, 97

13. Brathwaite, *Gods of the Middle Passage*, 9.

14. Brathwaite, *History of the Voice* 10, 7, his emphasis.

15. Ibid., his emphasis.

16. Brathwaite, *Contradictory Omens*, 7.

17. Brathwaite, *MR/1*, 77, 272. Readers familiar with Derek Walcott's 1974 essay "The Muse of History" will hear an echo in Walcott's claim that "the common experience of the New World . . . is colonialism" (36). For Walcott, emphasis on history tends to lead to a narrow focus on that past when what is called for is attention to the more urgent questions of writing poetry in the present.

18. Nicholas Brown offers a helpful counter to the theoretical positions of such theorists as Fredric Jameson and Franco Moretti that see postcolonial literature as merely adopting European forms to local materials, reading the development of those forms through colonialism rather than as a separate development.

19. Brathwaite, *ConVERsations*, 274.

20. Though I am inclined to attribute this lack of critical commentary to the difficulty of squaring Brathwaite's recent work with a politics of expression, Graeme Rigby's "Publishing Brathwaite" reminds us that part of the issue is reproducing the unorthodox SVS faithfully.

21. Brathwaite, *Ark*, xv.

22. Ibid.

23. Eliot, *The Three Voices of Poetry*, 6.

24. I am thinking here of Jonathan Culler's argument that because of the intertextual hermeneutic needed to decode an act of apostrophe, the trope always threatens to become merely an "invocation of invocation" (*The Pursuit of Signs*, 144).

25. Quoted in Rohlehr, *Pathfinder*, 66. Tracing Eliot's "influence" has also become a common critical move. Charles W. Pollard and Matthew Hart trace lines of relation between Brathwaite and Eliot in their respective *New World Modernisms* and *Nations of Nothing but Poetry*.

26. Nathaniel Mackey, *The Paracritical Hinge*, 269–70. As Mackey notes, there are "heterodox tradition[s] of the lyric" that "go counter to and are contrary to the very rationalist Cartesian order"; crucially for my purposes, he also points out that the lyric/antilyric arguments suppress or sideline those other traditions. I take this up more fully in chapter 3.

27. Brathwaite, "Timehri," 33.

28. Eliot, "Tradition and the Individual Talent," 39. For a different, polemical account of *nam*, I would direct readers to Pollard, *New World Modernisms*, 31–39 and 111–36. While Pollard rightly argues that SVS "has not yet established the conventions necessary to connect reliably orthography with orality, sign with sound, text with speech," which for him makes it a partial failure, my argument is that such "reliable connection" is beside the point. SVS deconstructs the lyric as a sign of presence, making expression opaque and writing transparent as a process.

29. I borrow this term from Dipesh Chakrabarty's *Provincializing Europe*, especially pages 90 and following. The term, like Ernst Bloch's "nonsynchronism," reminds us that other temporalities and other forms of creating the world coexist and are possible, if not mutually intelligible.

30. Brathwaite, *Gods of the Middle Passage*, 1; Brathwaite, "Caliban, Ariel and Unprospero," 44; Brathwaite, *Barabajan Poems*, 96.

31. His two *Magical Realism* volumes sustain a polemic against "missilic" cultures convinced they have a particular telos to fulfill.

32. Brathwaite, *Contradictory Omens*, 6.

33. His first published use of that aphorism is in "Caribbean Man in Space and Time," 11.

34. Brathwaite, *Contradictory Omens*, 22–24. Brathwaite is here implicitly engaging §59 of Immanuel Kant's *Critique of Judgment*.

35. Timothy Yu sketches this development in the 1970s, exploring differences between white and Asian American avant-gardes, arguing that "the question of race became central to the constitution of *any* American avant-garde" after 1970 and "that the communities formed by contemporary American writers of color can themselves best be understood in the terms we have developed for the analysis of the avant-garde" (2, his emphasis). While I would argue that the question of race was central to constitutions of the avant-garde prior to 1970 and that *white* artists became "increasingly aware of how their social locations inflected their aesthetics" (2) in that period, Yu's historical claims about the invention of categories of racial difference and his readings of how these social formations influence aesthetics are instructive.

36. These phrases come from Eliot, *The Three Voices of Poetry*, 7.

37. Brathwaite, *History of the Voice*, 30–31n41. In the main text, Brathwaite credits Eliot with introducing "the notion of the speaking voice, the conversational tone" (30).

38. "The term *riddim*, initially a localizing of the English word *rhythm*, has," musicologist Michael Veal notes, "taken on a distinctive meaning in Jamaican music over time, used to refer to these generic chord progressions and/or bass lines that have formed the basis of subsequent songs" (*Dub*, 48). Matthew Hart suggests a similar reading of Brathwaite's relation to Eliot, referring to it as a "competitive fusion" (*Nations of Nothing but Poetry*, 112).

39. Pollard, *New World Modernisms*, 2.

40. This, of course, is also Jameson's notorious error in his notorious "Third-World Literature" essay. For a very productive critique of Jameson's essay, see Brown, *Utopian Generations*, 7–9.

41. I am drawing on Hart's notion of a "synthetic vernacular" (*Nations of Nothing but Poetry*, 137–38).

42. Brathwaite, *Ark*, xv.

43. Ibid.

44. Brathwaite, *ConVERSations*, 104. Brathwaite is alluding to Hamlet's advice to a player in the play he commissions to "catch the conscience of the king," revising it to suggest, complicatedly, the nature of the historical "theater" in which he writes.

45. Culler, *The Pursuit of Signs,* 146, my emphasis.

46. Ibid., 149.

47. Derrida, *Psyche,* 44.

48. Retamar, "Caliban," 28. For a slightly different take on this debate and Retamar's essay, I would direct the reader to Spivak's *A Critique of Postcolonial Reason,* 117–18.

49. Brathwaite, *The Arrivants,* 192.

50. Ibid., 195.

51. Brathwaite, "Caliban, Ariel and Unprospero," 54. Brathwaite refers to her there as the one "in whom resides the quality of soul grit or kernel, known as *nam*" (44).

52. See note oo in chapter 1.

53. Doyle, *Bordering on the Body,* 5.

54. As with this capital "x" in "Sycorax," Brathwaite emphasizes the letter "x" throughout this version of the poem and much of the SVS work, sometimes for its phonic qualities but more often for its visual qualities. "Letter SycoraX" is in *Middle Passages,* 95–116. "X/Self xth letter from the thirteenth provinces" is in *Ancestors,* 444–56. Both revise "X/Self's Xth Letters from the Thirteen Provinces," collected in the first publication of *X/Self,* 80–87.

55. Hughes, *Collected Poems,* 215.

56. Braithwaite, *Ancestors,* 445, 454.

57. Ibid., 444.

58. Readers of *The Arrivants* may recall that one of its dramas is between the historical possibilities offered by Ariadne/Ananse (the silver thread being the line out of the labyrinth of confused or neglected history and modernity) and the open time of the covenant represented by Noah.

59. Brathwaite, *Ancestors,* 445, 455.

60. Ibid.

61. Ibid., 446.

62. Brathwaite, *The Arrivants* 68–69; Brathwaite, *Ancestors* 456.

63. Brathwaite, *History of the Voice,* my emphasis.

64. Brathwaite, *ConVERSations,* 177.

65. Brathwaite, "Timehri" 40. "Obeah blox" or "box," is X/Self's term for the computer's monitor.

66. Brathwaite, *ConVERSations,* 167, his emphasis.

67. Ibid.

68. Brathwaite, *Ancestors,* 72.

69. Ibid.

70. Hollander, "Breaking into Song," 83.

71. My reading here assumes an imitation of a discursive context in which a speaker could connote possession through inflection. One could plausibly read it in a similar to vein to "I writing" and understand the sentence to be changing abruptly from one grammatical form to another, but that does not strike me as plausible.

72. Mackey, "An Interview with Kamau Brathwaite," 23. Brathwaite speaks that phrase.

73. For an exemplary reading of this poem's themes, I direct the reader to Pollard, *New World Modernisms,* 111–26. I would also direct the reader to Brathwaite's own discussion of the poem and the importance of the name in *Barabajan Poems,* 234–65.

74. Brathwaite, *Shar,* n.p.

75. Figures 3, 4, and 5 each occupy an entire page.

76. Jameson, *Postmodernism*, 76.

77. Brathwaite, *DreamStories*, 95.

78. I would like to thank Caetlin Benson-Allot for deepening my understanding of video technology.

79. Brathwaite, *DS(2)*, 159.

80. Brathwaite, *DreamStories*, 95; Brathwaite, *DS(2)*, 160.

81. That apostrophe is a direct citation of calypso singer David Rudder's (one of the poem's dedicatees) "Haiti."

82. Brathwaite, *DS(2)*, 173.

83. Ibid., 189. Brathwaite commonly links Toussaint L'Ouverture with Legba, the *loa* of the crossroads and intermediary between mortals and divinities.

84. Ibid.

85. Ibid., 192. Brathwaite is repeating the language of one of his critics who complained that his work was made up of such purgatorial passages.

86. Ibid., 192, 193–96, his emphasis.

87. Ibid.,185, 189, my emphasis.

88. Brathwaite, *ConVERSations*, 166–76.

89. See, for example, Grant Farred who, observing the resonance of the eleventh day of the month in recent history, notes "that iconographic eleven upon which the whole of the United States' political now turns, 11 September, or, in the argot of this nation, '9/11.' A moment inaugurated, it could be argued, with that other 9/11: the overthrow of Salvador Allende by Augusto Pinochet in Chile in September 1973" ("Foreigners among Citizens," 141).

90. Brathwaite, *Ark*, 1.

91. Deren, *Divine Horsemen*, 38.

92. Brathwaite, *Ark*, 3.

93. Ibid., 9.

94. Ibid.

95. Ibid., 42.

96. Brathwaite, "Jazz and the West Indian Novel," 70.

97. Brathwaite, *Ark*, xvi.

98. For more on the concept of àxé, see Carol Boyce Davies's article "Àshé" in *Encyclopedia of the African Diaspora*, 119. She writes that "as a cultural definition, then, àxé moves across two large discursive fields: that of spirituality, and that of creativity, with its meanings and associations of what it is to be human in the world, questions of existence, the power to be, dynamic force in all things."

CHAPTER 3. Between Now and Yet

1. Jackson, *Dickinson's Misery*, 10. Jackson there engages Paul de Man's writing on the lyric.

2. Ibid., 100.

3. Major, *The New Black Poetry*, 18, his emphasis. For the authors in this chapter, the "essential energy" refers to the energy of that racial location rather than a stable racial identity. The energy is in its flux.

4. Nielsen, *Black Chant*, 33.

5. Here, I would mention Keith D. Leonard's *Fettered Genius*, a terrific account of the ways black poets from the Civil War era through the civil rights era adapted and revised traditional poetic forms to create a public space from which to express transgressive political desires.

6. Rankine, "The First Person in the Twenty-First Century," 134.

7. I draw this concept from Jacques Derrida's reading of French experimental writer and philosopher Maurice Blanchot. Derrida reflects on the distinction between the narratorial voice (an abstract grouping together of the various fictional elements and conventions central to the telling of a tale, including genre) and the narrative voice (the psychic density conjured as the agent of storytelling; the "point of view" in the vernacular, rather than technical, sense of the term). For Derrida, "the 'I'-less 'I' of the narrative voice, the 'I' 'stripped' of itself," in *La folie du jour*, ambiguously referred to as "a récit?," with the question mark, on the cover of the journal the story first appeared in rather than forthrightly declaring its genre, throws the narratorial voice into crisis. See *Acts of Reading*, 246.

8. Rankine, *Don't Let Me Be Lonely*, 23.

9. I have in mind Patricia J. Williams's discussion of then candidate Barack Obama, following the brouhaha when Oprah Winfrey endorsed him, and the "paradox of supposedly transcending race: "It means you can't be seen frolicking in the presence of too many other black people. You have to cut a noble lonely figure and act like you don't have a black friend in the world. A plurality of tokens gives jitters to those who fear, in numbers, a great slide toward the unwashed masses.... Three or more of even the most transcendental and otherwise adorable figureheads and it becomes an agenda, an affirmative action, a plot, a conspiracy, a tribe, a cabal, a balkanization, a separatist movement, a riot" ("The Power of One," 43–44).

10. Jennifer Ashton provides a helpful summary of those conversations, especially of the perspectives of Yopie Prins and Virginia Jackson, in the context of a broader discussion of (white) avant-garde poetry in her "Labor and the Lyric." Referring to the lyric mode rather than genre, I am essentially agreeing with Paul de Man's claim that "the lyric is not a genre, but one name among several to designate the defensive motion of understanding, the possibility of a future hermeneutics" (*Rhetoric of Romanticism*, 261). For my purposes, de Man's argument helps me hold apart the grammatical, phenomenological, and political notions of subject, whose conflation the hermeneutic project of the lyric encourages.

11. Rankine, *PLOT*, 60.

12. Rankine, "The First Person in the Twenty-First Century," 133.

13. I have in mind here Ruth Wilson Gilmore's definition of racism in *Golden Gulag*: "Racism, specifically, is the state-sanctioned or extralegal production and exploitation of group-differentiated vulnerability to premature death" (28). The threat of premature death looms over Rankine's and Kearney's work.

14. Dworkin, "The Fate of Echo," xxix. One target of Dworkin's polemic is what he sees as professionalized, overly conventional forms of writing, such as those encouraged by many MFA programs and related institutions of prestige and normalization. Dworkin and Goldsmith present their anthology, which includes authors as varied as Denis Diderot, John Cage, Jackson Mac Low, as well as the editors' own work, as a counterdiscourse valorizing "uncreative" writing against work thought too personal in narrow ways. The anthology highlights texts that mark their use of other texts as source material.

15. I am drawing Snead's "On Repetition in Black Culture." According to Snead, black culture builds "accidents" and repetition into its sense of itself and makes rooms for accident and rupture within that system.

16. This is not an entirely new concern, even if the scale of it has changed. Amy Abugo Ongiri has persuasively argued, for example, that the style of the Black Panthers "created an iconography whose power lay much more in its translatability to commodity culture than in

its distance from it" (*Spectacular Blackness*, 52). My point would simply be that in the postsegregation era the pace and extent of such "translation" have intensified.

17. Alexander, *The Black Interior*, 181.

18. Henderson takes the title of his preface from a Richard Wright lecture of the same name (collected in *White Man, Listen!*), which Wright in turn borrowed from Shakespeare's *A Midsummer Night's Dream*.

19. Henderson, *Understanding the New Black Poetry*, 10.

20. Ibid., 62, my emphasis.

21. I cite Theodor W. Adorno's famous definition of the lyric poem, which comes from a similar Hegelian-Herderian tradition of romantic nationalism to which Du Bois responds. See Adorno, "On Lyric Poetry and Society," 45.

22. In *Represent and Destroy*, Jodi Melamed argues that literary studies has been complicit in the production of such knowledge, the result of which is that the terms of racial critique cease to be radical and assume the form of liberal and neoliberal reconciliation and the "dematerialization" of race so central to certain forms of white ressentiment. "Neoliberal" is not the most helpful term, but it does encompass the shifts in the domains of culture, governmentality, and ideology—especially the personalization of systemic traits—of the era that followed decolonization and that were accelerated by the Cold War and the economic crises of the 1970s.

23. Ibid., 4, my emphases.

24. North, *Dialect of Modernism*, 182, his emphasis.

25. Hunt, "Notes for an Oppositional Poetics," 202.

26. The term "appropriate" merits brief comment, since one does not own culture the way one owns the commodities associated with culture. What is appropriated is a set of dispositions, behaviors, ways of being, and ways of making habitually associated with a racial group that, when we speak of appropriation, is likely to have no other property. In addition, the one adopting another's culture is likely to add to his or her wealth, while those with whom the cultural forms had been associated will continue to be dispossessed.

27. Rankine, "The First Person in the Twenty-First Century," 134.

28. Flescher and Caspar, "Interview with Claudia Rankine."

29. Nealon, *The Matter of Capital*, 146; Bell, "Unheard Writing in the Climate of Spectacular Noise," 93.

30. Here I endorse Antonio Viego's observation that critical race and ethnicity studies scholars, to the extent that we stress strong, whole, complete subjects, "fail to see how the repeated themes of wholeness, completeness, and transparency with respect to ethnic-racialized subjectivity are what provide racist discourse with precisely the notion of subjectivity that it needs" (*Dead Subjects*, 4).

31. Nealon, *The Matter of Capital*, 151.

32. Rankine, *PLOT*, 9, 80, 96, and 102.

33. Ibid., 9.

34. Ibid., 5, her emphasis.

35. Ibid., 43.

36. Rankine, *Don't Let Me Be Lonely*, 23.

37. Ibid., 130.

38. Shockley, *a half-red sea*, 4; Hayden, "Those Winter Sundays," 41.

39. Rankine, "The First Person in the Twenty-First Century," 134.

40. Rankine, *PLOT*, 43. I have reproduced the box that frames the text in the original.

41. Woolf, *To the Lighthouse*, 52.

42. Ibid.

43. Along these lines, it is significant that in a work invested in the meanings of words, "forgiveness" is redefined as a word for "a feeling of nothingness that cannot be communicated to another, an absence, a bottomless vacancy held by the living, beyond all that is hated or loved" (*Don't Let Me Be Lonely*, 48).

44. Ibid., 131.

45. Ibid., 119. This passage marks another important feature of *Don't Let Me Be Lonely*: the use of the conjunction "or" at the beginning of sections, adding to a fractured sense of time, or a list of examples being put forward without the discursive situation being made clear. Poetic images accumulate that are oriented toward emotional rather than logical clarity.

46. Ibid., 108.

47. Ibid., 121.

48. Ibid. 54.

49. Ibid.

50. Nealon, *The Matter of Capital*, 3.

51. Ibid. 34.

52. Ibid., 152.

53. Ibid.

54. Rankine, *PLOT*, 77.

55. Rankine, *Don't Let Me Be Lonely*, 55.

56. Rankine, *PLOT*, 61.

57. Rankine, *Don't Let Me Be Lonely*, 91.

58. Rankine, *PLOT*, 101. Ersatz, implied speaker of these lines, echoes Liv's earlier "Oh, Ersatz, my own, birth is the limiting of the soul."

59. I refer to Jacques Rancière's *Disagreement*.

60. Kearney, *The Black Automaton*, 16.

61. The Roots' lead MC, Black Thought, alludes to Kool Keith's verse on the Ultramagnetic MCs "Ego Trippin.'" I am borrowing the term "habitus" from sociologist Pierre Bourdieu who uses it to describe the habits of mind, dispositions, and schemes of perception and taste for a given class formation.

62. The curly brackets are being used here to suggest the typography of this line. The word "not" appears above the word "knot," and the whole line ("or knot / not Toby") appears below "to be," with a curly bracket uniting "to be" with "or knot / not Toby."

63. Addressing these questions from a different perspective, Greg Tate himself has edited a collection of essays entitled *Everything but the Burden*.

64. Baldwin, *The Cross of Redemption*, 42.

65. Kearney includes notes at the end of his volume, suggesting that he or his publishers did not take for granted the existence of such a reader.

66. Kearney, *The Black Automaton*, 35.

CHAPTER 4. "Sing It in My Voice"

1. It also assuages what Robert B. Stepto observed to be a long-standing ambivalence toward the written word: "Literature has developed as much because of [African American] cul-

ture's distrust of literacy as because of its abiding faith in it," making music a necessary mediating fiction in some accounts of black writing (196).

2. In her recent *Black Resonance*, Emily J. Lordi offers a necessary and productive critique of this "music-text hierarchy."

3. One important model for this way of reading the blues is Brent Hayes Edwards's essay "The Seemingly Eclipsed Window of Form."

4. Parks, *The America Play*, 9; Mullen and Keizer, "Incidents in the Lives of Two Postmodern Black Feminists," n.p.

5. In a similar argument, Aldon Nielsen refers to this as a blues-surrealism continuum (*Black Chant*, 163).

6. Here, I am drawing on Derrida's interpretation of Nietzsche in "Structure, Sign and Play in the Discourse of the Human Sciences."

7. Spillers, "The Idea of Black Culture," 9.

8. Baker, *Blues, Ideology, and African American Literature*, 3; McGinley, "Highway 61 Revisited," 88; Carby, "It Jus Be's Dat Way Sometime," 476.

9. Adorno, "The Perennial Fashion," 122.

10. Douglas, *Terrible Honesty*, 399.

11. Baldwin, "My Dungeon Shook," 295. I follow here Robin D. G. Kelley's arguments in *Freedom Dreams* that the critic must attempt to discern the unfulfilled dreams of freedom in prior generations rather than simply critique their failures or co-optation.

12. Mullen, *Recyclopedia*, 125.

13. In particular I have in mind Paul de Man's "The Concept of Irony." There, he defines irony as "the permanent parabasis [interruption] of the allegory of tropes," a way of reading and relating tropes to one another that "has its own narrative coherence, its own systematicity, and it is that coherence, that systematicity, which irony interrupts, disrupts. . . . [I]rony is precisely what makes it impossible ever to achieve a theory of narrative that would be consistent." I adapt and develop Andrzej Warminski's use of the zero as an example of something whose definition is given by its function but resists anything other than relational definition.

14. Jameson, *Postmodernism*, 17.

15. Cited in Carby, "It Jus Be's Dat Way Sometime," 476.

16. Mullen and Keizer, "Incidents in the Lives of Two Postmodern Black Feminists." In particular, Mullen cites Smitherman's 1977 *Talkin' and Testifyin'* and Clarence Major's 1970 *Dictionary of Afro-American Slang*, revised and republished as *From Juba to Jive*.

17. Mullen, "Hauling up Gold from the Abyss," 401; Hogue, "Interview with Haryette Mullen," n.p.

18. I discuss this in detail in the chapter 3.

19. Henderson, *Understanding the New Black Poetry*, 4.

20. To elaborate this discussion from the introduction, I am drawing here on Marx's discussion of double existence of the commodity in *Grundrisse*, 146–47.

21. Pinson, "An Interview with Lorenzo Thomas," 299.

22. Bedient, "The Solo Mysterioso Blues," 656.

23. Ibid., 665.

24. Ibid., 663.

25. Mullen, *Recyclopedia*, xi.

26. Spillers, "Mama's Baby, Papa's Maybe," 203.

27. Mullen, *Recyclopedia*, xi.

28. Ibid., 99.

29. Mullen, quoted in Perloff, *Differentials*, 171.

30. Jones, *The Muse Is Music*, 157.

31. Spillers, "Mama's Baby, Papa's Maybe," 229.

32. Williams, "'The Queen of Hip Hyperbole,'" 706.

33. Ibid.

34. Mullen, *Recyclopedia*, 109.

35. Ibid., 102, 130, 154.

36. Ibid., 132, 143, 154.

37. Another, more local, example of irony is "then I wouldn't be long gone | I'd be Dogon," a play on a Marvin Gaye lyric, a West African culture, and, by extension, those poets, like Nathaniel Mackey and Jay Wright, inspired by Dogon mythology and writing practices.

38. Mullen, *Sleeping with the Dictionary*, 9.

39. Hogue, "Interview with Haryette Mullen," n.p.

40. Mullen, *Recyclopedia*, 125.

41. Parks, *The America Play*, 4.

42. Derrida, *Of Grammatology*, 68.

43. Parks, *The America Play*, 12.

44. Parks, "New Black Math," 582, my emphasis.

45. Derrida, "Structure, Sign and Play in the Discourse of the Human Sciences," 292.

46. Brustein, *Millennial Stages*, 219, my emphasis. Brustein, in the same piece, reports an interview wherein Parks complained that "no one asks me about form." What his corrective underscores, then, is the difficulty of talking about both experimental form and race.

47. Johung, "Figuring the 'Spells' / Spelling the Figures," 40. The phrase "black suffering, loss, and misrepresentation through history" is Elinor Fuchs's, taken from a very valuable overview of Parks's work in *The Death of Character* (103). Helpfully, for my present argument for privileging form and the value of illegibility in this text, Fuchs refers to such suffering and so forth as motivic, highlighting the ways in which they are foregrounded as referents at least as much as themes.

48. Steven Druckman put this question to her in an interview, and Parks speculated that the problem is "what we allow black people to do and one of [those things] is not theory." See "Doo-a-Diddly-Dit-Dit," 61.

49. Parks, *The America Play*, 21.

50. Hartman, "Venus in Two Acts," 25. Hartman's essay, in part concerned with a problem she faced in writing *Lose Your Mother* as a challenge to historiography, has broadly informed my understanding of Parks and her project.

51. Parks, *The America Play*, 4–5.

52. The spelling of the character's name changes about halfway throughout the play, but she is listed as Momma at the beginning of the play.

53. Parks, "New Black Math," 579–80, her emphasis and omitted apostrophes.

54. Parks, *The America Play*, 16.

55. Roach, "Great Hole of History," 146. Here, the spell here makes the invocation of the dozens clear.

56. One finds something similar in a number of blues songs where someone expresses the sentiment "if I don't go crazy I believe I'll lose my mind."

57. Parks has said that the Third Kingdom is "that of fungi. Small, overlooked, out of sight, of lesser consequence. All of that. And also: the space between." Cited in Ben-Zvi, "Aroun the Worl," 193.

58. Parks, *The America Play*, 25.

59. Ibid., 26. Mokus, the mute robber, has no speaking lines and is only present on the page, in any event, when characters refer to him. Parks's plays feature very few if any stage directions, so were he not mentioned, he would not exist here.

60. Ibid.

61. Ibid., 31, 27, 28.

62. Ibid., 42, 43.

63. Ibid., 43.

64. Ibid., 44. The idiomatic "draw from" immediate shifts to a discussion of the dental extraction "the book says [Aretha is] due for."

65. Ibid., 56.

66. de Man, "The Concept of Irony," 178.

67. Spivak, "Learning from de Man," 33.

68. The original cast for this play consists of five actors who play all the roles of the play, irrespective of gender. For simplicity's sake, when pronoun use requires that the Seers' genders be specified, I do so in accord with gender of the opening-night actors: Over-Seer/Naturalist/Dr. Lutsky/Charles/Duffy (Peter Schmitz); Us-Seer/Veronica/Verona/Aretha Saxon/Mrs. Smith (Pamela Tyson); Soul-Seer/Robber/Miss Faith/Mr. Smith (Jasper McGruder); Kin-Seer/Molly/Mona/Blanca/Muffy (Kenya Scott); Shark-Seer/Charlene/Chona/Anglor/Buffy (Shona Tucker).

69. Parks, *The America Play*, 37.

70. Ibid.

71. Ibid., 57. According to Parks's glossary of "foreign words and phrases," "thup" is "([a]ir intake with sound placed in mouth; liberal use of the tongue.) Slurping" (17).

72. Garrett, "Figures, Speech and Form in *Imperceptible Mutabilities in the Third Kingdom*," 9.

73. Carpio, *Laughing Fit to Kill*, 196. Carpio reads the first section's "should I jump or what" as a statement that "would have been spoken first by the captive [i.e., Aretha] on the slave ship," though that section conjoins the experience of the slave ship with that of government housing projects.

74. Parks, *The America Play*, 39.

75. Ibid., 38, my emphasis.

76. Ibid., 55–56.

77. Ibid., 54. This dialogue is an abstraction and exaggeration of the literary conventions for representing African American Vernacular English, a play on the form of verbal invention rather than an imitation of it. A similar operation informs Kamau Brathwaite's notion of "nation language," considered in the second chapter.

78. Ibid.

79. Ibid., 57.

80. "Hottentot" was the colonial name given to the Khoikhoi or Khoisan people of present-day South Africa that, as Carpio points out, came to be a derogatory term meaning "stammerer" or "stutterer" (*Laughing Fit to Kill*, 193).

81. Elam and Rayner, "Body Parts," 274.

82. Warner, "Suzan-Lori Parks's Drama of Disinterment," 179.

83. Parks, *Venus*, 78.

84. Ibid., 166.

85. Iton, *In Search of the Black Fantastic*, 13. Hortense Spillers's "Mama's Baby, Papa's Maybe" makes a similar argument about black women.

86. Parks, *Venus*, 78. This claim, made in the play by the Chorus of the Court, is followed by a peal of laughter: "HAHAHAHAHAHAHAHAHAHHAHAHAHAHAHHAHAHAHAHAHAHAHA-HAHAHAHAHAHAHAHAHAHHAHAHHAHAHA."

87. Hartman, *Scenes of Subjection*, 81. The mismatch between my invocation of a text about U.S. slavery and the life of Saartjie Baartman is deliberate: New World slavery more than colonialism in South Africa overdetermines the discourse surrounding Baartman and *Venus* in the U.S.

88. Some critics, especially Jean Young, argue that Parks's effort was unsuccessful. See Young, "The Re-Objectification and Re-Commodification of Saartjie Baartman."

89. The Venus uses the past tense only once in the play, during her testimony to the Negro Resurrectionist at the end of the play, when she is telling him what he, essentially, already knows.

90. Parks, *Venus*, 99, her emphasis. The 8 Human Wonders also appear as the Chorus of the Spectators, the Court, and the 8 Anatomists.

91. Ibid., 159, her emphasis.

92. Ibid., 161.

93. Iton, *In Search of the Black Fantastic*, 8.

94. I am thinking here, in part, of Hortense Spillers's bracing essay "The Idea of Black Culture."

CHAPTER 5. Exploding Dimensions of Song

1. Mackey, *Discrepant Engagement*, 127.

2. Mackey, *Splay Anthem*, 46.

3. Mackey, *Eroding Witness*, 54.

4. I draw on Jacques Coursil's utopian claim that "what is happening now contains a part that has never been previously declared in the future tense in any past discourse" ("Hidden Principles of Improvisation," 64).

5. Mackey, *Bedouin Hornbook*, 16–18.

6. Neal, "And Shine Swam On," 653.

7. Mackey, *The Paracritical Hinge*, 82.

8. Baucom, *Specters of the Atlantic*, 24.

9. Spivak, "Time and Timing," 99.

10. Gilroy, *The Black Atlantic*, 37.

11. Ibid., 38.

12. Baldwin, *Collected Essays*, 340.

13. Jameson, *Valences of the Dialectic*, 415. Frantz Fanon speaks to this positioning of black culture as insurance in his acid observation in *Black Skins, White Masks* that "the Blacks represent a kind of 'humanity insurance' in the eyes of the Whites. When the Whites feel overmechanized, they turn to the Colored and request a little human sustenance" (108, translation modified).

14. Ibid., 434.

15. This notion of utopia runs counter to, say, Ernst Bloch's notion that utopian wish fulfillment is immanent to the objects of study; the interpretive project is located less in in-

stances of resistance or subversion than in the inchoate or ambiguous soundings of some other desire or potentiality that under other circumstances might be salvific rather than oppressive.

16. Lorca defines "duende" as "a power and not a behaviour" and adds that "it is a struggle and not a concept" ("Theory and Function of *Duende*," 92). In *The Paracritical Hinge*, Mackey notes that "the word means 'spirit,' a kind of gremlin, a gremlinlike, troubling spirit" marked by "a sound of trouble in the voice," and underscores the New World–Old World connection Lorca traces through these "black sounds" (182).

17. Mackey, *The Paracritical Hinge*, 292.

18. Ibid., 197–98.

19. Lorca, "Theory and Function of *Duende*," 92, 95–96.

20. Ibid, 103.

21. Mackey, *Eroding Witness*, 54.

22. Mackey derives this claim to an originary refused relation from the Kaluli myth of the boy who became a *muni* bird as related by Steven Feld in his landmark *Sound and Sentiment*.

23. Edwards, "Notes on Poetics Regarding Mackey's *Song*," 573. "Methodologic fissures" is Cecil Taylor's phrase.

24. Mackey, *The Paracritical Hinge*, 295.

25. Mackey, *Splay Anthem*, x. The combined "pre-" and "post-occupation" comes from *Song of the Andoumboulou 7*: "You really do seem to believe in, to hold out for some first or final gist underlying it all, but my preoccupation with origins and ends is exactly that: a pre- (equally post-, I suppose) occupation" (*Eroding Witness*, 50). The "speaker" of this epistolary prose section is the N. character at the center of the prose series.

26. Robert L. Zamsky reads *duende*'s objectless longing through a psychoanalytic framework of desire and the drive. For my reading *duende* has a more general function that is not strictly subjective, or related to the subject's desire for wholeness.

27. Mackey, *Eroding Witness*, 31.

28. Mackey, *Splay Anthem*, xi.

29. Ibid.

30. Mackey, *Whatsaid Serif*, 20.

31. Mackey, *Splay Anthem*, xi.

32. Mackey, *Eroding Witness*, 33.

33. "The European" is inquiring about a point of cosmology that the Dogon sage Ogotemmêli refuses to clarify for him, "a Nazarene" (*Conversations with Ogotemmêli*, 58, cited in *Eroding Witness*, 33).

34. Mackey, *Eroding Witness*, 34.

35. The open and generative "what" becomes thematic: the title *Whatsaid Serif* refers to the "what-sayer," who must receive and respond to any story for that story to be told. That function is internalized into the writing in an anticipated moment of reading or audience.

36. Edwards, "Notes on Poetics Regarding Mackey's *Song*," 588.

37. Naylor, *Poetic Investigations*, 85.

38. Mackey, *Eroding Witness*, 50. This is the first of the prose epistles from N. to the Angel of Dust.

39. Snead, "On Repetition in Black Culture," 20. For a different take on "the cut" in *Bedouin Hornbook*, see Moten's *In the Break*.

40. Mackey, *Bedouin Hornbook*, 9.

41. Ibid., 38.

42. Ibid., 42.

43. Ibid., my emphasis.

44. Mackey, *Discrepant Engagement*, 232. Mackey relates Feld to African American music through Orlando Patterson's description of slavery as "social death."

45. Mackey, *Eroding Witness*, 50, his emphasis. To be sure, N. could be using "your world" colloquially to describe the Angel of Dust's disposition.

46. Mackey, *Whatsaid Serif*, 28.

47. Mackey, *The Paracritical Hinge*, 303.

48. Ibid., 190.

49. Mackey, *Splay Anthem*, ix.

50. Mackey, *Whatsaid Serif*, 91. The phrase "words don't go there" is saxophonist Charles Lloyd's response to an interviewer who requested that he comment on a piece of his music. In this poem and more directly in prose coauthored with Art Lange, Mackey declares that "writers influenced by jazz have been variously rising to the challenge of proving him wrong" (*Moment's Notice*, ii).

51. Mackey, *School of Udhra*, 29.

52. There may well be an allusion to the ending of James Baldwin's "Sonny's Blues" and/or to the books of Isaiah (51:17 and 51:22) and Zechariah (12:2), both of which would fit the series' interests in movement and finding a new republic.

53. Zamsky, "A Poetics of Radical Musicality," 133.

54. Mackey, *Whatsaid Serif*, 69.

55. Ibid.

56. Ibid., 14.

57. Ibid., 19. The phrase is Cerno Bokar's, a West African Sufi teacher, who, according to Louise Brenner, strived in his teachings to "move 'beyond the letter' of the written word." The citation in full: "Language is a fruit of which the skin is called chatter, the flesh eloquence, and the seed good sense. Those whose profession it is to flatter the masses [i.e., the griots or *djeli*] know the uses of all these parts, and they employ them in a marvelous fashion" (Brenner, *West African Sufi*, 179).

58. Examples of these include "that" (ahtt, ttha), "star" (tsar, rast, rats), and, nearly, "alterably": "Holding air he was | holding the world, he intimated, | lolled his tongue, trailed | off into singing, Lebert | Aaly | the name he now took . . ." (*Whatsaid Serif*, 79). That name derives from an Art Ensemble of Chicago composition dedicated to Albert Ayler, for whose unspoken name "Lebert Aaly" is a near anagram.

59. Mackey, *Whatsaid Serif*, 30–31.

60. Mackey, *Whatsaid Serif*, 59. In the preface to *Splay Anthem*, Mackey says of Mu that it "carries a theme of utopic reverie, a theme of lost ground and elegiac allure" and goes on to write that the "places named in the song of the Andoumboulou, set foot on by the deceased while alive but lost or taken away by death, could be called 'Mu'" (x).

61. Mackey, *Eroding Witness*, 54.

62. Johnston, "Nathaniel Mackey and Lost Time," 563. Johnston uses this phrase in connection with an engagement with Julia Kristeva to describe language.

63. Mackey, *Splay Anthem*, 79.

64. Mackey, *Bedouin Hornbook*, 7.

65. Both "Naima," dedicated to Coltrane's wife at the time, and "Cousin Mary," dedicated

to a cousin, were initially released on Coltrane's *Giant Steps* album, which, as Lewis Porter points out, contains several such dedications, including one to band mate Paul Chambers ("Mr. P.C.") and a stepdaughter ("Syeeda's Song Flute"). See Porter, *John Coltrane*, 156.

66. Mackey, *Bedouin Hornbook*, 7.

67. Ibid., 9.

68. Ibid., 84. The context that gives rise to this conclusion is N.'s meditation on the use of "alienate" as a verb to describe the dispossession of Kenyan peoples by the English, giving historical specificity to the concern over words' part of speech and thereby underscoring the performative power of words.

69. Ibid., 88.

70. Lukács, *History and Class Consciousness*, 83. Lukács goes on to suggest that commodity exchange and its social forms greatly influence the "*total* inner and outer life of society," meaning that, using N.'s language, the commodity system has a quantum-qualitative effect to the extent that its presence in a given society is total. The eccentric "out" N. seeks, therefore, must be a correspondingly quantum-qualitative out, that is, a strategy.

71. Mackey, *Discrepant Engagement*, 235.

72. Ibid., 236.

73. Mackey, *Bedouin Hornbook*, 111.

74. Ibid., 112.

75. Ibid., 115.

76. Ibid., 116.

77. Ibid., 119. This episode also marks the first instance in *Perfume Bottle* of the "word balloons" that accompany many of the band's performances and records.

78. Ibid., 125.

79. Ibid., 137.

80. Ibid., 146.

81. Benjamin, "On the Concept of History," in *Selected Writings*, vol. 4, 389–400.

82. Edwards, "Notes on Poetics Regarding Mackey's *Song*," 586.

83. Mackey, *Djbot Baghostus's Run*, 97.

84. Mackey, *Bass Cathedral*, 45.

85. This latter attack afflicts Penguin, whose disappearance and reappearance sparks *Atet A.D.*'s central concern, namely, the appearance of comic word bubbles during performances.

86. Hartman, *Lose Your Mother*, 209. Hartman goes on to describe the popular lore that nets cast to "dredge for treasure" would yield the corpses of the enslaved "encased by thousands of shells, which covered the figure from head to toe."

87. Mackey, *Bass Cathedral*, 87.

88. Mackey, *Bedouin Hornbook*, 119, 121. Readers familiar with Eric Dolphy's playing will recognize this as a temporal claim. Like Billie Holiday, Dolphy had a tendency to play *tempo rubato*—rigorously in time with himself, but now ahead, now behind the ensemble.

89. Ibid., 123.

90. Ibid., 182–83.

91. Ibid., 195.

92. Ibid., 197.

93. Ibid., 204.

94. Mackey, *Djbot Baghostus's Run*, 148.

95. *Atet A. D.*, 122.

96. Ibid.

97. Ibid., 48.

98. Mackey, *Bedouin Hornbook*, 74.

99. Another instance of such "invisible hands" or police omnipresence occurs at the end of *Bedouin Hornbook*, in an after-the-fact lecture/libretto called "The Creaking of the Word," with that libretto's protagonist, Flaunted Fifth, being accosted by the police while urinating in a field at the outskirts of town, as his numb right hand, disembodied, caresses Djamilaa's "pantyless rump" through her cotton dress, a play on "outskirt" that suggests the body's place in spiritual or sentimental geographies.

100. Mackey, *Djbot Baghostus's Run*, 14.

101. Ibid., 14. Prior to Djamilaa's singing, the two women in the group play, the not (a Kashmiri drum) and the nay (an Iranian reed flute), in order to sound a punning rejection of the male drummer the band has been auditioning, thereby strengthening the implicit links between musical and linguistic signs that N. advances throughout the series.

102. Ibid., 16.

103. Mackey, *Bass Cathedral*, 6.

104. Ibid., 13.

105. Ibid., 6.

106. Ibid., 65. Though somewhat unorthodox, this approach to composition and arrangement, where certain "drift conduits" are made available to the players just prior to performance, calls to mind Lawrence "Butch" Morris's "conduction" and Anthony Braxton's Ghost Trance Music.

107. Ibid., 67.

108. Ibid., 68.

109. Ibid.

110. Ibid., 69.

111. The text specifies the version recorded by Julian "Cannonball" Adderley, with his brother Nat (who composed the song), Bobby Timmons, Sam Jones, and Louis Hayes.

112. One pertinent couplet suggests the crime is "being hungry and poor."

113. Mackey, *Bass Cathedral*, 74.

114. Ibid., 75, my emphasis.

115. Ibid., 77.

POSTSCRIPT

1. Baraka, "Black Art," 149.

2. Gourgouris, *Does Literature Think?*, 43. I am also thinking of Virginia Jackson's "Thinking Dickinson Thinking Poetry" and Simon Jarvis's "Prosody as Cognition." "Thought" may be a metaphor, but it underscores that ways of engaging literary material, like other social practices, involve a specific form of intelligence.

3. Alexander Weheliye reads these epigraphs alongside the romantic poetry it typically accompanies in terms of sampling and DJ practice (*Phonographies*, 73–105). Du Bois emphasizes in the form of the Senegambian song handed down phonetically from his grandfather's grandmother through generations in his family. Part of that song, "gene me gene me," David Levering Lewis has suggested, translates as "get me out, get me out" (*W. E. B. Du Bois*, 14).

4. Hanchard, "Afro-Modernity," 277.

5. Ibid., 285–96.

6. Castronovo, *Beautiful Democracy*, 108.

7. Major, *The New Black Poetry*, 16; Hollo, *Negro Verse*, 7. Major's anthology begins with an epigraph taken from Du Bois's 1899 "The Song of the Smoke." That poem, incidentally, would also appear in later anthologies such as Paul Breman's *You Better Believe It* and Arnold Adoff's *The Poetry of Black America* as a forerunner of the new black consciousness. Like Breman, Hollo understands "Negro poetry" as global, "openly conscious of, and committed to, its racial and cultural origins," which he relates to a lyric from an African American gospel song, "Go, and I Go With You": "Open your mouth, and I speak for you" (7).

8. Henderson, *Understanding the New Black Poetry*, 4.

9. Neal, "And Shine Swam On," 647.

10. Marx, *Economic and Philosophic Manuscripts of 1844*, 302.

11. Stewart, *Poetry and the Fate of the Senses*, 40.

12. Du Bois draws those examples from contemporaneous scenarios that illustrate the viciousness of racism—e.g., a "brown" daughter who commits suicide when she is not allowed to attend her white sister's wedding, a white woman who extorts money from a "colored lawyer [surrounded] on all the other sides [of a town square] by men who do not like colored lawyers" by threatening to scream if he refuses her ransom—to highlight the ways racism constrains the possibilities for black artists in the United States. Curiously, David Levering Lewis's *Reader* omits the literary examples but keeps the historical ones that tell the "untold tale" of colonialism and world events.

13. Richard Iton makes a similar point in his articulation of the "black fantastic" as an analytical term for the ways African American cultural production indexes the need to supersede the norms and arrangements of modernity: "The pursuit of genuine emancipatory schemes is not a simple matter of escaping or even resisting existing arrangements (in the manner, perhaps, that new world blacks could conceivably in some past time establish maroon communities). The processes of exclusion that have defined the black experience of modernity have not allowed those of African descent to avoid the transfiguring and scarring aspects of the extended moment or complicity in its present conditions. These dynamics have also demanded sensibilities that recognize that solidarities are always contingent and essentialisms at best pragmatic, positional, and strategic. Opting out, then, is not a viable—or available response" (*In Search of the Black Fantastic*, 15). This nexus of complicity and opposition informs my own sense of outfulness and of blackness as a category that comes into being only through the processes of colonialism and slavery. To say "black is beautiful" is to acknowledge, however indirectly, a long history of voices saying the opposite.

14. Du Bois, *Writings*, 995.

Bibliography

Adorno, Theodor W. "On Lyric Poetry and Society." In *Notes to Literature*, vol. 1, ed. Rolf Tiedermann, trans. Shierry Weber Nicholson, 37–54. New York: Columbia University Press, 1974.

———. "The Perennial Fashion—Jazz." In *Prisms*,120–32. Cambridge, MA: MIT Press, 1967.

Alexander, Elizabeth. *The Black Interior: Essays.* St. Paul, MN: Graywolf Press, 2004.

Alexander, Will. "Nathaniel Mackey: An Ashen Finesse." *Callaloo* 23.2 (2000): 700–702.

Althusser, Louis. *For Marx.* Trans. Ben Brewster. London: Verso Press, 2005.

Ashton, Jennifer. "Labor and the Lyric: The Politics of Self-Expression in Contemporary American Poetry." *American Literary History* 25.1 (2013): 217–30.

Baker, Houston A., Jr. *Blues, Ideology, and Afro-American Literature: A Vernacular Theory.* Chicago: University of Chicago Press, 1984.

———. *Modernism and the Harlem Renaissance.* Chicago: University of Chicago Press, 1989.

Baldwin, James. *The Cross of Redemption: Uncollected Writings.* Ed. Randall Kenan. New York: Pantheon, 2000.

———. "My Dungeon Shook: A Letter to My Nephew." In *Collected Essays*, ed. Toni Morrison, 291–95. New York: Library of America, 1998.

Baraka, Amiri [LeRoi Jones]. "Black Art." In *Transbluency: The Selected Poems of Amiri Baraka/ LeRoi Jones (1961–1995)*, ed. Paul Vangelisti, 142–43. New York: Marsilio, 1995.

———. *Black Music.* New York: Da Capo, 1998.

Barthes, Roland. *Writing Degree Zero.* Trans. Annette Lavers and Colin Smith. New York: Hill and Wang, 1977.

Baucom, Ian. *Specters of the Atlantic: Finance Capital, Slavery and the Philosophy of History* Durham, NC: Duke University Press, 2005.

Bayard, Caroline. *The New Poetics in Canada and Quebec: From Concretism to Post-Modernism.* Toronto: University of Toronto Press, 1989.

Bedient, Calvin. "The Solo Mysterioso Blues: An Interview with Harryette Mullen." *Callaloo* 19.3 (1996): 651–69.

Bell, Kevin. "Unheard Writing in the Climate of Spectacular Noise: Claudia Rankine on TV." *Global South* 3.1 (2009): 94–107.

Benjamin, Walter. *Selected Writings*, vol. 1: *1913–1926.* Ed. Marcus Bullock and Michael W. Jennings. Cambridge, MA: Harvard University Press, 1996.

———. *Selected Writings*, vol. 2, pt. 1: *1927–1930.* Ed. Michael W. Jennings, Howard Eiland, and Gary Smith. Cambridge, MA: Harvard University Press, 2005.

———. *Selected Writings*, vol. 2, pt. 2: *1931–1934*. Ed. Michael W. Jennings, Howard Eiland, and Gary Smith. Cambridge, MA: Harvard University Press, 2005.

———. *Selected Writings*, vol. 4, *1938–1940*. Ed. Howard Eiland and Michael W. Jennings. Cambridge, MA: Harvard University Press, 2003.

Benston, Kimberly W. *Performing Blackness: Enactments of African-American Modernism* London: Routledge, 2000.

Ben-Zvi, Linda. "'Aroun the Worl': Signifyin(g) Theater of Suzan-Lori Parks." In *The Theatrical Gamut: Notes for a Post-Beckettian Stage*, ed. Enoch Brater, 189–208. Ann Arbor: University of Michigan Press, 1995.

Best, Stephen, and Sharon Marcus. "Surface Reading: An Introduction." *Representations* 108.1 (2009): 1–21.

Brathwaite, Kamau. *Ancestors: A Reinvention of Mother Poem, Sun Poem, and X/Self*. New York: New Directions, 2001.

———. *Ark: A 9/11 Continuation Poem*. New York: Savacou North, 2004.

———. *The Arrivants: A New World Trilogy*. London: Oxford University Press, 1973.

———. *Barabajan Poems*. Kingston, Jamaica: Savacou, 1994.

———. "Caliban, Ariel and Unprospero in the Conflict of Creolization." In *Comparative Perspectives on Slavery in New World Plantation Societies*, ed. Vera Rubin and Arthur Tuden, 41–62. New York: New York Academy of Sciences, 1977.

———. "Caribbean Man in Space and Time." *Savacou* 11–12 (Sept. 1975): 1–11.

———. *Contradictory Omens*. Kingston, Jamaica: Savacou, 1974.

———. *ConVERSations with Nathaniel Mackey*. Staten Island: WE Press and XCP, 1999.

———. *The Development of Creole Society in Jamaica, 1770–1820*. Oxford: Oxford University Press, 1971.

———. *DreamStories*. London: Longman, 1994.

———. *DS(2) dreamstories*. New York: New Directions, 2007.

———. *Gods of the Middle Passage*. Kingston, Jamaica: Savacou Working Papers, 1982.

———. *Golokwati 2000*. New York: Savacou North, 2002.

———. *History of the Voice: The Development of Nation Language in Anglophone Caribbean Poetry*. London: New Beacon, 1984.

———. "Jazz and the West Indian Novel." In *Roots*, 55–110. Ann Arbor: University of Michigan Press, 1993.

———. *Middle Passages*. New York: New Directions, 1993.

———. *Mother Poem*. London: Oxford University Press, 1977.

———. *MR/1: Magical Realism*. New York: Savacou North, 1998.

———. *MR/2: Magical Realism*. New York: Savacou North, 1998.

———. *Shar: Hurricane Poem*. Kingston, Jamaica: Savacou, 1990.

———. "Timehri." In *Is Massa Day Dead: Black Moods in the Caribbean*, ed. Orde Coombs, 29–43. Garden City, NY: Anchor Bay, 1974.

———. *Sun Poem*. London: Oxford University Press, 1982.

———. *Trench Town Rock*. Providence: Lost Road, 1994.

———. *X/Self*. London: Oxford University Press, 1987.

———. *The Zea Mexican Diary: 7 September 1926–7 September 1986*. Madison: University of Wisconsin Press, 1993.

Brenner, Louise. *West African Sufi: The Religious Heritage and Spiritual Search of Cerno Bokar Saalif Taal*. Berkeley: University of California Press, 1984.

Brooks, Gwendolyn. Foreword to *New Negro Poets: USA*, ed. Langston Hughes and Arna Bontemps, 13–14. Bloomington: Indiana University Press, 1964.

Brown, Nicholas. *Utopian Generations: The Political Horizons of Twentieth-Century Literature.* Princeton, NJ: Princeton University Press, 2005.

Bruce, Dickson D., Jr. "W. E. B. Du Bois and the Idea of Double Consciousness." *American Literature* 64.2 (1992): 299–309.

Brustein, Robert Sanford. *Millennial Stages: Essays and Reviews, 2001–2005.* New Haven, CT: Yale University Press, 2006.

Carby, Hazel V. "It Jus Be's Dat Way Sometime: The Sexual Politics of Women's Blues." In *The Jazz Cadence of American Culture*, ed. Robert G. O'Meally, 469–82. New York: Columbia University Press, 1988.

Carpio, Glenda. *Laughing Fit to Kill: Black Humor in the Fictions of Slavery.* Cambridge, MA: Harvard University Press, 2008.

Castronovo, Russ. *Beautiful Democracy: Aesthetics and Anarchy in a Global Era.* Chicago: University of Chicago Press, 2007.

Chakrabarty, Dipesh. *Provincializing Europe: Postcolonial Thought and Historical Difference.* Princeton, NJ: Princeton University Press, 2000.

Clüver, Claus. "Reflections on Verbivocovisual Ideograms." *Poetics Today* 3.3 (1982): 137–48.

Coleridge, Samuel Taylor. "Shakespeare, a Poet Generally." In *The Complete Works of Samuel Taylor Coleridge*, vol. 4, ed. William Thayer Shedd, 46–49. New York: Harper and Brothers, 1853.

Coursil, Jacques. "Hidden Principles of Improvisation." In *Arcana III: Musicians on Music*, ed. John Zorn, 58–65. New York: Hips Road, 2008.

Cruz, Jon. *Culture on the Margins: The Black Spiritual and the Rise of American Cultural Interpretation.* Princeton, NJ: Princeton University Press, 1999.

Culler, Jonathan. *The Pursuit of Signs: Semiotics, Literature, Deconstruction.* 1981. Ithaca, NY: Cornell University Press, 2001.

Dash, J. Michael. *The Other America: Caribbean Literature in a New World Context.* Charlottesville: University of Virginia Press, 2008.

Davies, Carole Boyce. "Àshé. " In *Encyclopedia of the African Diaspora: Origins, Experiences, and Culture*, vol. 1, 118–19. Oxford, UK: ABC-CLIO, 2008.

———. *Black Women, Writing and Identity: Migrations of the Subject.* London: Routledge, 1994.

De Campos, Augusto. "Concrete Poetry: A Manifesto." Trans. John Tolman. In *Contemporary Poetics*, ed. Louis Armand, 213–14. Evanston, IL: Northwestern University Press, 2007.

de Man, Paul. "Anthropomorphism and Trope in the Lyric." In *The Rhetoric of Romanticism*, 239–62. New York: Columbia University Press, 1984.

———. *Blindness and Insight.* Minneapolis: University of Minnesota Press, 1983.

———. "The Concept of Irony." In *Aesthetic Ideology*, ed. Andrej Warminski, 163–84. Minneapolis: University of Minnesota Press, 1999.

Deren, Maya. *Divine Horsemen: The Living Gods of Haiti.* New York: Documentext, 1970.

Derrida, Jacques. *Acts of Literature.* Ed. Derrick Attridge. New York: Routledge, 1992.

———. *Acts of Reading.* Ed. Derrick Attridge. New York: Routledge, 1992.

———. *Counterfeit Money.* Vol. 1 of *Given Time.* Trans. Peggy Kamuf. Chicago: University of Chicago Press, 1992.

———. *Edmund Husserl's "The Origin of Geometry": An Introduction.* Trans. John P. Leavey Jr. Lincoln: University of Nebraska Press, 1989.

——. *Of Grammatology*. Trans. Gayatri Chakravorty Spivak. Baltimore, MD: Johns Hopkins University Press, 1997.

——. *Margins of Philosophy*. Trans. Alan Bass. Chicago: University of Chicago Press, 1982.

——. *Psyche: Inventions of the Other*. Vol. 1. Ed. Peggy Kamuf and Elizabeth Rottenberg. Stanford, CA: Stanford University Press, 2007.

——. *Specters of Marx: The State of Debt, the Work of Mourning and the New International*. Trans. Peggy Kamuf. 1993. Reprint, London: Routledge, 2006.

——. "Structure, Sign and Play in the Discourse of the Human Sciences." In *Writing and Difference*, trans. Alan Bass, 278–94. Chicago: University of Chicago Press, 1978.

Dinius, Marcy J. "'Look!! Look!!! at This!!!!': The Radical Typography of David Walker's *Appeal*." *PMLA* 126.1 (2011): 55–72.

Douglas, Ann. *Terrible Honesty: Mongrel Manhattan in the 1920s*. New York: Noonday Press, 1995.

Doyle, Laura. *Bordering on the Body: The Racial Matrix of Modern Fiction and Culture*. Oxford: Oxford University Press, 1994.

Draper, R. P. "Concrete Poetry." *New Literary History* 2.2 (1971): 329–40.

Drucker, Johanna. "Visual Performance of the Poetic Text." In *Close Listening: Poetry and the Performed Word*, ed. Charles Bernstein, 131–61. Oxford: Oxford University Press, 1988.

Druckman, Steven. "Doo-a-Diddly-Dit-Dit: An Interview with Suzan-Lori Parks and Liz Diamond." *Drama Review* 39.3 (1995): 56–75.

Du Bois, W. E. B. *The Autobiography of W. E. B. Du Bois: A Soliloquy on Viewing My Life from the Last Decade of Its First Century*. New York: International Publishers, 1968.

——. *Darkwater: Voices from within the Veil*. 1920. Reprint, New York: Washington Square Press, 2004.

——. *W. E. B. Du Bois: A Reader*. Ed. David Levering Lewis. New York: Henry Holt, 1995.

——. *Writings*. Ed. Nathan Huggins. New York: Library of America, 1986.

Dworkin, Craig. "The Fate of Echo." In *Against Expression: An Anthology of Conceptual Writing*, ed. Craig Dworkin and Kenneth Goldsmith, xxiii–liv. Evanston, IL: Northwest University Press, 2010.

Edwards, Brent Hayes. "Louis Armstrong and the Syntax of Scat." *Critical Inquiry* 28.3 (2002): 618–49.

——. "Notes on Poetics Regarding Mackey's *Song*." *Callaloo* 23.2 (2000): 572–91.

——. "The Seemingly Eclipsed Window of Form: James Weldon Johnson's Prefaces." In *The Jazz Cadence of American Culture*, ed. Robert G. O'Meally, 580–601. New York: Columbia University Press, 1998.

——. "The Uses of Diaspora." *Social Text* 19.1 (2001): 45–73.

Elam, Harry J. Jr., and Alice Rayner. "Body Parts: Between Story and Spectacle in *Venus* by Suzan-Lori Parks." In *Staging Resistance: Essays on Political Theatre*, ed. Jeanne Collerman and Jenny S. Spencer, 265–82. Ann Arbor: University of Michigan Press, 1998.

Eliot, T. S. *The Three Voices of Poetry*. New York: Cambridge University Press, 1954.

——. "Tradition and the Individual Talent." In *Selected Prose of T. S. Eliot*, ed. Frank Kermode, 37–44. New York: Mariner, 1975.

Fanon, Frantz. *Peau noir, masques blanc*. 1952. Paris: Seuil. 1995.

——. *Black Skins, White Masks*. Trans. Richard Philcox. New York: Grove Press, 2008.

Farred, Grant. "Foreigners among Citizens." *Cultural Critique* 67 (Fall 2007): 141–59.

——. "'Science Does Not Think': The No-Thought of the Discipline." *South Atlantic Quarterly* 110.1 (2011): 57–74.

Feld, Steven. *Sound and Sentiment: Birds, Weeping, Poetics, and Song in Kaluli Expression*. Philadelphia: University of Pennsylvania Press, 1982.

Flescher, Jennifer, and Robert Caspar. Interview with Claudia Rankine. *jubilat* 12 (2006): 14–28.

Foucault, Michel. "What Is an Author?" In *Michel Foucault Reader*. ed. and trans. Paul Rabinow, 101–20. New York: Pantheon, 1984.

———. "What Is Critique?" In *The Politics of Truth*, trans. Lysa Hochroth, 41–82. Los Angeles: Semiotext(e), 2007.

Frye, Northrop. *The Anatomy of Criticism: Four Essays*. Princeton, NJ: Princeton University Press, 1957.

Fuchs, Elinor. *The Death of Character: Perspectives on Theater after Modernism*. Bloomington: Indiana University Press, 1996.

Garrett, Shawn Marie. "Figures, Speech and Form in *Imperceptible Mutabilities in the Third Kingdom*." In *Suzan-Lori Parks: A Casebook*, ed. Kevin J. Wetmore and Alycia Smith-Howard, 1–17. London: Routledge, 2007.

Gilmore, Ruth Wilson. *Golden Gulag: Prisons, Surplus, Crisis, and Opposition in Globalizing California*. Berkeley: University of California Press, 2007.

Gilroy, Paul. "'After the Love Has Gone': Bio-Politics and Etho-Poetics in the Black Public Sphere." *Public Culture* 8.28–29 (1994): 49–76.

———. *The Black Atlantic: Modernity and Double Consciousness*. Cambridge, MA: Harvard University Press, 1993.

Gooding-Williams, Robert. *In the Shadow of Du Bois: Afro-Modern Political Thought in America*. Cambridge, MA: Harvard University Press, 2009.

Gourgouris, Stathis. *Does Literature Think? Literature as Theory for an Antimythical Age* Stanford, CA: Stanford University Press, 2003.

Griaule, Marcel. *Conversations with Ogotemmêli: An Introduction to Dogon Religious Ideas*. London: Oxford University Press, 1965.

Grosz, Elizabeth. "The Time of Thought." In *Time Travels: Feminism, Nature, Power*, 155–69. Durham, NC: Duke University Press, 2005.

Hall, James C. *Mercy, Mercy Me: African American Culture and the American Sixties*. London: Oxford University Press, 2001.

Hall, Stuart. "Race, Articulation and Societies Structured in Dominance." In *Black British Cultural Studies: A Reader*, ed. Houston Baker Jr., Manthia Diawara and Ruth H. Lindeborg, 15–60. Chicago: University of Chicago Press, 1996.

Hanchard, Michael. "Afro-Modernity." In *Alternative Modernities*, ed. Dilip Parameshwar Gaonkar, 272–98. Durham, NC: Duke University Press, 2001.

Harris, Wilson. "Adversarial Contexts and Creativity." *New Left Review* 154 (Nov./Dec. 1985): 124–28.

Hart, Matthew. *Nations of Nothing but Poetry: Modernism, Transnationalism, and Synthetic Vernacular Writing*. Oxford: Oxford University Press, 2010.

Hartman, Saidiya. *Lose Your Mother: A Journey Along the Atlantic Slave Route*. New York: Farrar, Straus and Giroux, 2007.

———. *Scenes of Subjection: Terror, Slavery, and Self-Making in Nineteenth-Century America*. London: Oxford University Press, 1997.

———. "Venus in Two Acts." *Small Axe* 26 (June 2008): 1–14.

Hayden, Robert. "Those Winter Sundays." In *Collected Poems*, ed. Frederick Glaysher, 41. New York: Liveright, 1997.

Hayes, Terrance. *Hip Logic*. New York: Penguin, 2002.

Hayes, Terrance, and Evie Shockley, eds. "African American Experimental Poetry Forum." *jubilat* 16 (2009): 115–54.

Heidegger, Martin. *Being and Time*. Trans. Joan Stambaugh. Albany: State University of New York Press, 1996.

Henderson, Stephen E., ed. *Understanding the New Black Poetry: Black Speech and Black Music as Poetic References*. New York: William Morrow, 1972.

Hogue, Cynthia. "Interview with Harryette Mullen." *Postmodern Culture* 9.2 (1999): n.p.

Hollander, John. "Breaking into Song: Some Notes on the Refrain." In *Lyric Poetry: Beyond New Criticism,* ed. Chaviva Hošek and Patricia Parker, 73–89. Ithaca, NY: Cornell University Press, 1985.

Hollo, Anselm, ed. *Negro Verse*. London: Vista, 1964.

Horkheimer, Max, and Theodor W. Adorno. *The Dialectic of Enlightenment: Philosophical Fragments*. Trans. Edmund Jephcott. Stanford, CA: Stanford University Press, 2002.

Hughes, Langston. *The Collected Poems of Langston Hughes*. Ed. Arnold Rampersad. New York: Vintage, 1994.

Hughes, Langston, and Arna Bontemps, eds. *New Negro Poets: USA*. Bloomington: Indiana University Press, 1964.

Hunt, Erica. "Notes for an Oppositional Poetics." In *The Politics of Poetic Form*, ed. Charles Bernstein, 197–212. New York: Roof, 1990.

Iton, Richard. *In Search of the Black Fantastic: Politics and Popular Culture in the Post-Civil Rights Era*. London: Oxford University Press, 2010.

Izenberg, Oren. *Being Numerous: Poetry and the Ground of Social Life*. Princeton, NJ: Princeton University Press, 2011.

Jackson, Virginia. *Dickinson's Misery: A Theory of Lyric Reading*. Princeton, NJ: Princeton University Press, 2005.

———. "Thinking Dickinson Thinking Poetry." In *A Companion to Emily Dickinson*, ed. Martha Nell Smith and Mary Loeffelholz, 205–21. Hoboken, NJ: Wiley-Blackwell, 2008.

Jameson, Fredric. *The Political Unconscious: Narrative as a Socially Symbolic Act*. Ithaca, NY: Cornell University Press, 1981.

———. *Postmodernism; or, The Cultural Logic of Late Capitalism*. Durham, NC: Duke University Press, 1991.

———. "Third-World Literature in the Era of Multinational Capitalism." *Social Text* 15 (1986): 63–88.

———. *Valences of the Dialectic*. London: Verso, 2010.

Jarvis, Simon. "Prosody as Cognition." *Critical Quarterly* 40.4 (1998): 3–15.

Johnston, Devin. "Nathaniel Mackey and Lost Time: 'The Phantom Light of All Our Day.'" *Callaloo* 23.2 (2000): 563–70.

Johung, Jennifer. "Figuring the 'Spells'/Spelling the Figures: Suzan-Lori Parks's 'Scene of Love (?)'" *Theater Journal* 58.1 (2006): 39–52.

Jones, Meta DuEwa. *The Muse Is Music: Jazz Poetry from the Harlem Renaissance to Spoken Word*. Urbana: University of Illinois Press, 2011.

Kearney, Douglas. *The Black Automaton*. Albany, NY: Fence Books, 2009.

Keller, Jim. *Writing Plural Worlds in Contemporary U.S. Poetry: Innovative Identities*. New York: Palgrave Macmillan, 2009.

Kelley, Robin D. G. *Freedom Dreams: The Black Radical Imagination*. Boston: Beacon, 2002.

———. "Notes on Deconstructing 'The Folk.'" *American Historical Review* 97.5 (1992): 1400–8.

Kinnahan, Linda A. *Lyric Interventions: Feminism, Experimental Poetry, and Contemporary Discourse.* Iowa City: University of Iowa Press, 2004.

Lange, Art, and Nathaniel Mackey, eds. *Moment's Notice: Jazz in Poetry and Prose.* Minneapolis, MN: Coffee House Press, 1993.

Leonard, Keith D. *Fettered Genius: The African American Bardic Poet from Slavery to Civil Rights.* Charlottesville: University of Virginia Press, 2005.

Lewis, David Levering. *W. E. B. Du Bois: Biography of a Race, 1868–1919.* New York: Henry Holt, 1993.

Lewis, George E. *A Power Greater Than Itself: The AACM and American Experimental Music.* Chicago: University of Chicago Press, 2008.

Llorens, David. "Seeking a New Image: Writers Converge at Fisk University," *Negro Digest* 15.8 (1966): 54–68.

Lorca, Federico García. "Theory and Function of *Duende.*" Trans. J. L. Gill. In *The Poetics of the New American Poetry,* ed. Donald Allen and Warren Tallman, 91–103. New York: Random House, 1973.

Lordi, Emily J. *Black Resonance: Iconic Women Singers and African American Literature.* New Brunswick: Rutgers University Press, 2013.

Lukács, Georg. *History and Class Consciousness.* Trans. Rodney Livingstone. Cambridge, MA: MIT Press, 1971.

Mackey, Nathaniel. *Atet A.D.* San Francisco: City Lights, 2001.

———. *Bass Cathedral.* New York: New Directions, 2007.

———. *Bedouin Hornbook.* 1986. Los Angeles: Sun and Moon Press, 1997.

———. *Discrepant Engagement: Dissonance, Cross-Culturality, and Experimental Writing.* Tuscaloosa: University of Alabama Press, 2000.

———. *Djbot Baghostus's Run.* Los Angeles: Sun and Moon Press, 1993.

———. *Eroding Witness.* Urbana-Champaign: University of Illinois Press, 1985.

———. "Interview with Kamau Brathwaite. In *The Art of Kamau Brathwaite,* ed. Stewart Brown, 13–32. Mid Glamorgan, Wales: seren, 1995.

———. *The Paracritical Hinge: Essays, Talks, Notes, Interviews.* Madison: University of Wisconsin Press, 2005.

———. *School of Udhra.* San Francisco: City Lights, 2001.

———. *Splay Anthem.* New York: New Directions, 2006.

———. *Whatsaid Serif.* San Francisco: City Lights, 2001.

Madhubuti, Haki R. (Don L. Lee). *Directionscore: New and Selected Poems.* Detroit, MI: Broadside Press, 1971.

Major, Clarence, ed. *From Juba to Jive: A Dictionary and African American Slang.* 1970. Reprint, New York: Penguin, 1994.

———, ed. *The New Black Poetry.* New York: International Publishers, 1969.

Marcuse, Herbert. *An Essay on Liberation.* Boston: Beacon, 1969.

Martin, Dawn Lundy. "The Language of Trauma: Faith and Atheism in M. NourbeSe Philip's Poetry." In *Eleven More American Woman Poets,* ed. Claudia Rankine and Lisa Sewell, 283–307. Middletown, CT: Wesleyan University Press, 2012.

Marx, Karl. *Economic and Philosophic Manuscripts of 1844.* In *Karl Marx, Frederick Engels, Collected Works,* vol. 3, ed. James S. Allen, Philip S. Foner, Howard Selsam, Dirk J. Struik, William W. Weinstone, trans. Clemens Dutt, 230–347. New York: International, 1975.

———. *Grundrisse: Foundations of the Critique of Political Economy.* Trans. Martin Niclaus. New York: Penguin, 1993.

McGann, Jerome. *Black Riders: The Visible Language of Modernism.* Princeton, NJ: Princeton University Press, 1993.

McGinley, Paige. "Highway 61 Revisited." *TDR: The Drama Review* 51.3 (2007): 80–97.

Melamed, Jodi. *Represent and Destroy: Rationalizing Violence in the New Racial Capitalism.* Minneapolis: University of Minnesota Press, 2012.

Melas, Natalie. *All the Difference in the World.* Stanford, CA: Stanford University Press, 2007.

Miller, Adam David. *DICES; or, Black Bones: Black Voices of the Seventies.* New York: Houghton Mifflin, 1970.

Mitchell, W. J. T. *The Language of Images.* Chicago: University of Chicago Press, 1980.

Morrison, Toni. *Beloved.* New York: Plume, 1988.

Moten, Fred. *In the Break: Aesthetics of the Radical Black Tradition.* Minneapolis: University of Minnesota Press, 2003.

Mullen, Harryette. "African Signs and Spirit Writing." *Callaloo* 19.3 (1996): 670–89.

———. *The Cracks Between What We Are and What We Are Supposed to Be: Essays and Interviews.* Tuscaloosa: University of Alabama Press, 2012.

———. "Hauling up Gold from the Abyss: An Interview with Will Alexander." *Callaloo* 22.2 (1999): 391–408.

———. *Recyclopedia: Trimmings, S*PeRM**K*T, and Muse & Drudge.* St. Paul, MN: Graywolf Press, 2006.

———. *Sleeping with the Dictionary.* Berkeley: University of California Press, 2002.

Mullen, Harryette, and Arlene R. Keizer. "Incidents in the Lives of Two Postmodern Black Feminists." *Postmodern Culture* 22.1 (2011), n.p., doi: 10.1353/pmc.2012.0008.

Nancy, Jean-Luc. *The Inoperative Community.* Trans. Peter Connor et al. Minneapolis: University of Minnesota Press, 1991.

Naylor, Paul. *Poetic Investigations: Singing the Holes of History.* Evanston, IL: Northwestern University Press, 1999.

Neal, Larry. "And Shine Swam On." In *Black Fire: An Anthology of Afro-American Writing,* ed. Amiri Baraka and Larry Neal, 637–56. 1968. Reprint, Baltimore, MD: Black Classic Press, 2007.

———. "Black Art and Black Liberation." *Ebony Magazine,* Aug. 1969, 54–56.

Nealon, Christopher. *The Matter of Capital: Poetry and Crisis in the American Century.* Cambridge, MA: Harvard University Press, 2011.

Nielsen, Aldon. *Black Chant: Languages of African American Postmodernism.* Cambridge: Cambridge University Press, 1997.

North, Michael. *The Dialect of Modernism: Race, Language, and Twentieth-Century Literature.* Oxford: Oxford University Press, 1994.

Oduyoye, Modupe. *Yoruba Names: Their Structure and Meaning.* London: Karnak House, 1982.

Omi, Michael, and Howard Winant. *Racial Formation in the United States: From the 1960s to the 1990s.* London: Routledge, 1994.

Ongiri, Amy Abugo. *Spectacular Blackness: The Cultural Politics of the Black Power Movement and the Search for a Black Aesthetic.* Charlottesville: University of Virginia Press, 2009.

Parham, Marisa. *Haunting and Displacement in African American Literature.* London: Routledge, 2008.

Parks, Suzan-Lori. *The America Play, and Other Plays.* New York: Theater Communications Group, 1995.

———. "New Black Math." *Theatre Journal* 57.4 (2005): 576–83.

———. *Venus*. New York: Theater Communications Group, 1997.

Patterson, Anita. *Race, American Literature, and Transnational Modernism*. Cambridge: Cambridge University Press, 2008.

Perloff, Marjorie. *Differentials: Poetry, Poetics, Pedagogy*. Tuscaloosa; University of Alabama Press, 2004.

———. "Poetry on the Brink: Reinventing the Lyric." *Boston Review*, May/June 2012.

———. *Unoriginal Genius: Poetry by Other Means in the New Century*. Chicago: University of Chicago Press, 2010.

Philip, M. NourbeSe. "Fugues, Fragments and Fissures—A Work in Progress." *Anthurium: A Caribbean Studies Journal* 3.2 (2005): 1–15.

———. "Ignoring Poetry." In *A Genealogy of Resistance and Other Essays*, 120–25. Toronto: Mercury Press, 1997.

———. *She Tries Her Tongue, Her Silence Softly Breaks*. Charlottetown, Canada: Ragweed Press, 1989.

———. "Zong #1." *Facture: A Journal of Poetry and Poetics*, no. 2 (2001). www.webdelsol.com/Facture/poems/mnourbesephilip.htm.

Philip, M. NourbeSe, as told to by Setaey Adamu Boateng. *Zong!* Middletown, CT: Wesleyan University Press, 2008.

Pinson, Hermine, and Lorenzo Thomas. Interview with Lorenzo Thomas. *Callaloo* 22.2 (1999): 287–304.

Pollard, Charles W. *New World Modernisms: T. S. Eliot, Derek Walcott, and Kamau Brathwaite*. Charlottesville: University of Virginia Press, 2004.

Porter, Lewis. *John Coltrane: His Life and His Music*. Ann Arbor: University of Michigan Press, 1999.

Pritchard, N. H. *EECCHHOOEESS*. New York: New York University Press, 1971.

———. *The Matrix: Poems 1960–1970*. New York: Doubleday, 1970.

Ramazani, Jahan. *A Transnational Poetics*. Chicago: University of Chicago Press, 2009.

Rancière, Jacques. *Disagreement: Politics and Philosophy*. Trans. Julie Rose. Minneapolis: University of Minnesota Press, 1999.

———. *The Emancipated Spectator*. Trans. Gregory Elliot. London: Verso, 2011.

———. *Politics of Literature*. Trans. Julie Rose. Cambridge, UK: Polity Press, 2011.

Rankine, Claudia. *Don't Let Me Be Lonely: An American Lyric*. St. Paul, MN: Graywolf Press, 2004.

———. "The First Person in the Twenty-First Century." In *After Confession: Poetry as Autobiography*, ed. Kate Sontag and David Graham, 132–36. Minneapolis, MN: Graywolf Press, 2001.

———. *PLOT*. New York: Grove Press, 2001.

Retamar, Roberto Fernández. "Caliban: Notes Towards a Discussion of Culture in Our America." Trans. Lynn Garofola et al. *Massachusetts Review* 15.1–2 (1974): 7–72.

Rigby, Graeme. "Publishing Brathwaite: Adventures in Video Sycorax Style." *World Literature Today* 68.4 (1994): 708–14.

Roach, Joseph. "The Great Hole of History: 'Natural' Catastrophe and Liturgical Silence." In *Reflections on Beckett: A Centenary Celebration*, ed. Anna McMullan and S. E. Wilmer, 134–52. Ann Arbor: University of Michigan Press, 2009.

Rodó, José Enrique. *Ariel*. Ed. Gordon Brotherston. 1900. Cambridge: Cambridge University Press, 1967.

Rohlehr, Gordon. *Pathfinder: Black Awakening in "The Arrivants" of Edward Kamau Brathwaite*. Tunapuna, Trinidad: Rohlehr, 1981.

Savory, Elaine. "Returning to Sycorax / Prospero's Response: Kamau Brathwaite's Word Journey." In *The Art of Kamau Brathwaite*, ed. Stewart Brown, 208–30. Mid Glamorgan. Wales: seren, 1995.

Shockley, Evie. "Going Overboard: African American Poetic Innovation and the Middle Passage." *Contemporary Literature* 52.4 (2011): 791–817.

———. *a half-red sea*. Durham, NC: Carolina Wren Press, 2006.

———. *Renegade Poetics: Black Aesthetics and Formal Innovation in African American Poetry*. Iowa City: University of Iowa Press, 2011.

Smitherman, Geneva. *Talkin' and Testifyin': The Language of Black America*. Detroit, MI: Wayne State University Press, 1977.

Snead, James A. "On Repetition in Black Culture." In *Racist Traces and Other Writings: European Pedigrees/African Contagions*, ed. James A. Snead, Kara, Keeling, Colin MacCabe, and Cornel West, 11–33. New York: Palgrave Macmillan, 2003.

Spillers, Hortense J. "The Idea of Black Culture." *CR: The New Centennial Review* 6.3 (2006): 7–28.

———. "Mama's Baby, Papa's Maybe: An American Grammar Book." In *Black, White and in Color: Essays on American Literature and Culture*, 203–29. Chicago: University of Chicago Press, 2003.

Spivak, Gayatri Chakravorty. *A Critique of Postcolonial Reason: Toward a History of the Vanishing Present*. Cambridge, MA: Harvard University Press, 1999.

———. "Ghostwriting." *Diacritics* 25.2 (1995): 64–84.

———. "Learning from de Man: Looking Back." *boundary 2* 32.3 (2005): 21–35.

———. *Outside in the Teaching Machine*. London: Routledge, 1993.

———. "Scattered Speculations on the Question of Value." In *In Other Words: Essays in Cultural Politics*, 154–75. New York: Routledge, 1988.

———. "Time and Timing: Law and History." In *Chronotypes: The Construction of Time*, ed. John Bender and David E. Wellbery, 99–117. Stanford, CA: Stanford University Press, 1991.

Stepto, Robert. *From within the Veil: A Study of Afro-American Narrative*. 1979. Urbana: University of Illinois Press, 1991.

Stewart, Susan. *Poetry and the Fate of the Senses*. Chicago: University of Chicago Press, 2002.

Tate, Greg. *Everything but the Burden: What White People Are Taking from Black Culture*. New York: Broadway Books, 2003.

Thomas, Lorenzo. "The Shadow World: New York's Umbra Movement and the Origins of the Black Arts Movement." *Callaloo* 4 (Oct. 1978): 53–74.

Vendler, Helen. *The Art of Shakespeare's Sonnets*. Cambridge, MA: Harvard University Press, 1999.

Veal, Michael. *Dub: Soundscapes and Shattered Songs in Jamaican Reggae*. Middletown, CT: Wesleyan University Press, 2007.

Viego, Antonio. *Dead Subjects: Toward a Politics of Loss in Latino Studies*. Durham, NC: Duke University Press, 2007.

Villarejo, Amy. *Lesbian Rule: Cultural Criticism and the Value of Desire*. Durham, NC: Duke University Press, 2003.

Walcott, Derek. "The Muse of History." In *What the Twilight Says*, 36–64. New York: Farrar, Straus and Giroux, 1998.

Waldrop, Rosemarie. "A Basis of Concrete Poetry (1977)." In *Dissonance (if you are interested)*, 47–57. Tuscaloosa: University of Alabama Press, 2005.

Walvin, James. *Black Ivory: A History of British Slavery*. London: Harper Collins, 1992.

Warner, Sara. "Suzan-Lori Parks's Drama of Disinterment: A Transnational Exploration of *Venus*." *Theatre Journal* 60.2 (2008): 181–99.

Warren, Kenneth W. *What Was African American Literature?* Cambridge, MA: Harvard University Press, 2011.

Watten, Barrett. "The Turn to Language and the 1960s." *Critical Inquiry* 29.1 (2002): 139–82.

Weheliye, Alexander. *Phonographies: Groves in Sonic Afro-Modernity*. Durham, NC: Duke University Press, 2005.

Williams, Emily Allen, and Harryette Mullen. "'The Queen of Hip Hyperbole': An Interview." *African American Review* 34.4 (2000): 701–7.

Williams, Patricia J. "The Power of One." *Black Renaissance/Renaissance Noire* 8.1 (2008): 43–45.

Woolf, Virginia. *To the Lighthouse*. 1927. New York: Harvest Books, 1989.

Wright, Jay. *The Guide Signs*. Bks. 1 and 2. Baton Rouge: Louisiana State University, 2007.

Yeats, William Butler. *The Collected Poems of W. B. Yeats*. Ed. Richard J. Finneran. New York: Simon and Schuster, 1996.

Young, Jean. "The Re-Objectification and Re-Commodification of Saartjie Baartman in Suzan-Lori Parks's *Venus*." *African American Review* 31.4 (1997): 699–708.

Young, Kevin. "Signs of Repression: N. H. Pritchard's *The Matrix*." *Harvard Library Bulletin* 3.2 (1992): 36–44.

Yu, Timothy. *Race and the Avant-Garde: Experimental and Asian American Poetry since 1965*. Stanford, CA: Stanford University Press, 2009.

Zamir, Shamoon. *Dark Voices: W. E. B. Du Bois and American Thought, 1888–1903*. Chicago: University of Chicago Press, 1995.

Zamsky, Robert L. "A Poetics of Radical Musicality: Nathanel Mackey's '-mu' Series." *Arizona Quarterly* 62.1 (2006): 113–40.

Index